FLORIDA STATE
UNIVERSITY LIBRARIES

NOV 19 1993

TALLAHASSEE, FLORIDA

Paradigms and Conventions

*Economics, Cognition, and Society*
This series provides a forum for theoretical and empirical investigations of social phenomena. It promotes works that focus on the interactions among cognitive processes, individual behavior, and social outcomes. It is especially open to interdisciplinary books that are genuinely integrative.

Editor: Timur Kuran

Editorial Board: Ronald Heiner
       Sheila Ryan Johansson

Advisory Board: James M. Buchanan
       Albert O. Hirschman
       Mancur Olson

**Titles in the Series**

Ulrich Witt, Editor. *Explaining Process and Change: Approaches to Evolutionary Economics*

Young Back Choi. *Paradigms and Conventions: Uncertainty, Decision Making, and Entrepreneurship*

# Paradigms and Conventions

## Uncertainty, Decision Making, and Entrepreneurship

Young Back Choi

*Ann Arbor*

THE UNIVERSITY OF MICHIGAN PRESS

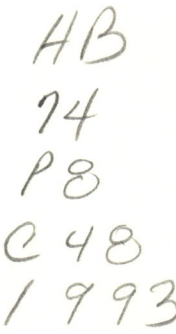
HB
74
P8
C48
1993

Copyright © by the University of Michigan 1993
All rights reserved
Published in the United States of America by
The University of Michigan Press
Manufactured in the United States of America

1996   1995   1994   1993      4  3  2  1

*A CIP catalogue record for this book is available from the British Library.*

Library of Congress Cataloging-in-Publication Data

Choi, Young Back, 1949–
    Paradigms and conventions : uncertainty, decision making, and entrepreneurship / Young Back Choi.
      p.    cm. — (Economics, cognition, and society)
    Includes bibliographical references and index.
    ISBN 0-472-10422-5 (alk. paper)
    1. Economics—Psychological aspects.  2. Paradigms (Social sciences)  3. Decision-making.  4. Consumer behavior.
5. Entrepreneurship.  I. Title.  II. Series.
HB74.P8C48   1993
330′.01′9—dc20                                           92-39840
                                                                  CIP

*to Daniel R. Fusfeld*

# Preface

In this book, I present a theory of human behavior reflecting decision making under conditions of uncertainty. The theory is designed to deal, among other things, with the phenomenon of the interdependence of human actions in society, often neglected in neoclassical economics.[1] Let me hasten to add that this is not another critique of orthodox economics or another shopping list of desired characteristics of an alternative theory yet to be developed. This is primarily a constructive exercise in theory.

The roots of the book are deep. Several years ago, I set out to explore the role of envy in economic activity as the bulk of my dissertation research. I was motivated by my interest in the issues of income distribution and discovery of how pervasive and yet latent and essentially unexplored was the matter of invidious comparisons in such discussions. But I soon learned that the neoclassical economics in which I was most trained has largely ignored not only envy but also the broader matter of interdependent utility, and such other important phenomena as X-efficiency and entrepreneurship. Eventually I came to the conclusion that it is the very *structure* of neoclassical economic analysis that precludes investigation into such phenomena, which seem to reflect the fundamental human condition of decision making in the face of uncertainty. It is not that neoclassical economists have ignored the fact of decision making in the face of uncertainty, but that the basic analytical structure of traditional economics has induced them to adopt a certain approach that overlooks the most basic characteristics of decision making under uncertainty. At this point, my inquiry took a quantum leap.

Now aware that addressing envy and other issues in a truly substantive manner required addressing the structure of the analytical framework, I began by studying the critics of the neoclassical school. Although many appeared to have pinpointed an inability to deal with the sorts of problems I have cited as a shortcoming of the traditional approach, unfortunately, few went beyond identification of the problem areas and criticisms to theoretical modi-

---

1. I use the term *neoclassical economics* interchangeably with traditional or orthodox economics to refer to the core theory of microeconomics, about which an overwhelming consensus exists in spite of substantial divergence elsewhere in the field.

fication and rectification. Moreover, those who *did* attempt to advance beyond the stage of criticism seemed to end up either offering explicit models of behavior designed to explain what they perceived to be the problem area or concluding that *no* theory, neoclassical economic or otherwise, can ever be adequate for the task of systematically exploring human perception and the decision-making process—the central facts of human action. Neither course seemed to offer a viable alternative to neoclassical economics.

In this book I offer a *third* possibility. This approach does not provide a behavioral model to explain a chosen set of observations. Nor does it delve into the inner psychology of every individual, preparatory to presenting a specific model of decision making under uncertainty. Rather, it takes as given the fact that we must all make judgments without being omniscient, and it then explores the implications both for individuals and for broader socioeconomic changes. This approach enables us to search for discernible patterns of human behavior and social tendency as necessary consequences of decision making in the face of uncertainty. The result, I hope, begins to provide the basis for a new framework of analysis that is both simple and powerful.

Of course, I probably overstate my case by calling it new: psychologists, philosophers, and linguists have already made sizeable inroads into related areas. In fact, I am greatly encouraged to note that the framework I develop here is based on premises in keeping with the frontiers of knowledge in psychology, where theorizing about the process of human reasoning has become a major growth industry, as indeed it has for many of the other social sciences as well.

I must emphasize at the outset, however, that this book is *not* a study in psychology. Instead, it is strictly a study of the logical implications of a few axioms of decision making in the face of uncertainty. Determining the degree to which my theory and psychological findings cohere will require further research, but I believe the prospect for success is a good one.

Not new, then, but novel, my approach is also consistent with the "evolutionary-behavioral economics" Viktor Vanberg recently suggested as an alternative to the "case-by-case maximization model."[2] The evolutionary perspective, he says, should provide a unified theory of human behavior that common experience tells us is functional and purposeful and that incorporates "evolutionary learning" to account for the process of adaptation.

I believe that my theory derives a system of reasonable propositions from a few basic axioms and develops a cogent framework of analysis that is consistent with other ongoing work in economics in particular and the social sciences as a whole, and is useful for explaining and understanding some of the problem areas in orthodox economics. But another word of caution is in

---

2. See Vanberg 1989.

order: parts of this study will doubtless appear to need further polish and clarification. In the absence of highly honed and established analytical tools with which to work, I have often had to improvise. Finally, I beg the reader to suspend his or her demand for "policy relevance" and judge the book for its cogency and its wealth of insights. Clarion calls for further research form an inevitable footnote to any analysis on the frontier.

Recently, Timur Kuran has observed: "We must guard against turning the [past] successes of neoclassical economics into a license to stop thinking. If a broader, more refined framework might prevent blunders and explain more successfully a wider set of phenomena, science mandates that we develop and explore it."[3] Progress in science occurs by constructing new analyses that work to resolve difficulties perceived in existing theories. That task, I believe, I have begun to accomplish here, work in progress, improvisation, and all. Let the reader proceed with the next iteration.

Before beginning to advance my theory, I acknowledge the help of the many people responsible for much of what is good in this volume, while accepting full responsibility for errors and incompleteness. First on the list of individuals whom I heartily thank is Colin Day, director of the University of Michigan Press. I had the good fortune to meet Mr. Day at the American Economic Association meeting held in Atlanta in 1989, and he kindly agreed to consider for publication the manuscript that had been languishing in the dust bin for several years. I am also indebted to Timur Kuran of the University of Southern California, Viktor Vanberg of George Mason University, and an anonymous reader of an earlier draft of this book for their thoughtful comments and helpful suggestions; to Nahid Aslanbeigui of Monmouth College, for her generosity with time and insight; to James M. Buchanan of George Mason University, Wolfgang Kerber of Walter Euken Institute, Gary Mongiovi of St. John's University, and Steven Pressman of Monmouth College for reading and commenting on the drafts of this book at various stages; and to Adele Wick of Greenland, New Hampshire, for editing the manuscript, thus rescuing me from infelicities of style. Finally, much of the study presented here would not have been possible without the encouragement and support of Daniel R. Fusfeld of the University of Michigan. I am especially grateful to him for allowing me to exercise my imagination, come what may, and to him I respectfully dedicate this book.

---

3. Kuran 1990, 18.

# Contents

Introduction   1

1. Decision Making under Uncertainty and the Concept of Rationality   11
2. A Theory of Decision Making under Uncertainty: The Paradigmatic Approach   27
3. The Decision-Making Process and Its Implications for Individual Behavior   45
4. Individuals in Society   63
5. Conventions and Social Institutions   87
6. Status   113
7. Envy   125

Conclusion   149

Appendix: Table of Propositions and Corollaries   155

Bibliography   157

Name Index   177

Subject Index   181

# Introduction

> ... [M]an [is] a mean between nothing and everything.... This is what makes us incapable of certain knowledge and of absolute ignorance. We sail within a vast sphere, ever drifting in uncertainty ... driven from end to end.
>
> —Pascal

People make decisions with information that is never perfect or complete. Indeed, decision making in the face of uncertainty is a given—so basic to human life that any serious effort to understand human actions and the social tendencies reflecting their interactions must address this condition directly. But the dominant tradition of economics, neoclassical economics, frequently fails to incorporate uncertainty into its models of human behavior.[1] The consequences are far from negligible.

In this book, I attempt to redress the balance by constructing an alternative analytical framework for economic analysis. It reflects as well both my fascination with how the human mind works, enabling individuals to manage their affairs in a variable environment that includes other people not unlike themselves, and my interest in how the collectivity of human actions—namely, social institutions—may also change over time.

The assertion that neoclassical economics has a fatal flaw might seem outrageous at first glance. Isn't economics the most rigorous of the social sciences by overwhelmingly common consent? Doesn't Stanislaw Andreski somewhat meekly exempt economics from his otherwise sweeping condemnation of the social sciences, whose work he excoriates for its prejudices and even its quackeries?[2] Articles in the discipline's learned journals often re-

---

1. The economics of uncertainty is actually a thriving branch of economics, but I shall argue, both subsequently and again in chap. 1, that its approach is inadequate for the problems I wish to investigate.

2. See Andreski 1972. Apparently, Andreski is not an isolated example. Hands 1987, 172–75 notes that a notable philosopher of social science, Charles Taylor, who harshly criticizes the social sciences for aping the natural sciences, somehow exempts economics from his attack.

semble work in theoretical mathematics, and its increasingly wide adoption by sociologists, anthropologists, and political scientists is surely evidence of the probity of the approach. Most law schools in the United States have by now added economists to their faculties, and even economists seem convinced that the neoclassical approach can enhance our understanding of ethics, marriage, and even the behavior of "Rotten Kids."[3] This "economic imperialism,"[4] if you will, implies that the health of neoclassical economics is hearty indeed.

This widespread extension of the theory to deal with problems beyond its traditional boundaries begins, however, to reveal some cracks in its very foundation. To the extent that economics is mechanistic and deterministic, leaving little room for uncertainty or genuine human interactions or the open-endedness of the evolutionary process, its very nature precludes fruitful explanation of such important phenomena as interdependent utility,[5] Leibenstein's X-inefficiency,[6] errors and regrets, habits and routines, entrepreneurial activities, and social institutions.

---

3. For a definition and discussion of "Rotten Kids" see Becker 1976.

4. See Hirshleifer 1985.

5. *Interdependent utility* is a term that economists use to describe a situation in which the utility (or satisfaction) of an individual is affected by the affairs of others. To understand its usage, imagine two friends, A and B, walking down an alley. Now compare the happiness of A in two alternative cases: (1) A and B walk straight through the alley; and (2) Before they are out of the alley, B picks up a gold coin. If A's level of utility in the second case is the same as that in the first case, A's utility is independent; if not, it is interdependent.

Another term in economics, *consumption externality*, may be construed as describing a similar sort of situation. But, by externality, economists usually have circumstances in mind where an individual's utility is affected by the other person's consumption of something like tobacco or loud music, which may create air or noise pollution. In these cases, an outside observer may be able to detect why the individual may suffer from other people's affairs, granted that different people have different levels of tolerance for noise or smell.

But the use of the term *interdependent utility* is much broader, as it includes situations in which one's utility is affected by others' affairs in less tangible ways. For example, the satisfaction a woman derives from her own dress may be affected by what other women wear. Or a worker's satisfaction from his or her own wage may be affected by a co-worker's wage level. Four kinds of interdependent utility are possible—envy, malice, sympathy, and benevolence. When an individual becomes less happy when another gains and exhibits behavior reflecting dissatisfaction, he or she is envious. When an individual becomes happier with another's relative loss, even though he or she may have suffered a loss in absolute terms, he or she is malicious. When an individual becomes less happy with another's loss, even though he or she may not have suffered any personal loss in absolute terms, he or she is sympathetic. When an individual becomes happier with other people's relative gain, even when he or she may not have gained a lot, he or she is benevolent. See the Introduction, chap. 6, and chap. 7 for further discussion of interdependent utility.

6. X-efficiency is a concept proposed by Harvey Leibenstein (1966). He argues that allocative efficiency, the central concern of neoclassical economists, is rather trivial, the welfare loss resulting from misallocation of resources being frequently no more than 0.1 percent of GNP. Much more important is another kind of efficiency loss, X-inefficiency, which is frequently higher

Economists have traditionally oriented their studies toward an examination of markets. Because the market process has been a powerful force in transforming the world, it has fascinated intellectuals for the last two centuries, and I have no wish to diminish the importance of this research. But the markets most traditional economists have analyzed have been stylized situations of equilibrium, where everything worth knowing in order to strike a bargain *is* known, so that the possibility of making mistakes or leaving profitable opportunities unexploited is nil. The central problems for traditional economics are thus those of static allocation, where social outcomes of Pareto optimality are the happy consequence of agents always doing the very best they possibly can.

In a world of this kind, relationships among people need not be personal; when social interactions are remote and impersonal, invidious comparisons disappear or become too trivial to merit the keen eye of analysis. Amounting to an additional and self-imposed constraint, interdependent utility would be an irrational waste of resources. It is no surprise, then, that economists working within such a frame of reference would remove interdependent utility from their domain: the dictates of internal consistency require its expulsion to other disciplines.[7]

There is also a historical dimension to this neglect. By deeming "unwholesome" the growing "desire for wealth as a means of display" and asserting that society would be vastly improved if personal behavior were "free from any taint of personal vanity . . . and envy,"[8] Alfred Marshall set the stage of a century's worth of disdainful treatment of interdependent utility. Not merely a moral derivative of the Victorian ethos, however, its exclusion from the analysis of other founders of the marginal revolution was also deeply rooted in their methodology. The basic orientation of such theorists as William Stanley Jevons and Leon Walras was to emulate the approach long proven efficacious by engineers, and adopting the scientific approach to social studies required the assumption that human beings can be treated much like physical objects that obey certain laws.

---

than 25 percent of GNP, according to Leibenstein. Determinants of X-efficiency include individual motivations, interplant motivation, external motivation, and nonmarket input efficiency. From the point of view of economic theory, the concept of X-efficiency renders questionable the validity of the concept of the production function, to the degree that the relationship between inputs and outputs is not determinate (see also Leibenstein 1976, 3–47). For further discussion of X-efficiency, see chap. 5.

7. Only to such poets as Emerson can consistency ever appear "foolish"—"the hobgoblin of little minds, adored by little statesmen and philosophers and divines." "Worldly philosophers" should not "dare to be misunderstood": "To be great is to be misunderstood" should not apply in the ranks of social scientists.

8. Marshall 1961, 136–37.

Such is the stature of this able trilogy of theorists that the tradition of the natural science analogy has continued to the present day. Just as apples obey the law of gravity, so, it is assumed, people harken to the law of maximization. Rocks tumble downward until they are blocked, resuming free fall when their path is cleared. So, it is argued, people seek happiness or pecuniary gain until they are hindered by a constraint, the removal of which results in their further and relentless pursuit of utility.

Is it any wonder, under these circumstances, that economics has had little, if any, room for interdependent utility? If helium cares not that an equal volume of oxygen has greater weight, should one college graduate be irked that another pounded the pavement to greater effect?

In fact, people *do* care about these differences, and a growing number of economists have begun to care that they care. No longer willing to acquiesce to the tradition of ignoring "invidious comparisons" in favor of scientific laws admirably taut, this group has started to examine such previously intractable topics as reputation, status, workplace norms and conformity, tradition, relative deprivation, and fairness.[9]

Unfortunately, these economists remain a minority—and one that still fails to be sufficiently radical in its departure from tradition. After appealing to common sense and the corroborative findings of sociologists and anthropologists, they remain strict adherents of the neoclassical approach, dealing with interdependence as simply another argument in utility functions that remain distinctly individual in nature. Adopting the hypothesis of maximization may be permissible when maximization is interpreted as somehow equivalent to "psychological egoism," but then it loses empirical content and interpretation degenerates to tautology. If maximization is, instead, considered more robustly as an empirical proposition, conceptual difficulties soon entangle the inquiry when interdependent utility is incorporated into the analysis.

After careful consideration of decision making and uncertainty, James Buchanan disputes the frequent assertion that neoclassical economics is a "science of choice."[10] Maximization is more appropriately the "logic of choice," taking as given the perception of a given situation. Maximization, therefore, is an inappropriate vehicle for the analysis of behavioral patterns that stem from our efforts to cope with the uncertainty that is ever present.

I also take issue with the orthodox application of maximization models indiscriminately to all entities, be they individuals, firms, industries, or the

---

9. See, for example, Feldman and Kirman 1974; Hamermesh 1975; Akerlof 1980; Frank 1984; Jones 1984.

10. Buchanan 1979, 39–63.

economy as a whole. Only individuals make decisions. Even with microfoundations, these macromodels rarely if ever make explicit the process by which individual decision making translates into group action. Accordingly, maximization in macroeconomic models lacks the methodological justification it has as the model of the logic of individual choice.

The individual is the basic unit of analysis in this study, and to understand an individual's action is to understand the judgment that led to this action. My discussions of social outcomes tend to be limited to areas in which they can be shown to emerge as the consequence of individual actions and interactions.

Some critics of neoclassical theory have urged us to examine the facts—especially those that traditional economics has so generally ignored. But facts do not speak for themselves.[11] Study must be guided by theory.

Other critics have emphasized the importance of habits, routines, and institutions, as well as decision making under uncertainty, as the basis for an alternative theory. But despite good intuitions, they have not advanced much beyond criticism or *ad hoc* explanations, partly because of their failure to pinpoint the source of the problems in neoclassical economics and partly because of the inherent difficulty in moving ahead after this identification has been made.

The contributions of the book in your hands are twofold. First, it provides a critical evaluation of neoclassical economics with a perspective that sorts out conflicting claims and identifies decision making under uncertainty a key area of mainstream analytical disregard. Second, by moving this condition of decision making in the face of uncertainty from the periphery to the center, I construct an alternative theoretical framework to underpin such important and also neglected aspects of human behavior as imitation, relative comparisons, routines, conventions, social institutions, and entrepreneurship.

Rationality and maximization are emphatically not the same concept,[12] and, in calling for an alternative framework of economic analysis, I am not resorting to "irrationality." The section on rationality in chapter 1 directly addresses this possible misunderstanding and endeavors to bury it in short order.

Of the many other frameworks advanced to address such problem areas in traditional analysis as "X-efficiency," mistakes, and regrets, it would appear that none is fully satisfactory for the purpose at hand. Surely, there is value and inspiration to be found in such concepts as Leibenstein's "inert

---

11. As a prominent judge once said, "What is a fact?" I state it baldly and boldly: "there is no such thing!"

12. Binmore 1987, 181.

area," Simon's "bounded rationality," Schelling's "multiple self," Heiner's "rule-governed behavior," and Kirzner's "selective attention."[13] But after examining these innovations, I end up improvising an approach that is unique in its ability to explore patterns of behavior as implications of individual decision making and avoids both the futile attempt to offer a specific model and the unnecessary philosophical step of nihilism.

Here is a summary of the basic argument. Economics concerns choices—decisions made in the face of uncertainty. This situation is *fact*. But careful consideration of "uncertainty" suggests that a general theory of decision making, whether normative or positive, may be beyond our reach. Rather than counsel despair, however, this insight may prompt us to ask what kind of behavior people exhibit when faced with uncertainty, and a systematic exploration of this question can provide a basis for a theory of behavior under such conditions.

How are we to inquire into the types of behavior people tend to exhibit? Here, my only recourse is to our native ability to reason. I neither take for granted the prevalent notion of the rationality of *Homo economicus* nor resort to irrationality as an explanation for observed anomalies. Instead, I base the study of behavior on the way in which the rational (or reasoning) mind should work in the face of uncertainty. The parallels between what I call the "reasoning process" and the descriptive cognitive propensities studied by psychologists are close.[14] The facts with which I deal, however, are more primitive, bordering, as they do, on the structural description of the judgmental process.

Individual judgment may be divided into *perception* (in the sense of intuitive cognition or discernment or understanding) of the given situation and *logical choice* within the perception. Traditional economic theory has worked out the implications of the latter component, but this "logic of choice" alone is insufficient to describe human behavior. We can and must also understand how the way in which perceptions and the very process of acquiring them influence our actions. Believing that the logic of choice is sufficient to understand human behavior is like believing that a dog is wagged by its tail.

But what can we say about human perception in general? Here, I sharply disagree with such economists as Israel Kirzner[15] and George Shackle,[16] who appreciate the place of perception in decision making but pronounce any effort to comprehend it untenable. In my view, the "logic of perception" is not

---

13. See Leibenstein 1976; Kirzner 1979; Schelling 1982; Simon 1982; Heiner 1983a.

14. As examples of cognitive propensities I have in mind such behavior as the habit of attributing causal relationships to phenomena. See Nisbett and Ross 1980; Markus and Zajonc 1985.

15. See Kirzner 1979.

16. See Shackle 1972.

impossible. Indeed, I base my theory on human perception as a precondition for rational choice and action.

The act of perception can be viewed as an exercise of our faculty of reason, loosely defined as our ability to compare different objects and to imagine something as something else. From this perspective, human perception amounts to identifying a situation to whose totality we lack direct access as a particular instance of some broader and better understood phenomenon. It thus consists of *modeling* the situation with enough confidence to support action.

To underscore our ability to learn from experiences, I shall refer to such a model as a *paradigm*.[17] Although Thomas Kuhn developed the term for scientists and I use it for human beings in general, the concepts are analogous: science is but one example of the human mind at work. The crucial differences between Kuhn and Popper regarding the development of scientific knowledge, for example, commensurability, are largely irrelevant here, where people are essentially practical and their criteria for judging paradigms are less their "truth" than their usefulness.

The "first fact" in my theory is that every human action presupposes an associated paradigm; its identification is the crux of decision making under uncertainty. A direct corollary, and "second fact," is that individuals will continue searching for a paradigm until they find one. Corresponding roughly to the statics and dynamics of perception and judgment, these two facts are the bases of my theory. The paradigmatic approach to decision making under uncertainty then becomes not only simple but also consistent (with this given of incomplete information) and fruitful in its implications for behavior.

There are also two strategies for exploring the logical behavioral consequences of adopting a paradigm. First, we can examine the logical implications of its general properties. Having identified paradigms with sufficient confidence to support action, individuals tend to be committed to what then amount to worldviews and their implied behaviors. Individual action is thus likely to be characterized by routines, habits, and certain inflexibilities. Changes, when they come, are likely to be discontinuous rather than smooth adjustments to disturbances. The model enables and even encourages us to inquire into such issues as selectivity of attention, the possibility of systematic

---

17. See Kuhn 1970; Popper 1972; Margolis 1987. My own chap. 2 contains an extensive discussion of these points, including the philosophical justification of the concept of paradigm. Neoclassical economists, of course, have their own paradigm, maximization, that they justify as an "as if" proposition, arguing thusly: this central assumption need not describe any one individual's behavior as long as it predicts social and economic outcomes better than any other working hypothesis. The winning track record they then trot out is really testimony to an uninspiring field of competition, and I hope my theory will soon enter the race.

error, and indeterminacy. It also leads us to expect certain results, for example, the possibility of human error or the existence of unexploited opportunities.[18] Second, we can explore the implications of paradigm seeking as we increase the complexity of our model from the simplest case of one individual acting in isolation to the most complicated case of several individuals interacting fully in society. This strategy leads to an understanding of various behavioral patterns, such as imitative behavior, interpersonal comparison making, and approval seeking in group situations. And it provides an explanation not only for *why* much behavior is governed by rules and norms, but also for *how* these guides to action are generated in the first place. Not the least of its virtues is that it allows us to understand envy as a reaction to disturbances in social relationships defined by social conventions.

People need paradigms to manage their lives; if they lack examples of viable practice, they will try to find them themselves, through experimentation or the more likely technique of trial and error. As we work through successively more complicated models by moving from the study of individuals in total isolation to cases of individuals in homogeneous, then heterogeneous, groups with minimal degrees of interaction, possibilities for vicarious experimentation, imitation, and interpersonal comparison also emerge as implications of this perpetual seeking of paradigms.

Indeed, on the social level, the interaction of paradigm-seeking individuals tends to generate regimes of conventions that govern and guide behavior. Social analogues to individual paradigms, conventions emerge largely as the unintended outcome of individual efforts to deal with uncertainty.

The tendency for conventions, like individual paradigms, to be stable implies that they are also likely to become suboptimal over time, even if they started out as "optimal" solutions. Their very stability sows the seeds of their own destruction, the culmination of which is a crisis. Therefore, the paradigmatic approach can provide a useful basis for the analysis of social change. It identifies unexploited potential (room for improvement) as an endogenous source of socioeconomic change. Social change does not come by itself. Even strong exogenous shocks may not be sufficient to precipitate a crisis, and the ability to overcome them is far from inevitable and certainly not automatic.

Applications of this model yield unconventional implications and interpretations. Status, for example, emerges as a matter less of taste than of practical significance, conferred on those whose practices set helpful precedents. Individuals seeking to identify a paradigm tend to emulate those with higher status or proven examples. Often, the competition for status results in

---

18. For further discussion of this basis for mistake making, see Hayek 1945; Kirzner 1979; and chap. 2.

using up considerable social resources without making anyone relatively better off. But can we call this "wasteful," as many social critics claim? I believe a more guarded judgment is called for.

Since the starting point of my theory is the durable interaction within groups where human relationships are multidimensional, the paradigmatic approach supports an analysis of market processes that is based on social institutions. Given their inertia, exploitable opportunities always exist, but they tend to be noticed and exploited by those with "unconventional" points of view—in other words, by entrepreneurs. That a conflict exists between the fundamental social tendency to try to preserve old ways and these convention breakers who want to try something new helps explain why entrepreneurial activities not only are the driving force of market activities and society as a whole but are also resented, envied, and ostracized by the society they disrupt and rejuvenate. The significance of property rights in the market process, that is, in the process of the entrepreneurial discovery of unexploited opportunities, then derives quite clearly from the power they convey to surmount the envy barrier to innovation.

The plan of the book is as follows. In chapter 1, I examine the concepts of decision making under uncertainty and economic rationality. I place them in literary context preparatory to proposing and justifying the "Paradigmatic Approach" to these matters in chapter 2. In chapter 3, I redefine decision making under uncertainty and then explore implications of the paradigmatic approach for the behavior of individuals in various contexts. These culminate in complexity in chapter 4 with a discussion of society as a system of interdependencies. In chapter 5, I then explore the implications of a regime of convention for both individual behavior and social tendencies. I provide a variety of applications and extensions of the theory in chapters 6 and 7 and summarize the basic arguments and suggest future research in the Conclusion.

CHAPTER 1

# Decision Making under Uncertainty and the Concept of Rationality

We are all doing it; very few of us understand what we are doing.
—Goethe

Life is not exactly "fair" to us: it requires us to make continuous decisions, holding us responsible for the consequences but denying us access to perfect information. Once we acknowledge the certainty of having to make decisions in the face of uncertainty, then the surprises and regrets, entrepreneurial opportunities and business failures we experience as regular personal or social events should cease to be surprising. Arming economic theory by incorporating the centrality of uncertainty in the decision-making process can enable us to understand even such phenomena as rueful or mistaken behavior that must otherwise be dismissed as "irrational" or "aberrational." The purpose of this chapter is to substantiate these assertions.

## Decision Making and Uncertainty

A brief foray into etymology may serve to clarify the extent to which decision making and uncertainty are inextricably linked. According to *Webster's New Collegiate Dictionary*, an *uncertain* state is indeterminate, problematic, dubious and doubtful; the English *certain* derives from the Latin *certus*, the past participle of *cernere*, which means "to sift, discern or decide."[1] This close connection in word origins supports the intuitive understanding that uncertainty is a state that requires decision making. It also means that decision making itself would be trivial without the uncertainty that makes choice a matter of deliberation. If information were perfect, the "logic of choice" would be the only construct necessary, and decision making would be a superfluous distinction.

---

1. *Webster's New Collegiate Dictionary* 1976, 1272.

## Risk versus Uncertainty

Frank Knight's distinction between risk and uncertainty can further our understanding of the concept.[2] In his parlance, the probable outcomes of a "risky" situation can be estimated, so that its actuarial value can be calculated and insurance is possible. An "uncertain" situation is unique or strategic. The possible outcomes and their probabilities cannot be estimated reliably. From the point of view of an individual decision maker, a circumstance can be classified as "risky" if it belongs to a very large sample or can be repeated and duplicated; it is "uncertain" if the relevant population is small and repetition is thus out of the question. Insurance is possible in the first, but not in the second, instance.

Consider the following. Although any specific outcome of the tossing of an unbiased coin is unknown before the toss, the mathematical expectation of heads is one-half: when the coin is tossed an infinity of times, it is likely that heads will show up 50 percent of the time. Although we, as individuals, do not know exactly how often or how seriously we shall be involved in automobile accidents, the relevant statistics for the population as a whole are readily available, enabling insurers to assign probabilities to different types of drivers and offer insurance at different rates. These situations are, thus, special cases of "risk" in general. Outcomes are less than perfectly certain, but probabilities are possible and individual risks can be reduced through pooling and insurance. All sorts of bets, lotteries, and insurance, in fact, belong to this category.

When a situation is genuinely uncertain, however, it is in some sense unique or strategic. One can hardly estimate mathematical expectations when the whole population of like events consists of very few data—or perhaps only one datum. Because there is no insurance against the failure of entire enterprises, entrepreneurs face uncertainty, and many (I shall argue most) of the situations that require decision making fall in this category.

Uncertainty can be reduced but not eliminated. We can go to the library and seek textbooks and data bases to reduce our ignorance when its origin is a void in our knowledge in engineering. Sometimes we can run a variety of experiments to gain insight into possible outcomes (provided experimentation itself has only a negligible effect on the conditions of decision making). Other times we can reduce uncertainty by efforts to control its source. For example, vertical integration often has as its *raison d'être* increased security of supply

---

2. See Knight 1921. This distinction has fallen into desuetude in modern economics, where uncertainty is often used to describe Knightian risk, sometimes at the cost of obfuscation. I shall resurrect it in this study.

or quality assurance. No amount of effort will suffice, however, to eliminate uncertainty.

## Sources of Uncertainty

The sources of uncertainty are fourfold. The coping mechanisms for each may be different, as discussed below.

*The relative complexity of calculation is one source of uncertainty.* Even situations that are, in principle, knowable in full may be perceived as uncertain by a decision maker whose abilities to calculate and to reason are not up to the task.[3] It is frequently impossible to be even aware of *all* possible outcomes at any given moment.

*Unpredictability of the future is a second source of uncertainty.* The determination of future events depends not only upon our actions but upon factors that are beyond our knowledge and control, and we have no guarantee that regularities observed in the past will hold in the future. Consider, for example, the problem of deciding whether or not to purchase a certain stock on a certain day. Its price "should" depend upon the value of its future income stream as discounted by the pertinent interest rates. The perfect knowledge of this stream and these interest rates is sadly beyond our reach as rational investors.

The future identity (preference structure, if you will) of the very person who makes the decisions is also obscure. We transform ourselves through work and experience, modifying our perceptions and changing our preferences and aspirations as we go. Earlier and later selves may thus not be the same, at least as they are reflected in behavior, and we cannot know the manner in which and rate at which our awareness will change.

The following Chinese fable of an old man in a fortress captures this wisdom nicely. An old man went out to the field and found a horse. He drove the horse to his home, where his son enjoyed riding it, and the old man said to himself, "Lucky me!" But one day the son fell from the horse and became lame, and the old man cried, "The horse has brought me a great misfortune!" Soon war broke out with the barbarians. Young men were drafted and went to war, whence many never returned, but the old man's son was exempted from

---

3. With the able analogy of a computer, Margolis describes the disparity between our calculating abilities and those demanded by the complexity of the environment.

In the case of human beings, the most obvious of the physical constraints requires that everything our brain does for us must be handled by an object small enough to fit inside the top of a human head. Within that constraint, we could not expect even approximately unlimited memory, or unlimited computational capability, or unlimited capability for handling input or output flows. (Margolis 1987, 26)

his duty because of his handicap. "After all," the old man thought, "the horse has been a good fortune."

*The interdependence of human actions is a third source of uncertainty.* Most social production is carried out by joint effort, and its worth is often difficult to ascertain. Consider, for example, the problem of evaluating the value of group input. Even if we assume, as is customary in the neoclassical theory of the firm, that the value of output is known, assigning the exact proportion that individual group members have contributed to it is still difficult, if not impossible. Furthermore, even if there were an exact relationship between contribution and remuneration *within* a firm, individual value would remain uncertain because of its dependence on whether the labor occurred within a high- or low-value producing team. (Janitors in General Motors factories may draw vastly higher wages than those doing essentially the same tasks in sweatshops.) Alfred Marshall coined the term *opportunity value* to designate the value of a team environment,[4] which becomes another element of uncertainty for individuals. To increase their value, should they work harder or find another production team?

Remuneration depends not only upon monetary wages and fringe benefits but also upon the value of the opportunities that any given job offers, and these are far from clear. But even if we knew exactly what we were getting in advance, the relationship between contribution and remuneration would remain unclear because of uncertainty about what we have given up in the process. Moreover, workers are capable of a wide range of exertions; this discretionary element of labor distinguishes people from machines and has been widely observed in all types of industrial studies.[5] In dealing with others, we are never sure whether or not they are doing their best and of how much more or less they are capable. No amount of effort, however sizeable, will eliminate this discretionary element from contract. Complete contract specification is impossible, even in principle, even under the system of slavery or servitude. And although managers can (in theory) monitor workers' actions completely within a firm, such oversight is often impractical. Labor relationships themselves rely on "implicit contracts" of willing cooperation, and the undesirable consequences of everyone "playing by the book" can be devastating.[6]

The binding rules of the economic game are uncertain because these rules are often implicit. Even if there were some codification upon which everyone could agree, we could still never guarantee against alteration, simple

---

4. Marshall 1961, 625.
5. See Shih 1944 as quoted in Mayo 1945; also Jones 1984.
6. See Akerlof 1982 and 1984; Leibenstein 1982b. "Working to rule" can often bring management to its knees more effectively than striking.

nonobservance, or even subversion. By definition, rules cannot be specific enough for every possible case. There is always room for interpretation. Genuine differences in interpretation and the willful distortion of rules to promote individual interests are, therefore, always possible and often very difficult to differentiate.[7] Scarcity and invidious comparisons make these problems of distribution decidedly nontrivial.

*The very nature of mental processes creates a fourth source of uncertainty.* We are not omniscient. Rather, we are endowed with certain mental faculties with which we must "make do," trying to uncover reality through the "cloud of unknowing."

Our problem thus becomes one of *inference.* Whatever the world is or is not, we can act only according to our understanding of it. I shall argue that *many* different worldviews are conceivable, depending upon our needs, desires, and experiences. We must somehow filter these diverse stimuli to construct our own global perspective and an understanding of the situation at hand.

To highlight the complexity of this problem, consider a relatively simple example. A tree has thousands and thousands of leaves in the summer. When we choose to see the tree "in its entirety," we observe no leaves in their particularity and fail to notice the insects that infest or inhabit some of them. If we focus, instead, on a single insect on a single leaf, the tree itself has now largely escaped our field of vision. If we hone in on one of the eyes of the insect, the leaf and the insect fall out of sight. This tree may also represent many different possibilities for artists, carpenters, and tired travelers. Its images can change even for one individual over time, and any attempt to rank their verity is absurd.[8]

Sometimes we speak as if uncertainty can arise only from too little information, but its source can also be too much. We cannot see all things at all times; we must *choose* and *create* images, else we are bound to be baffled.[9] The necessity of this sort of image selection, or rather image creation, is fundamental to the uncertainty that underlies the problem of decision making. It is therefore difficult even to imagine how uncertainty could be reduced by any optimal search rule, because searches themselves require the prior development of a viewpoint, whose validity is not warranted.

In rendering judgments, our method of inference is, more often than not,

---

7. See Kuran 1991a, 250–55, for a discussion of these two possibilities under the rubric of "creative" and "self-serving" interpretation.

8. See Shel Silverstein's children's story, *The Giving Tree,* for a poignant change of arboreal perspective as a child grows into a man.

9. If we *were* alert to all happenings, the "buzz of events," in philosopher William James's memorable parlance, would drive us mad. Note, in contrast, literary brother Henry's ambition to be one "on whom nothing was lost."

*post hoc ergo propter hoc*. In this confusion of correlation with causation, we are sometimes fortunate in our judgments, but sometimes we are not. Sometimes we try to revise our judgments based on experience and critical evaluations before we suffer the consequences of mistaken views. Sometimes we make these revisions after we experience some unpleasant consequences. All we can do is try. Insofar as causality is what the mind imposes on sensory data, uncertainty is always inherently present.

Of course, there are limits to the "fantasies" that can be sustained because the implications of those views, when carried out in action, come up against external realities. But as long as daily living proceeds more or less satisfactorily, there is little incentive to shake its very foundations for the sake of "truth." Laypersons, unlike scientists, are concerned less with the "objective truth" of their beliefs than with their practicality. Ordinary people act on the belief that they have grasped "reality" even though this is probably just a worldview they themselves have created while coping with their environment in all its physical, social, and cultural dimensions.

**Maximization**

The core of traditional theory is the paradigm of constrained maximization, whereby the agent selects, from the available alternatives, a course of action designed to yield the highest level of satisfaction. But when uncertainty is so pervasive, how helpful is neoclassical economics in understanding human actions as they reflect the problems of decision making?

The mathematical tool of maximization has many undeniably useful applications. Without mathematical programming, for example, it would be difficult to make the vast number of calculations required in underwriting municipal bonds. The principle of maximization is quite helpful in a deterministic, or semideterministic, environment, where the possession of perfect, or quasi-perfect, information can be taken for granted, objective functions are well defined, and alternatives and their expected values are known in full.

These conditions are not met when agents face genuine uncertainty, however. Then, as Frank Knight has observed, the real difficulty for decision makers involves formulating the problem to be solved.

> With uncertainty present, doing things, the actual execution of activity, becomes in a real sense a secondary part of life; the primary problem or function is deciding what to do and how to do it.[10]

Maximizing an incorrectly formulated problem can yield a solution that is very bad indeed. What the maximization paradigm really offers is either a

---

10. Knight 1921, 267.

## Decision Making under Uncertainty and the Concept of Rationality

hypothesis about the market outcomes on a social level, or "the logic of choice" on an individual level.[11] In neither case is it a model of decision making under uncertainty.

On the first level, as an empirical proposition, maximization is commonly applied to all sorts of entities—individuals, businesses, industries, and societies as a whole. This indiscriminate use is commonly justified by appeals to the "as if" propositions of no less an authority than Milton Friedman.[12] He argues that it does not matter how each and every individual, as an individual, makes decisions. That the hypothesis of maximization parsimoniously generates predictions that can be empirically verified, or at least not falsified, alone is important. But in this case, maximization is not meant to be a model of decision making. Only individuals make decisions, not aggregate entities, such as industries or economies. Maximization as an empirical proposition, therefore, is on a different level of logical abstraction than that of maximization as a model of individual decision making.

On the second level, that of individual decision making (which is the main interest of this book), maximization can be viewed as an idealization of the logic of choice.[13] Here, individuals motivated to become as happy or satisfied as possible make their choices in such a way that no other choice can yield a better result—*given* their assessment of preferences, resource availability, and information. But impounded in these givens are precisely the issues to be settled in decision making under uncertainty. Deciding upon the essential nature of a situation is the crucial step that must be taken before the logic of choice can be applied. This second step has its own form of rigor and use, but it cannot be a vehicle for investigating the decision-making process as a whole. To insist otherwise is to ignore the issue of how the decision maker forms beliefs and expectations and how his or her decisions are influenced by the process of obtaining the beliefs.[14]

### Expected Utility Maximization

As if reacting to this sort of criticism, neoclassical economists have recently begun to model the problem of decision making under uncertainty. Agents are now assumed to maximize *expected* utility, and this approach appears to be more realistic than the previous models of perfect information. Contrary to appearance, however, the expected utility maximization approach does not

---

11. Boland (1981, 1034–36) argues that maximization in economics is a metaphysical statement subject to neither logical nor empirical criticism.
12. Friedman 1953. Earlier, Alchian 1950 and Schumpeter 1934 also offered "as if" explanations.
13. Buchanan 1979, 39–63.
14. See Binmore 1987 and 1988.

qualify as a model of decision making in the face of uncertainty in the sense we discuss it here. At least three factors back up this assertion.

First, the model deals not with uncertainty in the Knightian sense we have elected to follow, but rather with risk. John Hey describes the approach as follows.

> *We assume that the individual* whose decision making we are studying perceives the lack of certainty as a situation of risk. That is, a situation in which the individual *can list all the possible states of the world . . . and can attach probabilities . . . to these various states of the world.*[15]

Second, this framework rests on such stipulations as "ordering of outcomes," "transitivity," "substitutability," and "applicability of probability rules" that have been shown to be counterfactual. For example, consider the seemingly innocuous assumption of transitivity. This assumption states that people are consistent in their behavior: If they prefer A to B and B to C, then they must also prefer A to C. Recent research on preference reversals suggests that this condition often does not hold. According to Paul Slovic and Sarah Lichtenstein, because choice depends strongly on the way information is presented, preference reversals can be created at will by appropriate framing devices.[16] As an example, consider two problems.

> *Problem One.* Imagine that you are given $200. If you are then given the choice between (A) a sure gain of $50 and (B) a 25 percent chance of winning $200 and a 75 percent chance of winning nothing, which one would you prefer?

> *Problem Two.* Imagine that you are given $400. If you are then given choice between (C) a sure loss of $150 and (D) a 75 percent chance of losing $200 and 25 percent chance of losing nothing, which one would you prefer?

Kahneman and Tversky found that most people chose A over B, *and* D over C. This, even though A and C, and B and D are identical in their outcomes. People appear to reverse their preferences in dealing with the two problems.[17]

Perhaps an even more fundamental objection to the expected utility theorem comes from Kahneman and Tversky, whose experiments disclose violations of the invariance of lottery space, the principle of stochastic dominance,

---

15. Hey 1979, 11; italics added.
16. Slovic and Lichtenstein 1983; see also Tverksy and Kahneman 1979.
17. Slovic and Lichtenstein 1983, 601–2.

and such basic rules of probability as those involving principles of conjunction.[18] According to Hey,

> [I]f economic theory is intended to provide a description of economic behavior . . . it is of little use to employ expected utility maximization in economic theory if economic agents do not obey the axioms of von Neumann–Morgenstern utility.[19]

Finally, the expected utility maximization approach complicates economic analysis without materially improving it. It still assumes away the question of how the decision maker arrives at the expectation based on what he or she maximizes.[20] The mathematical techniques are much more difficult, but the results are not materially different from those of traditional neoclassical theory.[21]

And because this model still fails to deal with genuine uncertainty, some rather commonplace phenomena still escape its purview. These problem areas can either be incorporated through further modifications of the model or dismissed as "irrational" or irretrievably intractable. I shall consider the second approach in the following section.

## The Neoclassical Notion of Rationality

Economists take great, perhaps even overweening, pride in their rationalistic tradition. According to Kenneth Arrow,

> An economist by training thinks of himself as the guardian of rationality, the ascriber of rationality to others, and the prescriber of rationality to the social world.[22]

But the meaning of "rationality" can often be obscured by the variety of possible interpretations. An individual's action may be quite rational from that individual's point of view, but not so rational at all from a social point of

---

18. Kahneman and Tversky 1984.
19. Hey 1979, 44.
20. Binmore 1987, 211.
21. Hey 1979, 118–19.
22. Arrow 1974b, 16. Gary Becker is Arrow's kind of economist, at least in this sense: he has described himself as one with perhaps "an irrational passion for dispassionate rationality." I thank Adele Wick for sharing Becker's oral remarks at a luncheon seminar at Tulane University in 1986. James Buchanan observes that he heard Frank Knight using the expression, "an irrational passion for dispassionate rationality," attributing it to John Bates Clark.

view.[23] Actions that appear rational when considered singly by separate individuals may result in outcomes that not one of them will find desirable.[24]

All definitions of rationality, however, do appear to share a sense of congruence between ends and means.[25] In its assumptions concerning human nature, propensities, and values, the rationality criterion basically judges actions in terms of their *consistency* with objectives, whatever they may be.

Many neoclassical economists assert that rational behavior is that which is consistent with the image of selfish and calculating economic agents. Rational individuals must pick the cheaper of two otherwise identical economic goods. Essentially indifferent to the circumstances of others, they derive satisfaction solely from their own consumption and possession. Demonstrable instances of altruism do not exactly refute "selfishness," because helping others can be a cost-effective way of promoting our own welfare.[26]

This relentless pursuit of selfish gain is the vehicle that leads to an economy where all opportunities are exploited in full. Perhaps neoclassical economists have held this assumption in order to support their basic tenet of the optimality of competitive equilibrium.[27] But is the traditional concept of *Homo economicus* useful in understanding social tendencies as well as individual behavior?

Kenneth Arrow has distinguished between the concepts of "weak" and "strong" rationality in neoclassical economics. In his view, the weak version applies to the "static world of certainty" and is "not easily refuted and therefore not very useful as an explanation, though not literally a tautology."[28] The strong version, on the other hand, applies "to a world in which time and uncertainty are real." Although it was designed to offer "explanations of empirically observed behavior . . . an important class of intertemporal markets shows systematic deviations from individual rational behavior."[29] As corroboration, Arrow cites case studies indicating that people do not always take advantage of obvious gains. For example, when the U.S. government was willing to provide flood insurance at rates well below their actuarial value, very few took advantage of the offer, despite the readily available information about its benefits. "The high costs of information" will not suffice

---

23. See Elster 1983b.
24. See Schelling 1978.
25. See Garelick 1971; Arrow 1974b and c; Sen 1977.
26. Frank 1989.
27. See Takayama 1974, 170. Do note that many economists seem to have become more and more dissatisfied with the utility maximization approach not so much because they find it inherently unreasonable as because their growing concern for externalities makes competitive outcomes increasingly appear to be suboptimal.
28. Arrow 1974, 1.
29. Arrow 1974, 3–4.

to rescue the expected utility maximization model from this predictive failure. Nor can it explain why outside speculators continue to enter the grain futures market when, according to Stewart's 1949 study, they consistently lose on average.[30]

The neoclassical concept of rationality, or consistency, is problematic since it tends to sweep under the carpet the question of how a decision maker arrives at his or her belief in the uncertain situations he or she faces on a daily basis. And however much rational explanations lean on the self-serving aspects of altruism and the high costs of information and enforcement, such phenomena as interdependent utility and X-efficiency disturb the traditional notions of selfishness and profit maximization or cost minimization. The more common such troublesome observations become, the less applicable and less relevant is the concept of rationality.

Efforts to modify rather than abandon "rationality" within the neoclassical framework of maximization may appear to rescue or redefine what previously presented itself as "irrational" behavior, but often at the cost of rendering the concept of *Homo economicus* inherently nonempirical. The point can readily be brought home by examining the structure of the neoclassical proposition, "If $M$, $U$, and $C$, then $P$," where $M$ is maximization, $U$ is preference, $C$ stands for constraints, and $P$ for proposition. Because neither $U$ nor $C$ is given explicit content at the outset, whenever not-$P$, is observed, economists can maintain the validity of $M$ by assuming $U'$ (quirky tastes) or $C'$ (oddities in information, transaction costs, or the extent of property rights). With these sorts of rescues possible, $M$ can be considered consistent with any observation whatsoever.[31] Any propositions involving the construct of *Homo economicus*, the personification of the maximization principle, by ceasing to be refutable, then cease to be empirical as well. They can still be the source of magnificent "finger exercises" that demonstrate splendid mastery of complicated techniques,[32] but they no longer provide a legitimate interpretation of the maximization hypothesis.[33]

---

30. Arrow Arrow 1974, 2.

31. At an economics seminar in 1983 at the University of Michigan, I remarked that neoclassical economics finds it difficult to explain such common experiences as mistakes, inefficiencies, uneven development, success and failure, and changing fortunes. A senior professor immediately and emotionally retorted that there was nothing neoclassical economics could not explain. This same professor later commented, "If a theory can explain everything, and anything, it is not a theory, but a tautology." I am in full agreement with the second observation.

32. With a candor as great as his jocularity, the late Ronald Teigen once remarked in my presence: "Economics is but a game, a game of building small machines, i.e., models, and cranking them again and again, hoping you get some publishable results. It is an illusion to think that one will understand the world by studying economics."

33. See Buchanan 1979.

Writing in the 1930s, at the depth of the Great Depression, William H. Hutt observed that "to admit to defending economic orthodoxy is to risk driving away readers with different opinions."[34] After asserting that one of economics's most important puzzles concerns why the public fails to accept the wisdom inherent in its doctrine, he offered his own understanding of the conundrum: Lay persons remain under the sway of the "nonrational thoughts," namely, "custom-thought" and "power-thought."[35]

Describing the public as nonrational is surely a strange response from an economist whose orthodox doctrine is premised on human rationality. Perhaps Hutt reasoned as follows. Neoclassical economics proposes policy based on both the assumption that people are rational and the doctrine that the economic system is efficient. But its wisdom is ignored by the public, who must therefore be irrational. Is he not in this way deeming agents irrational as judged by the very standard of rationality attributed to them in the first place? But what then becomes of the assumption of rationality and the ensuing policy recommendations?

Leibenstein argues that "if there is no general erosion of confidence in conventional microeconomics, there ought to be."[36] A more satisfactory course is to broaden the concept of rationality, as I propose to do in the remainder of this book. But first I will survey what other critics of neoclassical economics, namely Harvey Leibenstein, Israel Kirzner, Thomas Schelling, Ronald Heiner, and Herbert Simon, have offered by way of explaining the various problem areas of neoclassical economics.

### Alternative Views of Rationality

Harvey Leibenstein offers an explanation for X-inefficiency by proposing the concept of an "inert area" and a spectrum of rationality whose operational range is determined by competitive pressure.[37] Asserting that when this pressure is below a certain level, people will *knowingly* pass up better opportunities, he finds support in the observed persistence of habitual smokers despite their knowledge of the profound health hazards associated therewith. Examples that motivated formulating the concept of X-efficiency itself came from studies of productivity that disclosed the failure of some managers in the United States and less developed countries to minimize costs even when they had been clearly shown methods of improving productivity.

---

34. Hutt 1936, 39.
35. Even today, economists are often baffled by the lack of acceptance of their theories and policy suggestions.
36. Leibenstein 1976.
37. Leibenstein 1966 and 1976.

But the existence of a spectrum of rationality seems to imply a natural aversion to mental exertion. If so, simply adding the "cost of thinking" to the other factors considered within the neoclassical paradigm of maximization would make the model of "inert areas" fully compatible with traditional analysis. Interpreted thus, the concept of an "inert area" fails to establish a true alternative to the neoclassical assumption. But the problem of X-efficiency to which it has posited a solution still remains.

Nobel laureate George Stigler articulates the neoclassical viewpoint in his criticism of Leibenstein. "Waste is error within the framework of modern economic analysis, and it will not become a useful concept until we have a theory of error."[38] Until then, error or waste amounts to irrationality within mainstream economics, where the assumption is made, if only implicitly, that economic agents do not err. For example, the search theory that has gained popularity among economists is firmly grounded in the neoclassical approach of optimization.[39] This search theory, or the economics of information, could also be called a theory of the "optimal degree of ignorance." Its logical implication is that real mistakes, surprises, or unexploited opportunities are impossible.[40] We know differently, and so do entrepreneurs.

Israel Kirzner also objects to mainstream economics for excluding the possibility of error. Both the possibility of *learning* and the *tendency* toward equilibrium have been eliminated by models that assume exogeneity of ends and means and begin their analysis in states of market equilibrium.[41]

For Kirzner, human action is always rational in the sense that it is intended to achieve definite goals. Human beings act purposefully. They are rational *ex ante*, but can err *ex post*. As Kirzner's teacher, Ludwig von Mises, has argued,

> Error, inefficiency, and failure must not be confused with irrationality. He who shoots wants, as a rule, to hit the mark. If he misses, he is not "irrational"; he is a poor marksman.[42]

---

38. Stigler 1976, 216.
39. See Stigler 1961.
40. Indeed, this is precisely like Socrates' account of Menon's paradox of learning. "You look on this as a piece of chop-logic . . . as if a man cannot try to find either what he knows or what he does not know. Of course he would never try to find what he knows, because he knows it, and in that case he needs no trying to find; or what he does not know, because he does not know what he will try to find" (Plato 1956, 41). As Socrates points out, the possibility of learning can resolve this paradox, which exists solely when one considers only what is.
41. Kirzner 1979, 22-27.
42. Ludwig von Mises, quoted in Kirzner 1979, 121.

According to the Kirzner, the existence of uncertainty is central not only to the distinction between mistake making and irrationality, but also to a true understanding of market processes.[43] Indeed, the Austrian conception of error is imbued with a sense of knowledge as a process of selective and limited awareness. As Kirzner observes that,

> where ignorance consists not in lack of available information but in inexplicably failing to see facts staring one in the face, it represents genuine error and genuine inefficiency. . . . [T]he initial imperfection in knowledge is [thus] to be attributed not to lack of some needed resource, but to failure to notice opportunities ready at hand.[44]

Why would we fail to take advantage of "opportunities ready at hand"? Kirzner responds that our focus is not always a conscious decision.

> Alertness . . . appears to possess a primordial role in decision making that makes it unhelpful to treat it in the analysis of decisions, like any other resource.[45]

In other words, if some datum falls, *inexplicably*, outside our purview, perforce we ignore it. Believing in the inherent unpredictability of "inner biography" and its changes, Kirzner stops at this stage. We will continue, however.

While Leibenstein explains error as a consequence of inert areas and Kirzner highlights preoccupation with other wants, Thomas Schelling conjectures that seemingly irrational behavior is the outcome of alternating and competing goals and desires.[46] In this framework, people stay in bed on a cold morning, even when they know that they should be "up and at 'em" because they listen to a self that desires a warm bed. The self that is an income earner knows this behavior is "mistaken," but is overruled by the voice of self-indulgence. An error in Kirzner's sense can thus occur in Schelling's world because of preoccupation with other wants: a business manager may fail to take advantage of a profitable opportunity because he or she has been pursuing another interest that has little to do with dollars and cents. But Schelling's mode of explanation is largely unacceptable; Stigler's criticism of Leibenstein seems to be equally applicable here. Much like deferring to differences of taste—*de gustibus non est disputandum*—the notion of competing selves can explain not

---

43. See Hayek 1945.
44. Kirzner 1979, 131-32.
45. Kirzner 1979, 131.
46. Schelling 1984.

only some puzzling behavior, but any sort of behavior whatsoever. As an explanatory device, the approach is thus *ad hoc*.

Turning to Ronald Heiner, we find the perspective that error is possible because people deliberately restrict their flexibility in response to uncertainty, choosing to adhere to predetermined rules that do not necessarily suit each instance perfectly.[47] While Kirzner focuses on behavior that emanates from conscious and explicit decisions, Heiner examines all sorts of actions, not just by human beings but also by animals and micro-organisms. Examining the generalized findings from "signal detection experiments," he asserts that the greater the uncertainty (or, rather, the gap between the complexity of decision problems and our ability to calculate), the stronger is our (and lower beasts') incentive to adhere to rules and thus the more behavior is "rule governed." Given what can be gained and lost by taking a certain action, the reliability of any action that deviates from the rule must approach perfection as the probability of making the correct choice decreases below a certain point. Accordingly,

> . . . an agent's repertoire must be limited to actions which are adopted only to likely or "recurrent" situations. Thus a general characteristic of such a repertoire is that it excludes actions which will in fact enhance performance under certain conditions.[48]

Although his focus is a bit different and the range of his observations assuredly broader, Heiner's efforts to explain our common failure to maximize on a case-by-case basis actually broadens rather than overthrows the maximization approach. His formulation is essentially quite similar to that of Leibenstein and, thus, succumbs to the same form of Stiglerian criticism. We shall have to look to Herbert Simon for an alternative to the neoclassics.

Simon's "satisficing" model is based on the concept of "bounded rationality." He asserts that our ability to calculate falls short of the power demanded by certain complicated problems and that we therefore rely on simplified solution rules that yield "satisfactory" solutions in many instances.[49] The procedure he proposes is to set a satisficing result and then look for a solution that will make that goal or aspiration possible.

It is easy to see how a model like this can generate errors in the sense we have discussed. A satisficing individual would arrive at an optimal solution in

---

47. Heiner 1983a.
48. Heiner 1983a, 567.
49. Simon 1957.

any given situation only by fluke, having ceased the search for anything better upon finding an answer that was "good enough." Indeed, the difference between satisficing and maximizing can be easily clarified by the following mental experiment. Suppose that the solutions under the two models coincide in a given situation. Now change that situation ever so slightly. Maximization will generate a new solution, but satisficing will not.[50] Langlois observes that Simon's satisficing approach can be interpreted as the optimal course of action when computation is costly. Again, this interpretation would make satisficing compatible with maximization.

Simon is, without question, a pioneer in criticizing the neoclassical assumption of maximization as a model of decision making in complicated situations, but his influence has been more in the design of practical solutions than in the study of behavior under uncertainty *per se*. Perhaps this slant reflects his concern for the development of decision rules that can be implemented by businesses or government bureaus in a sort of "science" of management, rather than for the broader science of human behavior as a whole.[51]

My concern, however, is exactly to explore this vast terrain. Chapter 2 advances a theory concerning the manner in which people learn and deal with life. Developing the process of decision making under uncertainty in frontal fashion, it helps us to understand in broader context the heretofore puzzling phenomena confronted by Leibenstein, Kirzner, Heiner, and Simon, and perhaps those of Schelling as well.

---

50. Langlois 1986, 226.
51. Loasby (1989) expresses a view similar to mine.

CHAPTER 2

# A Theory of Decision Making under Uncertainty: The Paradigmatic Approach

By means of the old, we come to know the new.

—Confucius

In chapter 1, I argued that decision making under uncertainty is a fundamental ingredient of human action, and that a general theory of individual behavior and social tendencies must incorporate this essential given. Those who agree on the importance of this issue have reacted either by offering decision-making models that describe and proscribe or by denying the possibility of delving into the nature of this problem. An intermediate step is in the paradigmatic approach I shall develop. I first examine more traditional approaches.

## Models of Decision Making Under Uncertainty

Let us first consider the approach of modeling decision making in the face of uncertainty. Uncertainty is a state of doubt. It describes an indeterminate relationship between us and the environment we face. We are uncertain when we lack a definite idea of the course of action to take in a situation that appears unfamiliar, obscure, conflicting, or generally confusing. The very existence of uncertainty presupposes the need for judgment and decision making that will resolve this state.

The essence of decision making lies in making up our minds about the "reality" of the situation or choosing one representation from the many that compete for this status. That is, the essence of decision making lies in inference, and our efforts here become part of the attempt to model human inference as a whole.

Can we succeed in a general theory of inference? Central to this broader "science" is concern with the logical status of generalization based on known facts or experiences, described by Karl Popper as Hume's (logical) problem of induction. "Are we justified in reasoning from [repeated] instances of which we have experience to other instances [conclusions] of which we have no experience?"[1] The answer is negative: no inference follows by logical necessity. If this view is correct—and I believe it is—then any attempt to formulate a normative theory of inference is doomed to failure. Popper argues that once it has been seen that Hume's problem must be answered negatively, the invalidity of any "principle of induction" becomes perfectly obvious.[2] To the degree that the essence of decision making in the face of uncertainty is inferential and the possibility of a general theory of inference is denied, the aim of modeling decision making in general will remain unfulfilled. I therefore come to the radical conclusion that it is impossible to discover and present a rule of inference as either a prescription for, or a description of, decision making under uncertainty. The very word *uncertainty* stands for the absence of any universally valid rule of inference.

So much for efforts to model decision making under uncertainty! Indeed, the status of expected utility maximization, commonly interpreted as a model of decision making under uncertainty, should be reevaluated from Hume's perspective as well as from mine: it is untenable as well due to the patent illogic of offering a universally valid rule of inference. In neoclassical economics, human beings are assumed to be endowed with the problem-solving algorithm of optimization. But I have already suggested that optimization is only the logic of choice, whose exercise presupposes a perception of the situation we face. The model merely assumes that we have expectations based on which we maximize; it says nothing about how we have formed them.[3] But the essence of decision making, or inference, lies in identifying which rules of action to apply. The *real* problem of decision making is, therefore, that of deciding whether the case at hand warrants the application of maximization principles and probability calculus or some other *modus operandi* instead. For the model of expected utility maximization to be a model of decision making under uncertainty, Bayes's rule must be seen as the rule of inference. But is the Bayesian approach the optimal rule of inference?[4] Along with Karl Popper, I doubt that it, or anything else, can be. Indeed, Ken Binmore argues that the standard contemporary interpretation of the model of expected utility maximization as a prescriptive theory of decision making in the face of uncertainty is naive.[5] He says that Savage's theory of (subjective) expected utility maximization is "entirely and exclusively a *consistent* theory."

---

1. See Popper 1979, 4. Boland (1981, 1032) observes that "everyone knows today [that] there is no inductive logic which could supply a proof whenever the amount of information is finite or it is otherwise incomplete (for example, about the future)."
2. Popper 1979, 28.
3. Binmore 1987, 211.
4. See Edwards 1982, 361.
5. Binmore 1987, 209–12.

It has nothing to say about how decision makers come to have beliefs ascribed to them: it asserts only that, if the decisions taken are consistent . . . then they act *as though* they maximize expected utility relative to a subjective probability distribution.[6]

The naïveté of the contemporary interpretation "lies in supposing that the prior [beliefs] can be chosen from a limited stock of standard distributions without much . . . in the way of soul-searching" (Binmore 1987, 210).

> Naive Bayesians . . . [tell] us *nothing whatever* about how scientific inferences should be made. . . . [The] problem of scientific inference [is swept] under the carpet by absorbing the relevant issues into the *wholly unspecified* adjustment process by means of which primitive snap judgments are massaged into a consistent belief system. Once the problem is under the carpet . . . it can then be conveniently forgotten altogether.[7]

The naive Bayesians create the illusion that the problem of inference is somehow dealt with, when in fact the problem is ignored. Therefore, the view that the model of expected utility maximization is a more realistic than simple maximization in modeling decision making in the face of uncertainty is an erroneous one. As Hume and Popper concluded, I conclude as well: a general theory of inference is not tenable.

Experimental research by several psychologists questions more concretely the behavioral or descriptive truth in the optimality of revising existing probabilities or expectations about the state of nature in specific ways as new experiences provide new data.[8] Actual studies reveal, on the contrary, a systematic deviation of human inference from Bayesian predictions, thereby casting doubt on the probity of the approach.

> The usefulness of the normative Bayesian approach to the analysis and the modeling of subjective probability depends primarily not on the accuracy of the subjective estimates, but rather on whether the model captures the essential determinants of the judgment process. . . . [Perhaps] man . . . is not Bayesian at all.[9]

In their own examination of "judgmental heuristics," or the descriptive patterns of human inference, Kahneman and Tversky have discovered, in-

---

6. Binmore 1987, 209.
7. Binmore 1987, 211.
8. Nisbett and Ross 1980, 144; Binmore 1987.
9. Kahneman and Tversky 1982a, 46.

stead, certain heuristic rules of inference that lead to systematic biases. For example, when people are asked to assess the possibilities of an individual's occupation from a list of possibilities (e.g., farmer, salesman, airline pilot, librarian, or physician) after describing the individual's characteristics (e.g., shy and withdrawn, very helpful but with little interest in people), people tend to assess the possibilities by the degree to which the individual is a representative of the stereotypes of different occupations, ignoring the base rate probabilities of the occupation. This tendency is called the "representativeness" heuristic rule.[10] Consider another example. People often make judgments from a starting point (either suggested by the formulation of the problem or arrived at as a tentative conjecture based on preliminary consideration) that is adjusted to yield the final verdict. But this adjustment is often insufficient, resulting in biases. This tendency is called "anchoring."[11] Other identified heuristic rules include "availability," "causality," and "covariance."[12] These designations remain controversial;[13] even if they are descriptively valid *ex post*, they still provide the decision maker with no guidance about the *ex-ante* choices of which one or ones to apply, in what order.[14] In other words, they fail to address the basic nature of uncertainty itself.

Are these observations counsel for despair? Should we agree with Israel Kirzner that inquiry into the implications of decision making under uncertainty on human action is unviable, that all we can say under these circumstances is that uncertainty leads to selective attention and, therefore, to mistakes and unexploited opportunities?[15] I think not. Our inability to support a general theory of inference does not preclude our ability to discover useful information about individual behavior and social tendencies through a systematic exploration of the formal structure of decision making under uncertainty.

### The Structure of Decision Making Under Uncertainty and Two Concomitant Facts

My starting point in this endeavor is to discuss a purely formal structure of decision making under uncertainty. Every decision, a necessary antecedent to human action, must involve two structural elements: an idea or understanding of a given situation,[16] and, given that understanding, a selection of the most desirable course of action.

---

10. Kahneman and Tversky 1982a, 4–5, 69–98.
11. Kahneman and Tversky 1982a, 14–18.
12. Nisbet et al. 1982; Tversky and Kahneman 1982b; Jennings et al. 1982.
13. Einhorn, for example, calls some heuristics metaheuristics, or "rules on how to generate rules." See Kahneman and Tversky 1982, 271.
14. See H. Vaihinger's view (1965) that thought is more an art than a science.
15. Kirzner 1979.
16. Dewey 1933.

We shall consider the latter, the logic of choice, so admirably, nay exhaustively, studied in standard microeconomic theory, nonproblematic in this study, on the assumption that once an understanding of a given situation exists through the decision-making process, the appropriate course of action becomes rather obvious and noncontroversial. Consider, in this regard, the example of an individual faced with options definitely worth $1.00, $5.00 and $10.00 on net. A wealth maximizer will select the last, and do so with ease. The difficulty inheres instead in estimating the net values or in *understanding* the situation in the first place. And here we shall further assume that individuals never pose problems too difficult to solve: it is the task of the process of understanding itself to simplify in order to manage, and to do otherwise is counterproductive.[17]

Decision making must therefore hinge on the former element in the process: the conceptualization and understanding of situations. From this, then, comes our first fact of decision making under uncertainty. *In order to make decisions, individuals must have an understanding about any given situation, and hold this idea with sufficient confidence to follow the course of action it suggests.*

What, after all, is uncertainty but the absence of such an understanding, so that individuals are faced with unfamiliar and baffling situations of which they can make neither head nor tail? This state must somehow be transformed into one in which a way out is more or less obvious—one in which we have an idea of what to do. Are we *absolutely* certain about our ideas? Not necessarily. But when we act upon an idea, we are *certain enough*, for our precious life is at stake.

In our faculty of reason and imagination, we are fortunately endowed with the means of coping with uncertainty. We can make inquiries, deliberate about the variety of actions possible in any set of circumstances, and find those that are best suited to the particulars.[18] Once discovered, ideas transform states of doubt into those that support action. Indeed our second fact is that, *under uncertainty, individuals seek ideas that enable them to deal with given situations, terminating this search only when such understandings have been obtained.*

Because these two facts provide the basis for much of what follows, their further exploration is surely in order. In the next section, I explore how

---

17. Vaihinger (1965), it is true, argues that philosophers tend to pose for themselves (metaphysical) questions that are too difficult to solve. But I am concerned with laypersons who are primarily concerned with managing their daily affairs. Perhaps I, like Oliver Edwards in Boswell's *Life of Johnson*, am inherently too optimistic to be a philosopher: "somehow, I don't know how, the cheerfulness [keeps] breaking in."

18. People are, after all, said to be "tool-making" animals, and ideas are the most effective of all tools (see Vaihinger 1965, xxx).

individuals tend to formulate their understandings. This exploration is the "paradigmatic approach" to decision making under uncertainty.

**The Paradigmatic Approach**

As Howard Margolis has observed, "Creatures that must act in the world to survive cannot be continually open to taking a closer look at their cognitions."[19] To capture this sense of the *urgency of action*, compared to which the impulse for reflection and speculation tends to pale, the first step in our investigation into the decision-making process is to speak of "paradigms" instead of "ideas" or "understandings" to describe what we use to reflect our realities.

Derived from the Greek *paradeigma*, "to set up as an example," itself from *para*, "beside," and *deiknynai*, "to show," paradigm is defined as "a model or pattern." Recognized examples of good (or bad) form, paradigms thus provide guides for action, acquired through experience and embodying (implicit) lessons regarding permissible or viable actions and their contraries.[20]

The selection of paradigm in the development of my theory thus reinforces Margolis's perspective that places action in the foreground and reasoning in the background. This is not to say that reason is unimportant, but rather to emphasize a demand for action so keen that we are forced to make up our minds in a primitive fashion[21]—paraphrasing Hume, reasoning is a handmaiden of the will to live.

Like "hypothesis" or "rule," "paradigm" conveys the sense that concepts are integral aspects of the reasoning process, but it also implies that we have a looser and less explicit hold on our ideas. Although similar to Nelson and Winter's "skill",[22] it will play a very different role in our analysis. For Nelson and Winter, skill works to provide a substantive description of "simple rules," à la Herbert Simon, that operate (in the main) to provide an organizational analogue to genetic makeup and on which they build an evolutionary study of industries. For me, on the other hand, paradigm works to center mental activity in the analysis.

---

19. Margolis 1987, 139.

20. In his lectures on Roman law, Vico noted that "punishments were called paradigmata by the Greeks in the same sense in which Latins call them exempla; that (is) exemplary chastisements."

21. Binmore (1987, 204–9) also notes that, in seeking the perfect answer to a question, the "Turing machine," equivalent to a perfectly rational individual, may calculate forever. But in that event, the machine is not very useful. To insure that a conclusion is reached within a time limit, a "stopping rule" must be installed.

22. Nelson and Winter (1982, 24) acknowledge the similarity between their "skill" and others' terms such as plan, script, habit, routine, and program.

Although terms like *schema* in psychology at first glance appear to be similar in meaning to paradigm, none conveys so well the important nuances of both how urgent the demand for action is and how much we learn from past experiences. The vocabulary of schema, inference sets, hypotheses, theories, scripts, themes, frames, categories, prototypes, and attitudes reflects an almost exclusive focus on "the organization of knowledge in *static* terms."[23] Especially when I focus on the *dynamic* aspects of decision making, paradigm suits my purpose better than the terms used by cognitive and social psychologists to capture features of static cognitive structure.[24]

Real-world problems rarely, if ever, present themselves explicitly; their solutions are usually implied by the way problems are perceived and questions posed. All the paradigmatic approach really assumes is that people deal with the uncertainty inherent in any given situation by identifying an associated paradigm, the implicit rules of which suggest an appropriate course of action. A story about the young Karl Friedrich Gauss well illustrates the importance of identifying paradigms for (mental) action. When children in his class were asked to sum the numbers one through ten, most used the procedure $1 + 2 = 3$, $3 + 3 = 6$, $6 + 4 = 10$, . . . , $45 + 10 = 55$. Depending upon their proficiency in addition, some were speedy and some were slow; some were accurate and some were not. Karl Friedrich conceived of the problem instead as one with five 10s ($1 + 9, 2 + 8, 3 + 7, 4 + 6$, and 10) and one 5. He was quick to reach the answer not necessarily because of his facility in addition, but because he saw the situation differently than his classmates.

It is paradigms that provide viewpoints enabling us to distinguish what is relevant for the purpose at hand from what is not. Identifying paradigms is like making inquiries: no answers can be given before questions are posed. Within a theoretical context, scientists specify the precise relationship between outcomes and attributes, causes and effects. Ordinary people lay out these relationships as well, albeit implicitly. Practical in the sense of being sustained more by action than by armchair speculation or critical reasoning, they often find it sufficient to know what to do and what to expect in a given situation.[25] For scientist and layperson alike, however, the essence of reasoning consists of the ability to *make comparisons*. It is this that makes possible

---

23. Nisbett and Ross 1980, 28.
24. Markus and Zajonc 1985, 143; see also Nisbett and Ross 1980, 28.
25. The outcome of our actions and our views about their causes sometimes have little in common. We base our actions on paradigms we find suitable, with little guarantee that they are correct. All too often, outcomes surprise us, and, even when our expectations are realized, the cause may differ from that on which we based our action. As decision makers, we must acknowledge *ex post* that the outcome of our actions depends on many forces beyond our awareness, much less our control. See Leontief 1971 and Roll 1978 for a discussion of the disparity that also exists between theory and practice and may be the underlying rationale for Hall's law about the gap between acceptable and actual behavior.

the drawing of inference, deduction, and analogies, and the creation of allegory and metaphor. But comparison making itself requires a basis, and that basis is paradigm. As Pascal has said, "If we wish to prove examples which we take to prove other things, we should have to take those other things to be examples."[26] Examples constitute our very mental process, and examples are, literally, paradigms.

The choice of terminology reflects both my intellectual debt to Thomas Kuhn and my methodological predilection for treating the history of science (and of ideas in general) as a testing ground for the theory of behavior under uncertainty.[27] To Thomas Kuhn and the role paradigm has played in the philosophy of science, I therefore now turn.

## Kuhn's Theory of Scientific Paradigm

It is Kuhn who gave the term *paradigm* modern currency. Introduced to the sphere of the philosophy or history of science as "some accepted examples of actual scientific practice . . . [that] provide models from which spring particular coherent traditions of scientific research,"[28] a paradigm can refer to *both* the "disciplinary matrix" and the "exemplars"—the former being the entire constellation of symbolic generalizations, values, and techniques, and the latter being an "element in the constellation, the concrete puzzle-solution which, [when] employed as model or example, can replace explicit rules."[29]

Given how people actually learn science—by doing it—*paradigms must be prior to explicit rules*. Scientific disciplines are identified, in part, by shared paradigms because paradigms define cognition and because people can be classified with respect to their behavior only insofar as their perceptions of the world are similar. Because paradigms are ways of seeing or dealing with the world, they elicit the commitment of their users, and members of a scientific community who share a paradigm call their science "normal."[30]

---

26. Pascal 1941, 15.

27. Margolis's concept of pattern is very close to my concept of paradigm, and this similarity is little cause for wonder: we have both been influenced by Kuhn. The main difference between his approach and mine consists in how we use the history of science—to illustrate arguments regarding the pattern-recognizing aspect of human cognition (Margolis) or to explore the implications for people's behavior and social tendencies (Choi). See Choi 1986; Margolis 1987.

28. Kuhn 1970, 10.

29. Kuhn 1970, 187.

30. Methodologists have shown strong reservations about Kuhn's concept of paradigm, in the sense of the "disciplinary matrix," because it appears to imply incommensurability or even incommunicability between different schools. To make the situation worse, some academics have often used the term *paradigm* to bolster positions that are otherwise difficult to maintain intellectually. But the fact remains that two sincere people may be committed to two incompatible

To Kuhn, the practice of science *always* presupposes a paradigm. "The decision to reject one paradigm," he says, "is always simultaneously the decision to accept another."[31]

> Once a first paradigm through which to view nature has been found, there is no such thing as research in the absence of any paradigm. To reject one paradigm without simultaneously substituting another is to reject science itself.[32]

Science without paradigm is unthinkable.

### Scientific versus Lay Paradigms

What Kuhn claims for the practice of science, I also claim for the practice of laypersons. On the face of it, surely, there are noticeable differences between scientists and ordinary folks. Scientists are more explicit about their reasoning, their education is more structured, and they deal with a more precisely and narrowly defined range of problems and test each hypothesis with great rigor. Ordinary folk are educated for life with very little structure; they deal with their various daily problems with little critical evaluation of their paradigm, and test not its truth, but its viability, with practice.

The main difference between scientists and laypersons is perhaps the reflection of the differences in the situations they face, especially with respect to the urgency of action. Scientists often have the luxury of delaying action and critically evaluating their hypotheses; laypersons do not. As an illustration, Einhorn makes the following observation.

> [C]onsider a waiter in a busy restaurant. Because he doesn't have time to give good service to all the customers at his station, he makes a prediction about which customers are likely to leave good or poor tips. Good or poor service is then given depending on the prediction. If the quality of service has a treatment effect on the size of the tip, the outcomes "confirm" the original predictions. Note that the waiter could perform an experiment to disentangle the treatment effects of quality of service from his predictions if he was aware of the task structure; that is, he could give

---

positions. Even Popper (1979) argues that the pursuit of science requires that people be willing to defend their positions or hypotheses.

31. Kuhn 1970, 77.

32. Kuhn 1970, 79. Perhaps this is the kind of thinking that explains why Arrow (1974a) believes that "the starting point [for economic analysis] . . . must still be the much abused neoclassical theory, [since no] really cohesive alternative which aspires to the same level of completeness exists."

poor service to some of those he judged to leave good tips and good service to some of those he judged to leave poor tips. However, note that the waiter must be willing to risk the possible loss of income if his judgment is accurate, against the learning that his judgment is poor.[33]

Even so, the difference between a scientist and a practical individual is one of degree, not of kind. Is not scientific research really but the refined and extreme example of our minds at work in solving problems, that is, in dealing with uncertainty?[34]

Indeed, we have good reason to believe in a certain commonality among our various activities because all are *stamped by the human mind*. Donald McCloskey quotes Wayne Booth to the effect that "the process developed in the law is codification of reasonable processes that we follow in every part of our lives, even the scientific."[35] According to Michael Polanyi, scientific knowledge is no different in kind from personal knowledge.[36] Albert Einstein found that "the whole of science is nothing more than a refinement of everyday thinking."[37] Both science and practical affairs are human activities of inquiry, understanding, and judgment; the comparison between scientist and practical person is made in terms of *more* or *less*, not either/or.[38]

According to Brian Loasby, the idea of viewing ordinary folks as scientists has a venerable tradition, reaching back at least to Adam Smith.[39] But it was psychologist George Kelly who was most explicit in considering people as scientists, that is, as pattern-seeking and inquiring individuals, instead of considering them as responding to stimuli or drives.[40]

While we focus primarily on the layperson's practical paradigms as a basic framework for studying the implications of decision making for individual behavior, drawing the parallel between the scientific and the lay paradigm provides a distinct advantage. It allows us to regard the history of science as a testing ground, thus granting us access to a large collection of informative

---

33. Einhorn 1982, 282. It would therefore seem mistaken to measure the layperson's inferential ability by the benchmark of the scientist, but this is a metric some psychologists appear to employ.

34. Margolis (1987) also notes the close parallel between scientific activity and human cognition as a whole in what he calls "pattern recognition." Also see Nisbett and Ross 1980, 8–13.

35. McCloskey 1983, 501.

36. M. Polanyi 1962.

37. Albert Einstein, quoted in Maital 1982, 8.

38. According to Amos Tversky, "there is no inferential failure that cannot be demonstrated with untrained undergraduates that cannot also . . . be demonstrated in somewhat more subtle form in the highly trained scientist" (Nisbett and Ross 1980, 14).

39. Loasby 1986, 45–46. See also, Earl 1983, 117–23.

40. Earl 1983; Loasby 1986.

psychological experiments about the very topic of our concern. Without such access, we would confront a dearth of data, and not solely for lack of interest. One of the main difficulties in studying a layperson's behavior is that much of the associated thought is implicit; and even when it is explicit, the actual process is seldom revealed. Moreover, the findings from experimental psychology concerning people's inferential processes are fragmented and often contradictory, primarily because the experimental settings deviate from real-life situations by eliminating the urgency of action. Lacking sufficient and consistent evidence sometimes forces us to resort to our own introspection, the derived insights from which are rarely considered sufficiently "scientific."[41] In this context, the possibility of being able to learn from the examination of the reasoning processes of scientists, who think out loud, or at least louder than a layperson, is quite appealing. Such examination can yield relatively clear examples of how scientists cope with uncertainty, and the history of science can therefore serve as an excellent source of data dealing with the question of decision making under uncertainty.[42]

Based on these considerations, I advance the following proposition.

*Proposition 1 (Paradigmatic Approach).* People decide and act in a given situation based on a paradigm identified as appropriate for that situation. Without a paradigm there will be no decision and no action.

Proposition 1 is really just a restatement of our first fact. Paradigms are examples. They are "good" if they bring success, and "bad" if they bring failure. They are, in other words, examples of viable and unviable practice.

So defined, paradigms are guides for action. Their function is especially clear under conditions of uncertainty, when there can be no action without a guide for action.[43] Just as scientists approach their subject with a paradigm formed on the basis of previous experiments and studies, practical people deal with the environment by using a paradigm formed from past experiences.[44] A paradigm is the integral part of the reasoning processes through which judgments are rendered and decisions are made.

Because individuals must deal with diverse situations, they may have a

---

41. McCloskey (1983) notes that economists rely heavily on introspection, which has no place in their "official rhetoric."

42. For example, Margolis (1987) gives a detailed account of the Darwinian discovery and the Copernican revolution.

43. Transitory states, when paradigms to handle uncertain situations are actively sought, provide an exception, but even then not one wholly exempt from the network of paradigms. See chap. 3.

44. Popper (1979) conjectures the existence of the "World 3" as a product of science that acts upon scientists' behavior; the practical person's analogue is culture.

constellation of paradigms, each suitable for a separate set of circumstances. Paradigm X might tell us to speak English to an American and Korean to a Korean, while Paradigm Y tells us to act one way toward our families and another toward our business associates. Paradigms may be hierarchical in the sense that some paradigms govern choices among paradigms, instead leaving the choice to chance.[45] The array of paradigms may be hierarchical, ranging from simple table manners and rules for a chess game, to maxims and beliefs, to the language games of Ludwig Wittgenstein. We shall assume that people find hypothetical correspondence between external reality and one of the paradigms in their constellation.[46]

Neither Kuhn's "scientific" nor my "practical" paradigm is justified *a priori*. Kuhn's hypothesis is derived from an investigation of how scientists are educated, how they choose topics and methods, and how they make, accept, or reject discoveries. Mine is based on an analysis of the decision making and behavior under genuine uncertainty of creatures endowed with reason (and not excluding scientists). Kuhn presents a vision of the history of science that purports to explain, among other things, anomalies within the context of the philosophy of science. I advance a perspective on individual behavior and social tendencies that tries to explain anomalies within the context of neoclassical economic theory and is offered as a general theory of human behavior.

## Implications of the Paradigmatic Approach

Proposition 1 is not just a description of how we make decisions under uncertainty. It also has predictive value—implications for the *kinds* or *patterns* of behavior individuals tend to exhibit—and it is the purpose of this section to explore these implications. (Predictions about the *specific* actions any one individual will actually undertake in a specific situation require many more details—information that is both unavailable and unnecessary at this level of abstraction.[47])

> *Corollary 1a (Indeterminacy)*. The paradigmatic approach implies that there is no necessary or unique way of acting in any given situation.

---

45. This search method may be called an "assignment paradigm."
46. To heighten our understanding, we can liken paradigms in the paradigmatic approach to games in game theory. In that field, games characterize the relevant structure of situations, and the behavior of players depends quite strongly upon the game with which they identify a given situation. Similarly, in my approach, the actions of people rely heavily on the paradigm they have chosen as best "corresponding" to the circumstances.
47. See Einhorn 1982, 268.

Individuals may act in a number of different ways in any given situation; each specific action depends upon the paradigm they have elected to adopt. Nevertheless, anything does *not* "go." Even if paradigms were the products of wild imagination, only those that have withstood the tests of practice are retained and harkened unto.

Everyone operates within the context of two kinds of environments: the natural and the social. Nature imposes certain restrictions on what we can endure without perishing; we may call these constraints a lower bound to behavior. Society further constrains our possibilities by the requirement that we interact with fellow beings; call this an upper bound to our behavior. Within these bounds, there is much latitude for individual variation, and the choice of paradigms cannot therefore be characterized as uniquely determined by the environment.[48]

*Corollary 1b (Selectivity).* The paradigmatic approach implies that an individual will have selective vision.

A paradigm reflects a certain understanding of, or special way of viewing, a given situation. Causes and effects, inputs and outputs, revenues and costs are all different sets of vocabulary or perspectives we can bring to bear, for there are many ways to perceive or approach the same problem. That an individual follows one particular paradigm instead of another implies a singular understanding or vision of the situation that precludes any other; the paradigmatic approach implies selective vision.

*Corollary 1c (Veracity).* Those who hold the selective vision implied by a paradigm will regard it as a true representation of reality.

Paradigms elicit our faith that their implied vision is true because our livelihood depends upon action, and our action depends upon our paradigms. We cannot even entertain the possibility that the basis of our action is false *ex ante*. In other words, we posit faith in the veracity of our viewpoint.[49] We may doubt the veracity of the selected paradigms, but only *ex post*.

Perhaps there are times in selecting a paradigm when we are less than fully certain about the veracity of the implied view. Perhaps we are not at all

---

48. Fang (1991) observes how even theories in physics depend on the theorists' sense of beauty, and surely different people have different senses of beauty.
49. See also Kahneman and Tversky (1982) for a discussion of a "representative heuristic" that describes the tendency of people to regard a small sample as representative of reality for the purpose of prediction. The motivation to reduce the disparity between experience and belief is therefore strong indeed; this view is corroborated by work in the psychology of cognitive dissonance.

sure why one paradigm should be preferred over others. But if this is indeed the case, by what means can we decide? If we decide to roll a die instead of flipping a coin or relying on an oracle, then what we have selected is not any of the alternatives A, B, C, corresponding to one dot, two dots, three dots, but the rolling of a die. If we are to act based on the outcome of rolling a die, then there can be no doubt that rolling it is the proper paradigm to follow.

> *Corollary 1d (Commitment).* The paradigmatic approach implies that an individual will be committed to the selective vision reflected in the paradigm.

Paradigms tend to have normative as well as predictive implications for the individuals who adopt them. For people who must act, the line between "is" and "ought" is not clearly demarcated.[50] Nor are scientists wholly exempt from this tendency. In their field, a paradigm or theory must be treated as provisionally and potentially true, unless or until proven false. Although scientists are required to abandon a theory if it compares unfavorably to another, they are not obliged to abandon it at the first sign of trouble. As Popper himself would argue, even scientific discourse requires the existence of committed proponents of competing theories.[51] One of the chief reasons for adhering to a hypothesis is the lack of a better hypothesis. But it is often impossible to prove that one theory is better than another all around. At any rate, an instantaneous adjustment in expectations at the hint of the slightest of difficulty is logically inconsistent with a conjectural approach by hypothesis. This is the case even for scientists whose professed aim is to find the truth. Thus, Nisbett and Ross capture the essence of Michael Polanyi's ideas.

> Theories are useful because they structure knowledge into coherent wholes, organize experience, and facilitate supplementation of the data given with information that can be retrieved readily from memory. The implication of this position is that conservatism with respect to theories is often advisable. Neither the layperson nor the scientist should readily dispose of a well-established theory because it happens to conflict with some new evidence. It is often proper to look askance at, or even totally ignore, reports of virgin births or new cancer cures. It may even be proper to dismiss evidence collected by reputable scientists if it conflicts with some powerful, parsimonious, and integrative theory.[52]

---

50. People are law-making animals who often legislate the laws they should obey.
51. Popper 1979.
52. Nisbett and Ross 1980, 168.

Neoclassical economists may be tempted to conjecture that commitment itself is rational.[53] But Nisbett and Ross argue that although "a hesitancy in approaching new evidence may be justified, it is difficult to rationalize certain types of response to new evidence . . . [that] sometimes may be quite inappropriate."[54]

The paradigm initially chosen must have appeared better than any other, in view of the evidence then available, and people of action can ill-afford criticism and speculation unless events force them to reevaluation.[55] The paradigmatic approach therefore implies commitment.

*Corollary 1e (Inflexibility).* The paradigmatic approach implies that an individual's behavior will tend to exhibit a degree of inflexibility, or persistence, in the face of changing circumstances.

That individual behavior will be less than perfectly flexible or adaptable to changes follows directly from commitment.[56] The first evidence of a paradigm in trouble may not be sufficiently strong to tilt the balance of reason that weighted toward its selection in the first place, even though it is entirely possible that another paradigm might have been chosen in the first place if the sequence of events had been different. The evidence is ample that people tend to persist in their beliefs, and attendent actions, in the face of new information that should discredit their beliefs. We have already seen this persistence in scientists. Laypersons are no different, as evidenced by the following experiment.

Lord, Ross, and Lepper (1979) presented two empirical studies on the value of capital punishment in deterring future crime to a group of Stanford University students who had already indicated their beliefs on this matter. The first report supported capital punishment; the second did not. The experimenters discovered that

> subjects found whichever study supported their own position to be significantly "more convincing'" and "better conducted" than the study opposing their position. . . . The subjects thus treated the evidence in a highly asymmetric way: supportive evidence was handled with kid gloves; opposing evidence was mauled.[57]

---

53. This viewpoint would also justify the tenacity with which they hold on to orthodox economic theory; see Arrow 1974a.
54. Nisbett and Ross 1980, 170.
55. Earl (1983, 132) observes that if a scientist kept returning to the first principle, he would not advance very far.
56. Heiner's "rule-governed behavior" implies a similar inflexibility.
57. Nisbett and Ross 1980, 170–71.

If the study confirmed the students' initial positions, their initial beliefs were strengthened. But a contradictory study failed to dislodge their views, and, indeed, affected them very little.

In another experiment, Ross, Lepper, and Hubbard (1975) asked their subjects to distinguish authentic suicide notes from fictitious scribblings. First given contrived feedbacks leading them to believe that their performance in this task was inferior, average, or superior, the subjects were later told that they had been manipulated to believe their performance rating, and even shown how this manipulation had been achieved. They were then asked to rate their actual performance on this task, their probable performance on future, related tasks, and their own ability in such tasks.

> The results revealed a remarkable degree of post debriefing perseverance. Even after debriefing, subjects who had initially been assigned to the "success" condition continued to rate their performance and abilities far more favorably than did subjects whose initial feedback had indicated average performance, while subjects initially assigned to the failure condition showed the opposite pattern of results, continuing to rate themselves unsuccessful and lacking the ability for the experimental task and for other, similar ones.[58]

These people maintained their beliefs in significant measure even after they were told that they had been misled and that the evidence on which they had based their beliefs was carefully calculated deception. Joseph Schumpeter found this tendency sufficiently pronounced to label it *Wieser's principle of continuity*: "The data may change . . . But everyone will cling as tightly as possible to habitual economic methods and only submit to the pressure of circumstances as it becomes necessary."[59]

> *Corollary 1f (Possibility of Mistakes).* The paradigmatic approach implies the possibility of error.

The selective vision implied by the paradigmatic approach is an ingenious way of coping with a complicated world. It has served us well: humanity has proliferated and prospered. But it is not perfect. Selective vision, by definition, deliberately ignores some data, and the omissions might prove significant. It could thus be a source of errors and regrets, and such is the moral of Aesop's fable of the "One-Eyed Doe."

---

58. Nisbett and Ross 1980, 177.
59. Schumpeter 1934, 8–9.

A one-eyed doe used to graze near the sea. She kept her blind side towards the water from whence she did not anticipate danger. With her sound eye she watched the country as she fed. She felt safe, until an improvising hunter took a boat and silently approached her from the sea and shot her. She cried in agony: "O what a misfortune it is. I received a mortal wound from the blind side, from where I expected no harm, not from the side that I watched."

In this case, the doe's strategy—literally, her selective vision—had worked well, but proved her undoing in the last instance. The paradigmatic approach is consistent with Kirzner's view that the selectivity of attention is the source of errors and regrets.[60]

*Corollary 1g (Possibility of Systematic Error).* The paradigmatic approach implies the possibility of systematic error.

The commitment to selective vision is also the commitment to a biased viewpoint, and thus makes possible systematic errors in judgment. This corollary follows from corollaries 1e and 1f, namely, inflexibility and the possibility of mistakes. Its *raison d'être* is that it takes more in the way of effort and observation to convert an individual committed to one way of viewing and doing to a new approach than to establish this perspective *de novo*.

For example, suppose that, on the basis of linear regression on a sample of observations, an individual has estimated the following trend: $Y = A_1 + B_1 X + e$. He has committed himself to act on the basis of this estimate, paradigm, or hypothesis. Any future observation $Y_i^*$ that deviates from the expected $Y_i = A_1 + B_1 X_i$ is likely to be treated as random deviation for a long time before our modeler begins to reflect seriously on the possibility that the original sample was biased and that all these $Y_i^*$'s should be incorporated into a new equational guide. Even with steady updates and revisions—$Y = A_2 + B_2 X + e_2$ in the second period, $Y = A_3 + B_3 X + e_3$ in the third, and so on—this individual will be making systematic mistakes if the true model is something like $Y = A + BX + CX^2 + e$. Not only the sample but the regression model as well must ultimately be reexamined, and the time and energy this task requires are sufficiently onerous to postpone the day of (re)judgment.

Our view should be contrasted to Selten's "trembling-hand" explanation of mistakes, which says that mistakes are random deviations from perfect rationality.[61] As Binmore points out, the possibility of systematic error is a

---

60. Kirzner 1979, 120–36.
61. Binmore 1987, 182–84. Also see Sugden 1989, 92.

direct reflection of the fact that we act systematically, not haphazardly. We act systematically, or rather act in such a way that certain patterns are discernible, because we act according to the paradigms we identify.

*Corollary 1h (Discontinuity).* Changes in the pattern of individual behavior will be discrete and abrupt.

The discontinuous nature of changes in individual behavior follows from proposition 1 (paradigmatic approach) and corollary 1e (inflexibility). Individuals tend to be quite loyal to their paradigms and to revise them only over time and at the margin—that is, within the context of other paradigms to which they hold fast. This is not to say, however, that individuals will never forsake their paradigms. They are not genetic codes built into our natural makeup, but rather mental equipment we have chosen to help manage our lives. They can be and will be replaced—just not continuously or even continually. When these changes finally come, in brief, they come much like a shift in gestalt.[62] The behavioral patterns we actually observe as a consequence of this sort of revision of paradigms should, therefore, exhibit great continuity for a time, followed by great discontinuities, leaps to new patterns of action that will themselves prove stable for a considerable stretch before yielding to new ideas of being.

---

62. Margolis's discussion of "hill climbing" vs. "hill jumping" captures much the same essence as the distinction I draw between making adjustments within a paradigm and actually replacing it. See chap. 3 and Margolis 1987, 33, 219.

CHAPTER 3

# The Decision-Making Process and Its Implications for Individual Behavior

Coldness or warmth is known only to the one who feels it.
—Buddha

This chapter continues the exploration of the behavioral implications of decision making under uncertainty. After redefining uncertainty in the context of the paradigmatic approach, I shall relate this approach to the processes of decision making and learning and then discuss the general tendencies of individual behavior in an analysis beginning with the simplest case of an isolated individual and building to homogeneous, then heterogeneous, groups with minimal degrees of interaction.

**The Decision-Making Process**

*Definition (Uncertainty).* A situation is uncertain if one cannot identify an appropriate paradigm to associate with it.

Uncertainty is a state of doubt surrounding a situation for which one has yet to identify a paradigm to support action. It may arise when an individual is placed in unfamiliar circumstances that require the formulation of an initial paradigm. It may also arise in the midst of ordinary and repeated circumstances when customary outcomes no longer seem satisfactory, and a new approach seems potentially more appropriate. What may be obvious to one person may confound someone else. Uncertainty is subjective.

Uncertainty is also transitory. We refuse to tolerate it. Our lives require actions, and our actions require paradigms. We will do whatever is necessary to establish and believe in them.

*Definition (Decision Making).* To make a decision is to resolve uncertainty by identifying an appropriate paradigm.

Once a paradigm is identified, the appropriate course of action is clear. Doubt is no longer entertained, and uncertainty is resolved.[1]

Many of the daily situations we confront have elements of both familiarity and novelty. The majority probably resemble past events closely enough to enable us to cope on the basis of the paradigms to which we have grown accustomed. However, even these nonproblematic cases, for which we can identify and follow a paradigm without much thinking, go through a decision-making process. We must decide that other paradigms are not even worth considering before making judgments within the context of the already-adopted paradigm and acting accordingly.

In somewhat more problematic situations, we are not fully satisfied with the paradigms we customarily summon and can think of others that may be equally or more appropriate. In this case, sticking to the old paradigm will probably yield a customary result, but perhaps following an alternative would better the outcome. If we stick to old ways and they prove substandard, we have committed what statisticians call a "Type I" error. If we mistakenly switch, we have succumbed to a mistake of "Type II."[2]

Our propensity to become more proficient as we go considerably complicates the analysis of when to shift paradigms. The longer we hold a paradigm, the more skillful we are likely to be in using it and, therefore, the less likely we are to search for another. In other words, the more comfortable we are with a certain way of viewing and therefore coping with the world, the more likely we are to stick with that paradigm, whether or not it is truly effective.[3]

In part, the matter of shifting paradigms then becomes one of short-run versus long-run efficiency. Consider, for example, an individual who has used paradigm X so often that he or she is quite adept in its application—so adept that, in the short run, X yields better results than Y, even though, in the long run, with sufficient practice, paradigm Y would be the better tool. When should one make the switch?

Suppose, as another example, that an experienced farmer knows the ins and outs of cultivating his or her land—the soil, the climate, the market, and

---

1. Are we *absolutely* certain about the veracity of our paradigm? Not necessarily. But when we act according to a paradigm, we had better be certain enough, since our lives are at stake.

2. In a similar vein, Margolis (1987, 27–28) discusses how our limited mental capacities may make us either "hesitate too long in seeking the best response" or "jump too soon," thus committing, respectively, Type I and Type II errors. Heiner's discussion of the dilemma faced by an agent who adopts a simple, and imperfect, rule is also on point. See Vanberg 1989, 12; see also Einhorn 1982, 276–82.

3. Kuhn discusses this phenomenon among scientists. Also relevant is Keynes's discussion of the nature of economic modeling (see Hausman 1984, 300–302). I will pick up and expand the point in a discussion of the process of social change and the agents thereof in chap. 6.

so on. His or her income is lower, on average, and more varied than that of a merchant with comparable years of experience. Should he or she make a career switch? In the short run, at least, the income comparison is between an experienced farmer and a novice merchant; the farmer has invested years in farming, not in commerce. In assessing his or her immediate chances for success in agriculture versus the merchant trade, he or she will tilt toward the *status quo*. The tradeoff between Type I and Type II errors must be made, but perhaps in a purely subjective fashion. In many situations, people will tend to stick to their old ways (corollary 1e, inflexibility), but sometimes they will change, and do so abruptly (corollary 1h, discontinuity).

Only when a situation is truly problematic are we open to all sorts of suggestions. Desperately seeking a paradigm and paralyzed until we find one, in the face of genuine novelty, we are free of preconceptions, commitments, and inflexibilities.

*Proposition 2 (Paradigm Seeking).* When faced with uncertainty, an individual will search for a suitable paradigm; the search will continue until one is identified and uncertainty is resolved.

This merely restates the necessity of action and its impossibility without paradigms. The process of paradigm seeking is also the process of decision making.

*Corollary 2a (Learning).* The decision-making process is a learning process.

Learning is the process by which we acquire understanding of, or the ability to deal with, a situation that we could not make sense of, or deal with, before. When we are faced with an unfamiliar situation, for example, we are driven to search for a paradigm to cope with the novelty. Once the process is completed and an appropriate paradigm is identified, the decision is made. The situation is no longer regarded as uncertain, since we know how to act. Note that we can now deal with a situation we could not handle before. A decision-making process is, therefore, a learning process.

The novelty of a situation consists in our failure to identify a suitable paradigm—perhaps because we have none at our disposal or perhaps because our "assignment paradigm" has yet to come up with one we have already filed. Faced with uncertainty, we begin to search either by "stretching" existing paradigms or by acting randomly. The former is the more likely approach, consistent with how we deal with a variety of problems by means of reason and imagination; it may also resemble the process by which we understand metaphors (see below). In the end, we add a new paradigm to the file or restructure the assignment paradigm. And because we now know what to do in what used to appear to be a baffling situation, we have gained understanding or "learned" from our experience.

In the sense here of involving the process of identifying a paradigm, learning does not take place in a vacuum. It is both enabled and restricted by prior learnings—by the paradigms already in our possession. We come to understand and deal with novel situations by using paradigms we have already acquired, and our understanding and coping styles are limited to what is possible within the context of our existing paradigms, however imaginatively and creatively we may impose them.[4]

For example, consider how we add to our vocabulary. We understand a speech or a situation by means of examples or paradigms we have already registered. When someone says "horse," we take the statement to mean one of the equine species we have seen or heard of before. But if someone talks about a "kkokkam" and we have neither seen nor heard of one before so that we have registered no appropriate paradigm, we do not and *cannot* understand. We may form an idea if someone offers a further explanation: A "kkokkam" is something much more menacing than even a tiger; it is so scary that a crying child will stop crying as soon as it is so much as mentioned. Based on this explanation, we may form a vague (and wild) idea about "kkokkam." But our idea would be closer to truth if someone tells us that it is similar to something we have seen before, or shows us a "kkokkam" itself.[5]

The manner in which we learn and seek new paradigms can be likened to a dialogue we carry on with ourselves. When faced with a novel situation, we ask ourselves such question as "What is this? What should I make of this? What should I do about it?" We must base our answers on what we already know, even though we apply the results in ways that reflect new circumstances.

---

4. Imaginative and creative they are indeed! Unless computers can be programmed to imagine (that is, to think allegorically, by analogy or metaphor), they will remain mere machines, processing the commands we give them. If ever artificial intelligence can truly mimic human thinking, it will then be liable to make (systematic) mistakes, just as we are.

5. Consider a Korean fable. Once upon a time, a tiger came close to a farmhouse and overheard what went on inside the house. A child was crying quite loudly. The mother said, "If you do not stop, I will spank you." The child did not stop. The mother then said, "If you don't stop now, a tiger will come and carry you away." The tiger said to himself, "The baby will be too scared to cry!" But the child continued, to the amazement of the tiger. Then, in desperation, the mother said, "O.K. Here is a kkokkam!" The child stopped instantly and the house became quite. The tiger reasoned as follows: "If this kkokkam can scare the child more than a tiger, it must be a really terrifying creature; I should be careful when I encounter this creature in the future." *Kkokkam* is a dried persimmon in Korean.

When we inquire about nature, we act as if we have a dialogue with nature. When nature "speaks" to us, we understand it through our existing paradigms and act accordingly.[6] But when it speaks to us in a strange tongue, that is, when we face a less-familiar situation, we try to find its meaning within the existing constellation of paradigms by means of analogy and simile. Once we discover a way to understand its intentions, that is, the situation, the constellation of paradigms is transformed, however slightly. This is the process of learning.

What do we do if someone whom we take as serious and honorable utters something that appears false within the context of our given paradigm set? Our response to statements like "Man is a dog" is to reject the literal meaning (the direct application of existing paradigms) and to search for a figurative meaning (a way of stretching the paradigms). We project ourselves into what we believe to be the speaker's viewpoint, and once we feel that we understand the statement, by perceiving the common attributes alluded to in metaphor, we register it as another example of the figurative use our language allows and even encourages. In this, we resemble the scientist, who responds to the discovery of a false speech of nature (evidence that beyond doubt appears to refute accepted hypotheses and theories) by endeavoring to adopt the natural "viewpoint" (a new paradigm or framework within which the puzzling datum can be interpreted as "natural").

This learning process must be involved in people's dealings with novelty, their decision making under uncertainty. The methods they employ may be less striking than those of scientists or poets, but the underlying structure is the same. In all these cases, people deal with uncertainty by means of existing paradigms and their reasoning faculty, bridged by imagination. Indeed, as the acquisition of something new, learning is but the flip side of the paradigm-seeking coin, or decision making under uncertainty.

### The Learning Process of an Isolated Individual

Having made this identification, we are now ready to explore the individual behavioral consequences of proposition 2, paradigm seeking, by first examining the simplest case: that of an isolated individual faced with novelty. Although our starting point is justified mostly by considerations of analytical tractability, the setup is not so farfetched as it may at first appear. The perception of isolation is largely subjective, and "the loneliest person is the person in the crowd" is not just sophomoric in sentiment. "The individual in isolation"

---

6. St. Augustine spoke of the soliloquy of the truth seeker as the dialogue between "Man and God" (1963, bk. 10, esp. 235).

may live in a city of millions, but may feel as if he or she is playing a solitary game against nature. How will he or she respond to a novel situation that requires action?

> *Proposition 3 (Experiment).* When faced with uncertainty, an individual will use a trial-and-error approach to find a paradigm deemed suitable for the given situation, testing the most promising paradigm first and expecting certain outcomes. If this initial test brings the anticipated results, the individual will stop the search. If it fails, he or she will try another promising paradigm, continuing this search until attaining success.

Our hypothetical individual is very much like a lone scientist. Both have only nature to reckon with. Just like the scientist, the isolated individual will survey the stock of knowledge, determine the most promising paradigm, and act as if the identified paradigm is valid. The layperson's experiments, however, are much more "serious" than those of the scientist in that they involve all of life, not just the subset of work. In many real-life situations, an individual acts boldly as a subject-participant, not tentatively as a third-party observer. Scientists can often use expendable resources, such as measuring rods. Only occasionally are there lay parallels, such as Noah's use of doves to test for the existence of dry land. More often than not, lay situations require the commitment of the whole person or a significant proportion of his or her personal possessions; there is no dress rehearsal in the "unbearable lightness of being."[7]

Only the most promising paradigm is tried in this mental experimentation, and the process of determination is unlikely to be completely random. Individuals broaden the interpretation of antecedent paradigms with mental exercises like those used to create and interpret analogies or metaphors. Moreover, even though the potential perspectives on any given situation are infinite, people tend to consider only a tiny subset of possible variations as worthwhile candidates, and they tend to "choose" this initial set in much the same experiential way that chess players consider only a few strategies from a cast of thousands.[8] Of course, a choice among the initially chosen must also be made. I maintain that we try the most promising one first, the second most promising if the first fails, and so on until we find one that succeeds. We then adopt it as our paradigm, and cease the search.

The preferred method of this experimentation is, of course, a critical

---

7. The phrase comes from the title of Milan Kundera's novel.
8. In this choice of paradigms, a personal sense of beauty and propriety seem to play important roles (Fang 1991).

(mental) evaluation that eliminates weak candidates before their implementation, thus avoiding the probable consequences of error. Given the urgency of action, however, ordinary people can often ill afford tentative (scientific) attitudes. The dictum they face is "practice or perish."

Life becomes relatively easy after a successful paradigm has been identified. If the setting seems sufficiently stable, we may have located a practice to insure survival. This practice will then become *habitual*. Unfortunately, the existence of uncertainty eliminates the possibility of any guarantee.

*Corollary 3a (Unpredictability).* In a novel situation, the course of action any one individual will actually undertake is largely unpredictable.

The lay search process is essentially creative: it involves both imagination and leaps of logic, for all that it is based on is existing paradigms. The paradigm actually identified as suitable in an unfamiliar situation is therefore in good measure impossible to determine precisely beforehand. The perceived novelty of the initial situation precludes exact replication of old ones, and, because the search process will cease at the first sign of viability, the new paradigm may not be the very "best" available from global inquiry. The result is a strong element of unpredictability in anyone's action in unfamiliar circumstances.

The imprecision in our ability to predict the actions of others is heightened by the fact that there are many different ways to accomplish the same (broadly defined) goals. All people deprived of food for a period of time will try to overcome their hunger, but some will do so by hunting while others will proceed to gather fruit. Hunters will split off in their choice of prey, some pursuing deer, others rabbits, turkeys, or whatever. Even the deer hunters will differ by their choice of weapon, be it stones, traps, guns, or bows and arrows. And once the prey is caught, it can be skinned and cooked in a variety of ways. The possibilities for dealing with hunger, in brief, sum to a figure of almost unimaginable proportion. Is it any wonder that we are frequently taken by surprise by the strange customs of people in remote areas?

Although individuals can chose from countless possibilities in novel situations so that the likelihood of predicting their precise actions is unlikely in the extreme, many social scientists have led us to believe otherwise. Chief among them in this regard are economists, whose claim to being able to predict people's behavior, at least in principle, rests *inter alia* on the assumption that the choice-space is invariant. In other words, the underlying assumption (when neoclassical economists predict human behavior) is that individuals are aware of the nature of the situation, which is itself invariant. However, it is entirely possible, and even likely, that similar individuals could choose very different practices in the same situation, depending upon their perception of the event, which in turn depends on their past experiences and the way in which they sequence their experiments.

The possibility of affecting our judgment by different presentations of the same problem is daily affirmed by the efficacy of advertising. This casts considerable doubt on the invariance of choice-spaces. If describing a glass as half-filled elicits a different response from describing it as half-empty, then neoclassical predictions about human behavior are on shaky ground. Kahneman and Tversky have created tremors with exactly this sort of experiment.[9] Refuting some fundamental axioms of expected utility maximization by "advertising" the same phenomena in disparate ways, they have shown that individuals will switch their choice from A to B as descriptions of these multifaceted options vary from 1 to 2.

*Corollary 3b (Precedents).* Precedents have an important influence on later action.

The set of previously chosen paradigms has significant sway over the decision maker's subsequent practices. We are spellbound by visions of our own choosing because paradigms dictate which facts are relevant and worthy of attention (corollary 1b, selectivity). Even later searches for better practices are likely to lead less to new paradigms than to marginal improvements of those that already exist in the decision maker's file. For example, military commanders are less apt to overhaul overall strategies than to improve upon tactics within the framework of ones already adopted. Turntable manufacturers are less likely to question the very concept of turntables than to address various difficulties associated with turntables by improving their mechanics of shock absorption, noise reduction, and so forth. We grow committed to our viewpoints and diverge substantially from them only when the gap between them and "reality" becomes truly glaring (corollary 1e, inflexibility).

Psychology presents a parallel in the concept of "primacy effects." As Nisbett and Ross observe, "in impression formation . . . early-presented information has an undue influence on final judgment," and "several decades of psychological research has shown primary effects are overwhelmingly probable."

> [P]rimacy effects in information processing are the rule because people are "theorists" in their approach to information about the social and physical world. Early-encountered information serves as the raw material for inference about what the object is like. These inferences, or theories about the nature of the object, in turn bias the interpretation of later-

---

9. Kahneman and Tversky 1982.

encountered information. . . . [T]heories about the nature of the object are revised insufficiently in response to discrepancies in the later-presented information.[10]

In our terms, individuals faced with uncertainty adopt paradigms that provide circumstantial viewpoints and support action. Even in novel situations, subsequent action will be influenced by present action. The role of precedents provides continuity in observed behavior.

*Corollary 3c (Local Optima).* The chosen practice (paradigm) is, at best, locally optimal.

Although individuals put forth their best effort in choosing paradigms, their choices will be globally optimal only by chance. There is no assurance that the view implied by the paradigms is true, or that the practices they support are the very best possible. That a better perspective on, and therefore response to, the situation might exist follows easily from the initial choice of paradigm, which is experimental and arbitrary (proposition 3, experiment).

Moreover, even if this starting point is globally optimal when first selected, it may become only locally optimal at a later date because individuals tend to stick to their choices even as circumstances change. This inflexibility (corollary 1e) implies that paradigms in use at any particular time are likely to yield results that are locally optimal at best, and seriously defective at worst.

We have seen a few implications for individual behavior that follow directly from the paradigmatic approach to decision making under uncertainty. These include unpredictability, the impact of initial practice, less than perfectly adaptable behavior that may be only locally optimal, and the possibility of systematic error. None is supported by traditional economic views of human propensities based on the concept of rationality. Neoclassical economists usually hold that, for rational individuals, there is a unique solution for each situation, one globally optimal choice that cannot fail to be recognized. The implication is that, with enough data, social scientists can predict individual behavior precisely. The paradigmatic approach suggests otherwise.

To the extent that paradigms provide expectations, this approach can also be compared, albeit indirectly, to theories of adaptive and rational expectations.[11] The model of adaptive expectations holds that an individual continually updates expectations in light of the difference between what was

---

10. Nisbett and Ross 1980, 172.

11. The comparison is indirect because the existing theories about expectations try to explain the aggregate—the average behavior of the entire population—while the paradigmatic approach concerns that of the individual.

expected in the past and what actually happened. The implication is that persistent bias is possible, and some economists have objected to the generation of systematic error forever. Offered in its place, therefore, is the school of rational expectations, which asserts that people have expectations that are borne out *on average*, so that when an actual realization deviates from the expectation, they treat it as occasioned by a random shock and continue to hold their expectations. The trouble is that one cannot know whether a given realization represents a random deviation within the assumed economic model or an important structural change. Even Robert Lucas admits that people with rational expectations can be "fooled" by unexpected changes, but he argues that they cannot be fooled systematically.[12] The paradigmatic approach implies, on the contrary, the possibility of persistent systematic bias, at least on the level of individual behavior, and the implications for the aggregate are quite similar.[13]

Having analyzed the behavior of an isolated individual, we are now ready to consider the behavior of an individual in a group. To promote orderly analysis, I shall begin with the case of *minimal interaction* among members, deferring to the next chapter a discussion of individual behavior in the context of full interaction and interdependence.

**The Individual in a Group**

Consider an individual in a group. Observing what others do and what happens to them can be helpful in his or her paradigm seeking. He or she can use them as a means of experimentation.

> *Proposition 4 (Vicarious Experimentation).* When faced with uncertainty, individuals in a group will conduct vicarious experiments as a means of finding serviceable paradigms.

The vicarious experiment is a method of inference that allows one individual to identify a paradigm by observing others' behavior. The underlying assumption is that one can expect the same effect from the same cause.[14] Without access to any inner psychology, one can glean such useful information as who is successful, who gets higher wages, who gets fired, promoted, or ruined. These data are sufficient for the experimenter whose interests lie not so much in the personal fortunes or misfortunes of strangers as in the outcomes of different actions in the same environment, so that it is possible to infer, from the affairs of others, which behavior is responsible for which

---

12. See Lucas 1981.
13. See chaps. 4 and 5.
14. Asch 1987, 388–91.

outcome and what can and cannot be expected from different courses of action.

Vicarious experiments allow the individual to avoid mistakes from the kind of direct (mental) experiment in paradigm choice the individual in isolation must undertake by force of circumstance (proposition 3, experiment). Vicarious experiments will always be preferred to the direct experiments I discussed earlier. Unfortunately, they are not always readily available, even in a group context.

This context in which vicarious experiment is feasible can be further divided into homogeneous and heterogeneous groups. Implications of the simpler case of homogeneity will be considered first.

## Homogeneous Groups

*Corollary 4a (Imitation).* In a homogeneous group, individuals imitate others when faced with uncertainty.[15]

A homogeneous group provides a splendid setting for vicarious experimentation. If many people share relevant attributes, our paradigm-seeking individual can be well assured of replicating outcomes by replicating actions.[16] (Keep in mind that, for analytical tractability, I am postponing until the next chapter such interactions and interdependences among group members as the peer pressure to conform.)

But how can there be any action when everyone is trying to use everyone else in the group as a guinea pig and is hesitant to act before analyzing the consequences of others' actions? The answer here is that our analysis in this section is based on the artificial setting of a group *without interaction*, where, for the most part, people with limited mental capabilities are *compelled* to take action before exhausting all the possibilities in thought experiments. Sooner or later, someone is bound to act, thus becoming a subject of vicarious experimentation, however inadvertently.[17] It is impossible to take "no action." "Doing nothing" is its own form of action. As Lao-tzu said: "If no-action is called no-action, then that is no no-action."

---

15. It is quite tempting to speculate that imitation is an increasing function of uncertainty. After all, without uncertainty there is no need for vicarious experimentation. If certain, individuals should pay no attention to alternatives and simply do what they *know* to be best. As the degree of uncertainty grows, we tend to rely more and more on vicarious experiments and imitation of successful behavior.

16. Even this sort of aping requires a certain amount of intelligence. Asch (1987, 390–91) discusses Koehler's experiment where one chimpanzee bootlessly imitated another in moving a box.

17. This first mover will not necessarily fare less well than the more patient observer-experimenters. Situations like the preemptive game may favor speedy action, and followers in games of procrastination may be at great disadvantage.

56    Paradigms and Conventions

In a group setting, we therefore have ample and greatly beneficial opportunity to learn from others. Timur Kuran has made the following observation.

> [T]he individual cannot formulate an opinion and then take a position on every human issue. To protect his nervous system from overload, he must be very selective in choosing what information to seek and process . . . [deferring] on most matters to the judgments and choices of others.[18]

With benefits this great, it should come as no surprise that the tendency to imitate is often and easily observed. Children are constantly aping the behavior of others, and adults behave no differently when faced with the unfamiliar. In Kenneth Arrow's example of low-cost flood insurance mentioned in chapter 1, the salient characteristic of those few who did take out the insurance was their knowledge of other people who had already bought the insurance.

The behavior of investors in the stock market is usually described in terms such as the *herd instinct* and *mass psychology*, but the explanations for this behavior vary considerably. Scharfstein and Stein, for example, argue that managers tend to imitate one another to avoid being oddballs, because they know that their board of directors is likely to evaluate their performance by comparing it with the performance of others.[19] But why does not the board make an absolute, instead of a relative, assessment, and why do the managers not rely on their own judgments and try to outperform the pack? Paradigm seeking in a group setting can provide a unified and persuasive answer.

The paradigmatic approach also provides good reason to study history. The majority of problems that arise in our daily lives have some sort of precedent in history, if not in personal experience, and our predecessors can provide a rich source of vicarious experimentation and paradigms. The response to uncertainty may thus include imitation of previous historical choices—or the choices one believes should have been made. As Santayana has said, "those who do not remember the past are condemned to repeat it."[20]

While the tendency to imitate others fully accords with our daily experience, it is quite at odds with the behavioral implications of neoclassical economics. When the choice is obvious, there is little room for imitation. But when the choice is unclear, when there is uncertainty, imitation finds a place. For example, when given a choice, no strings attached, between two checks

---

18. Kuran 1990, 13.
19. Scharfstein and Stein 1990, 465–67.
20. This historical perspective confirms the possibility of bias in group behavior. It also opens up some interesting questions about customary conformance to norms, path-breaking innovation, entrepreneurs, and elites. I shall explore these issues in subsequent chapters.

different only in denomination, we should always pick the $100 check no matter how many other people selected the $10 check. But when confronted with strong thirst and two different unidentified liquids to quench it, we shall observe the first people to sample a glass, keeping a keen eye on the results.

Indeed, the more uncertain a situation, the more the predictions of the paradigmatic approach will tend to dominate those of the neoclassical approach. This assertion could be tested by the following type of study. Design a series of tests descending in difficulty from nearly total obscurity to near transparency and reward the subjects of this study with a prize for each correct answer in the series. First, isolate them for the tests and record the results. Then place them in a room with someone whose behavior is controlled, run the same series of tests, and reveal at the end of each test how each person answered and why, having already arranged that the control will be the only person to answer the initially very difficult questions correctly. The goal is to demonstrate and establish this person's superiority, while making all others highly doubtful. If this aim is accomplished, the experimenter can then manipulate the situation so that the uncontrolled subjects will later abandon even their correct answers to relatively easy questions in favor of those chosen by the control, who may purposely have chosen an incorrect answer.[21]

The situation then becomes one where people imitate what they consider to be a superior paradigm. If they incur losses by aping someone else's behavior even for problems they could have solved fairly easily by themselves, their approach is one of paradigm seeking rather than maximization, and the neoclassical economists are in trouble. How many times have you personally heeded expert council even when you have doubts about its wisdom?

*Corollary 4b (Precedents).* Precedents are important determinants of group behavior.

If the search for a paradigm through vicarious experimentation results in imitation of someone else's early success, that success will set the tone for the entire group's behavior, because not just one individual, but every individual, can imitate it. Corollary 4b (precedents) suggests that the behavior of a newly formed group without consensus or precedent will be largely determined by the first mover. This implication is supported by the experiment by Kahn et al. (1982) on how groups decide among equity, equality, and other possible allocative schemes.

---

21. A slight variation of the Ross, Lepper, and Hubbard study (1975), mentioned previously, may be sufficient. Psychologists are likely to have undertaken experiments of this kind already, but I am not sufficiently well versed in psychology to be able to cite such a study.

> The (group) choice of allocation norm appeared to be determined by who spoke first, how much that person said, and what norms that person suggested.[22]

This choice is also consistent with corollary 4a (imitation).

> *Corollary 4c (Group Bias).* A group's behavior may be just as biased as the precedents its members imitate.

As long as a precedent appears good enough for survival, individuals within a group may use it as their paradigm. If these followers are sufficiently numerous, it may gain respectability and credibility, even if it is not the best paradigm going. Nothing succeeds like "success," especially if shortcomings are not immediately apparent. Therefore, there is no assurance that imitation leads to optimality.

John Conlinsk claims that, because individual optimization can be costly, imitation may be better than optimization for some people in a group composed mostly of optimizers. The implication of "rationalistic imitation" is that everyone in the group will behave optimally one way or another.[23] But whence comes the rational imitator's ability to discern whether or not the other's action is optimal? The paradigmatic approach is less conclusive. Perhaps not one optimizer will exist in a given situation. If so, the entire population could end up imitating a suboptimal practice set by the first mover. The imitative approach provides no way of knowing whether the response is mass hysteria or mass dispassionate rationality. Examples of disastrous imitation abound, from the tulip mania of the seventeenth century to the savings and loan debacle of the 1990s.

### Heterogeneous Groups

Vicarious experimentation is more difficult in this case, where the individuals facing the same situation are no longer identical in every respect.[24] Our paradigm seeker can no longer simply extrapolate but must first control for differences. What now for the paradigm-seeking process?

---

22. Kahn et al. 1982, 3.
23. Conlinsk 1980. Other economists seem to share this view; see, for example, Matthews 1984.
24. I continue to ignore the complication that may arise from the fact that others' actions alter the situation we face. Imagine, instead, a situation where we observe the behavior of a prior generation in circumstances similar to those we now face.

*Proposition 5 (Interpersonal Comparisons).* When faced with uncertainty, people will compare themselves to others as a precondition for vicarious experimentation and imitation.[25]

Vicarious experiments in heterogeneous groups make little sense without the interpersonal comparisons that enable us both to control or correct for individual differences and to identify others who are sufficiently similar in their relevant attributes for their practices to serve as paradigms. Individuals with comparable abilities, appearances, and qualifications, for example, provide data similar to those from vicarious experiments in a homogeneous population. When their relevant attributes are somewhat but not greatly different from our own, we can still "guesstimate" the value of alternative courses of action by allowing for these variations. But any case that does not resemble our own sufficiently closely should be ignored.

Comparison itself is essential to the process of reasoning. Even in the neoclassical paradigm of maximization, one compares the values of known alternatives, given goals and constraints, and then selects the highest value. For example, if an individual goes to a supermarket to buy an apple and sees the sign, "One dollar each," he or she will select the largest one if all other qualities are equal. But if the sign reads "One dollar per pound," the best choice may not be the largest. Depending upon the intensity of the individual's preference for apples, his or her appetite, and the values he or she expects from the alternative uses for money, the best choice may turn out instead to be the smallest piece of fruit, and the comparison in this case will be made among the (marginal) values of apple consumption and all other goods.

Here, however, we are talking about *interpersonal* comparisons that yield otherwise unobtainable information to help individuals in heterogeneous groups cope with an uncertainty that obscures the relationship between action and consequence. How are we to act when we are unsure about what is optimal? We seek a guide, and preferably a reliable guide, to action, and we find it through vicarious experiments controlled by interpersonal comparison.

Consider individual X. If isolated, Mr. X may procure a paradigm by performing a mental experiment or extending the applicability of existing paradigms. If he is desperately hungry for fruit and approaches a stand with unlabeled items that resemble apples, Mr. X may "solve" the selection problem with an "apple paradigm," picking the fruit that is especially large, hard, and red. The proof of the paradigm will be in the eating. If the bite is bitter, the choice of "apple paradigm" was a bad one, if the flavor is acceptable, the

---

25. Again, it is tempting to ponder whether relative comparison is an increasing function of uncertainty, just as imitation may be. Both speculations will be deferred for future research.

paradigm is good, or at least not too bad. It is altogether possible, however, that, had Mr. X acted upon a "peach paradigm," he would have picked an even tastier piece of fruit.

Now suppose that Mr. X's isolation is broken just before his hesitant choice is made. Someone else, Ms. Y, approaches the stand and, with no attention to X, decisively selects an item that looks sour to his "apple paradigm" mind-set. How will Mr. X act? He can now either dismiss Ms. Y or credit her with knowledge superior to his own.[26] If X were already certain of the truth and efficacy of his own paradigm, he would probably ignore or scorn her as a fool. But if X is very tentative about adopting the apple paradigm, he will compare himself to Y and ask which of them is more likely to be informed in these special circumstances. If the sign on the stand read "Tropical Fruit" and Y wore a T-shirt from Tahiti, X might even abandon his notion about apples and simply follow her lead, assuming that he will enjoy by imitation an outcome similar to hers.

Robert Axelrod's experiments illustrate the strength of this tendency to make interpersonal comparisons. Axelrod repeatedly instructed students to be concerned only with their own payoff in the paired game of Prisoner's Dilemma,[27] only to report the following results.

> These instructions simply do not work. The students look for a standard of comparison to see if they are doing well or poorly. . . . People tend to resort to the standard of comparison that they have available—and this standard is often the success of the other player relative to their own success.[28]

Notwithstanding explicit instructions to the contrary, the students wanted to know how they stacked up relative to the others. Why? When the population is heterogeneous, interpersonal comparison of performance is an essential ingredient of vicarious experimentation aimed at gleaning information from other people's experiences. To qualify as an experiment, these experiences must resemble one's own case in respects that are relevant to the case at hand. Those that meet this standard will provide the most useful prediction of an individual's own actions, and he or she will then watch for relative performance that may indicate the possibility for betterment.[29]

---

26. Mr. X may not suspect that the stranger's grounds for adopting, say, a "prune paradigm" is any less secure that his foundation for adopting the "apple paradigm."

27. See chap. 5 for a discussion of the Prisoner's Dilemma game.

28. Axelrod 1984, 111.

29. See Schoemaker's (1980) survey of "nonholistic" approaches to decision making under risk. Unlike the present study, these approaches seem to aim at establishing specific rules of inference. Agreeing with Popper's negative solution to "Hume's problem," however, I find this

*Corollary 5a (Peers 1)*. As a precondition for vicarious experimentation, people will compare themselves with those who are similar in relevant attributes.[30]

The aspects of a problem that are deemed relevant constitute a basis of comparison. Some are obvious and some not. For example, when a co-worker is promoted, the other workers are not always certain whether this advancement occurs because of personal charm, proven ability, future potential as perceived by the manager, racial or sexual prejudice, or other factors. Even obscure choices gain clarity from repeated comparison—but only if the situations are truly comparable. Blue-collar workers cannot gain much insight into the process of promotion by comparing themselves to movie stars or executives. Economics professors involved in salary negotiations do not look to the wages of professors in medical schools or English departments. Useful comparisons are made, instead, with others who constitute a comparable group in some sense, and this group acts as the paradigm for the individual within it.[31]

*Corollary 5b (Equality)*. Insofar as interpersonal comparisons are controlled vicarious experiments, people expect similar "effects" from similar "causes".

Once a paradigm has been identified, the relationship between cause and effect is perceived as one of logical necessity. It is therefore natural to expect the same "effect" from the same "cause." To illustrate this point, consider a worker who compares herself with others deemed similar in the attributes relevant for the situation at hand. If their tasks are alike, she will expect like remuneration. If their wages are the similar, she will conclude that similar performance is sufficient. Other workers are her paradigms, and she acts as if she has inferred, through comparison, a certain relationship between performance, $X$, and remuneration, $Y$. In the language of mathematics, $Y = f(X)$, with $\partial y/\partial x > 0$.

---

ambition bootless on philosophical grounds: I fail to see the *logical* basis of inference as a whole. See Popper 1979, 4–31; my discussion of Hume's problem in chap. 1.

30. This point has a precedent in Leon Festinger's Social Comparison Theory (see West and Wicklund 1980). Based on the postulate that people possess the drive to evaluate their abilities and opinions correctly, Festinger hypothesizes that, in the absence of objective measures, they make these evaluations through comparisons. Festinger is implicitly dealing with an aspect of decision making under uncertainty, namely, the information-gathering process. I thank Professor James Jackson, now the Associate Dean of the Rackham School of Graduate Studies, University of Michigan, for this reference.

31. See also work in sociology concerning the theory of reference groups; West and Wicklund 1980.

A problem will be perceived, however, if the result of the comparison renders untenable the paradigmatic relationship between "cause" and "effect." A disturbance, whether permanent or temporary, may arise in a hitherto stable structure. For example, the initial situation may find $A$ and $B$ with similar attributes and salaries. The paradigm is thus upheld since $f(X_a) = f(X_b)$ where $X_a = X_b$. If $A$ now receives a raise, promotion or bonus, and $B$ does not, $B$ is bound to perceive a problem. Her expectations are frustrated because, at this point, $f(X_a) > f(X_b)$, while $X_a = X_b$.

The problem may be resolved in any of four different ways. First, following Albert Hirschman's "tunnel vision" hypothesis,[32] $B$ may expect that she too will receive a like reward, soon. This trusting expectation is based on the assumption that the existing paradigm, $Y = f(X)$, is essentially correct, and calls for no paradigm revision. Second, $B$ can maintain her faith in the paradigm, expect no improvement in her own situation, suspect foul play, and feel unjustly treated. $B$ will then probably demand some sort of immediate action for redress or explanation. In this case, the vicarious experiment based on interpersonal comparison results in envy, and this state of mind leads to envious behavior, as $B$ tries to reduce the disparity between the paradigm $Y = f(X)$, assumed to be correct, and the actual realization, $f(X_a) < f(X_b)$, when $X_a = X_b$. $B$'s third possibility is to lessen but not relinquish her hold on the paradigm, now accepting it only nominally and acquiescently, after expectations have been repeatedly frustrated. Even if the problem persists, $B$ finds the situation absurd and gives up any effort to deal with it. This case may be described as a state of *accidia*, a feeling of helplessness stemming from the perception of an impossible gap between reality and self.[33] Finally, $B$ may abandon the old paradigm and adopt a new one, such as $Y = g(X)$, so that $g(X_a) < g(X_b)$, when $X_a = X_b$. The last type of response, changing one's view to fit the reality, instead of the other way around, as in the second case, is often cited in the cognitive dissonance literature.

I shall discuss the envy inherent in the second response further in chapter 7. In chapter 4, however, I turn to the social implications of paradigm seeking on the part of individuals. At this juncture, I enrich and complicate the model by allowing full interaction and interdependence among the individuals in the group.

---

32. Hirschman 1981.
33. Shoham 1974.

CHAPTER 4

# Individuals in Society

> It is thus that man, who can subsist only in society, was fitted by nature to that situation for which he was made.
>
> —Adam Smith

In the preceeding chapters, I have discussed the implications of paradigm seeking for the behavior of isolated individuals and individuals in homogeneous or heterogeneous groups with minimal interaction. All of these cases can be perceived as games against nature. Now it is time to introduce into the analysis interactions and interdependencies—in a word, society. In a social setting, we shall see, individuals play games mainly with or against one another.[1]

**Individuals in a Group with Interaction**

In a social setting, paradigm-seeking individuals are faced with two distinct sorts of decisions: one concerning their own actions, which may affect other people, and the other involving their reaction to other people's actions, which may in turn affect them. I shall consider each in turn, beginning with the former.

*Proposition 6 (Approval Seeking).* Faced with uncertainty, individuals will seek approval and avoid disapproval.

People are easily swayed by public opinion. Signs of social approval range from faint smiles to such rewards as praise, gifts, and shared time. Social disapproval can be as simple as shrugs and as devastating as death. Regardless of the amplitude or severity of the response, we have long been observed to seek the positive and eschew the negative reaction to our own

---

1. To quote Johansson: "[As] human beings learned cooperatively to change and modify natural environments, they began to construct increasingly elaborate systems that were further removed from natural systems and thus more and more dependent upon the creation of cultural information processing" (1988, 177).

actions. Indeed, well before he wrote the *Wealth of Nations*, Adam Smith had an eye to this sort of behavior in *The Theory of Moral Sentiments*.

> Nature, when she formed man for society, endowed him with an original desire to please, and an original aversion to offend his brethren. She taught him to feel pleasure in their favorable, and pain in their unfavorable regard. She rendered their approbation most flattering and most agreeable to him . . . and their disapprobation most mortifying and most offensive.[2]

Smith is willing to argue that approval seeking underlies a large part of human action, including wealth seeking. Our striving for wealth is not so much because it helps us obtain material advantages, but rather because we improve our standing in others' eyes.[3]

I should like now to advance a theory to fit this long-standing observation of our dependence on others. We have already seen that individuals faced with uncertainty seek paradigms that can identify viable courses of action. Consider now the possibility that we seek approval of our actions in order to increase our own confidence in a paradigm choice that has been quite tentative. Social acceptance makes us feel better about the propriety of our decision. Community disapproval, on the other hand, tends to weaken our commitment and perhaps force a reexamination of the issue.

Adam Smith has again hit the mark.

> The agreement or disagreement of the sentiments and judgments of other people with our own, is, in all cases, it must be observed, more or less important to us, exactly in proportion as we ourselves are more or less uncertain about the propriety of our own sentiments, about the accuracy of our own judgments. . . . When [man] is perfectly satisfied with every part of his own conduct, the judgment of other people is often of less importance to him. Our uncertainty concerning our own merit, and our anxiety to think favorably of it, should together naturally make us desirous to know the opinion of other people concerning it.[4]

Illustrating the point by comparing the degree to which an upstart poet and a mathematician might care about others' approval, Smith observed that "Nothing delights [the poet] so much . . . as the favorable judgments of his friends and of the public; nothing mortifies him so severely as the contrary," while the

---

2. Smith 1976b, 116.
3. Smith 1976b, 50–51.
4. Smith 1976b, 122–23, 126.

mathematician is "frequently very indifferent about the reception which [he meets] from the public."[5] The difference, of course, stems from the greater degree of uncertainty in ascertaining the value of the poet's work.

Not only our confidence in our actions but also their viability depends, *inter alia*, upon the reactions of others. If others respond as we expect them to, with favorable disposition, our decisions are supported and more likely to "work" than if they thwart our expectations with disapproval.

Each action, moreover, becomes part of our reputation. We are judged and treated in the future on the basis of past and present actions. They work their way, as it were, into other people's paradigms about us. In the future, life will be easier with the support of others than without it; all the more reason to seek approval today.

In sum, people may seek approval and eschew disapproval in part because they are pleased by the first and pained by the second. But, in the face of uncertainty, social approbation and its contrary also provide useful information about the propriety of our decisions and the viability of future actions.[6] Paradigm-seeking individuals come to feel themselves in the assembly of fellow human beings, as it were. They respond as if the approval of others, for whatever reason, vindicates their choice of paradigm, while disapproval is seen as the verdict of the assembly that the decision has been found wanting.

The trouble with approval seeking, however, is that both approbation and disapprobation tend to follow actions, while decision making must precede them. To arrive at a decision with reference to public opinions and reactions is somewhat like putting the cart before the horse. How can we, as paradigm-seeking creatures, deal with this problem?

*Corollary 6a (Imagined Spectators).* In making decisions, individuals in society will seek the approval of imagined spectators and avoid their disapproval.

To choose a course of action likely to meet the approval of others, decision makers may conduct *mental experiments* by imagining an assembly of spectators. Initially, the most promising paradigm will be brought to the assembly for a trial. If this candidate meets the approval of this assembly, it will become the paradigm of choice. If, on the contrary, it fails to meet approval, the paradigm will be discarded and a different candidate brought to the "assembly within." In acting in accordance with the imaginary judges, we shall feel proud for having behaved properly. Going against the imaginary

---

5. Smith 1976b, 123, 124.

6. One consequence of this practical attention to the (dis)approval of others, as we shall see below, is to reduce individual differences, at least in the public domain.

judgment, on the other hand, would make us feel shame and guilt for having acted improperly. The imagined spectators are, in brief, our *conscience*.

The imagined assembly may not be an exact replica of actual spectators. Rather, it is likely to be the synthetic product of our lifetime learning. Children become accustomed to being watched and judged for good or ill by adults. As they grow up, some of these adults may be replaced, in part, by friends, heroes and movie stars. Whether or not they are "alive," episodes involving significant others become paradigms and take up residence in our mind as a highly subjective assembly of spectators. According to Ross and Anderson, people tend "to see their own behavioral choices and judgments as relatively common and appropriate to existing circumstances while viewing alternative responses as uncommon, deviant, and inappropriate."[7] This "false consciousness" or "egocentric attribution bias" is a necessary implication of the individual judgmental process involving imagined spectators.

We do try, however, to make this assembly as impartial and disinterested as possible. What we really want is not so much the approval of others, or that of the imagined others, as the correct choice of paradigm. The verdict of a favorably biased assembly may be pleasing, much as flattery from an assembly of sycophants is pleasing. But a biased assembly would be an unreliable instrument of determining the correctness of our judgments.[8] Therefore, we try to imagine an assembly of impartial spectators when we seek an appropriate paradigm.

Nonetheless, in the end, our inner assemblies remain subjective. As a reflection of an individual's lifetime experiences in all their eccentricities, pain, and glory, they remain unique to the individual, perhaps as widely variant as the difference in individual backgrounds.

If so, the paradigms identified as appropriate in a given situation by two individuals could be different, leading to different actions. This may be a source of interpersonal conflicts. Also, a paradigm approved by the imagined assembly, that is, an action according to the dictates of our conscience, may fail to meet the approval of the people around us, the actual spectators.[9] Decision making in society is, therefore, no easy matter.

I shall postpone my discussion of the implications of interaction among individuals with imagined impartial spectators that are subjective and poten-

---

7. Ross and Anderson 1982, 140.

8. See Smith (1976b), who builds his moral theory on the concept of an "impartial spectator."

9. Kuran (1990, 18) observes that "it is possible for [an individual decision maker] to have a troubled conscience" and that the neoclassical framework "fails to account for the fact that individual choice can be a harrowing experience." He suggests that "personality" is itself a matter of nature and nurture, which explains our different needs or preferences for "decisional autonomy." What Kuran organizes around the concept of preference, I group around cognition.

tially incongruent to the second half of this chapter. First, let us consider the manner in which we evaluate other people's actions, as a precondition for our reaction to them.

> *Corollary 6b (Empathy).* We evaluate others' actions by placing ourselves (or, rather, our imagined spectators) in their shoes. We tend to approve of their action if, in their shoes, we should have acted similarly and disapprove if we would have acted differently. Empathy is vicarious experimentation within a social context.

When people around us act, we must respond, or react, to their actions in one way or another. Whatever form of response we decide to take (and ignoring them is one), it must be based on our assessment of the other's actions. We "invite" favorable responses from others and others invite favorable responses from us. To disregard this invitation for response is to act, or rather react, inappropriately.

How are we to judge another's action and respond appropriately? Which paradigm should we adopt for our own action? Our mental experiment may take a form of *empathy*. Recreating in our own minds that person's circumstances as closely as possible, we may try to identify an appropriate paradigm that would have been identified, if we had been in the individual's shoes.[10] Though we cannot hope to replicate exactly another's circumstances, including his or her knowledge and feelings, we try our best.[11] In empathizing, it is we (not the individual in question) who summon the imagined spectators. If we conclude, based on this *mental experiment*, that we would have behaved similarly, then we tend to approve of the individual's action and respond favorably. Otherwise, we tend to disapprove and respond unfavorably. To do otherwise is to disapprove of our own conscience.

Approval or disapproval does not, therefore, hinge only on the personal, utilitarian consequences of other people's actions.[12] Indeed, we can approve of actions that harm us and disapprove of actions that benefit us. In judging our own and others' behaviors, we are bound to rely on the council of imagin-

---

10. *Empathy* is the central concept in Smith's *The Theory of Moral Sentiments*, but he used the term *sympathy* to express it. This was an unfortunate word choice since many people have erroneously interpreted sympathy as man's phylogenetic disposition to be benevolent or altruistic, leading to what Germans used to call *Das Adam Smith Problem*, a pseudoproblem (see Choi 1990).

11. We can more easily empathize with people who are near to us than with those who are far because we are better able to recreate the circumstances of the close ones, we can more fruitfully conduct a mental experiment for them than for those at a considerable remove.

12. Smith (1976b) provides many examples to show that the basis of our approval is not utilitarian consideration.

ary spectators that constitute our conscience. A murderer, for example, can actually approve of his own execution, in the sense of concluding that he or she too would have called for it if he or she were in the position of others. This judgment hinges on his or her ability to empathize strongly enough (though too late, we must say) with the dead and bereaved, the government responsible for enforcing the law, and a public that is fearful, outraged by the injustice, and interested in revenge and deterrence. When Katherine Howard was ordered to be beheaded by Henry VIII for infidelity, she "extolled the virtue of the king and the justness of the sentence and asked those remaining to be good and obedient subjects of the king."[13] This sort of sentiment, if genuine, presupposes her ability to empathize with Henry VIII and to appreciate the principle of succession of the crown as a matter far more weighty than any individual life. Without this sort of ability to empathize, prisoners will consider it unjust for them to be on death row.[14]

## The Emergence of Conventional Practices

Over time, the paradigm-seeking individuals in society tend to work out a system of interactions to support coordination and cooperation among members. These conventional practices are based on a degree of predictability in individual behavior and eventually constitute a social order.[15]

> *Proposition 7 (Conventional Practices).* Conventional "solutions," or social paradigms, exist for many of the problems that arise in the process of social production and distribution. These conventions resemble individual paradigms in their role of enabling individuals to cope with uncertainty. They differ in usually being the simple by-product of separate individuals seeking their own paradigms rather than a deliberate social choice.

Individuals in isolation or in minimally interactive groups may adopt any paradigm they choose, as long as it meets the bare requisites of biological survival. This latitude presents problems for theory, which should be able to

---

13. Katherine Howard, paraphrased in Randell Bartlett 1989, 184.
14. To the degree that empathy is the basis of moral judgments, the proper excercise of empathy should be the cornerstone of moral education and penal codes.
15. "Conventions" and "social norms" are synonyms for "conventional practices," and the concept of their existence is in no way original to this study. Leibenstein (1982b) and Field (1984) have both discussed the role of conventions in solving social situations that take the form of Prisoner's Dilemmas. New to economics are, rather, the emphasis and examination of how these conventions are actually generated by paradigm-seeking individuals.

impose some constraints on paradigm choices, but the formal approach adopted in this book makes it impossible to go beyond what has been accomplished in the previous two chapters.

Our saving grace is that people live in a society full of interactions and interdependencies. If society is defined as a system of human interaction over time,[16] the viability of one individual's paradigm depends upon the paradigms of all the other individuals with whom he or she must interact. Because only at our peril can we choose any idiosyncratic paradigm whatsoever, this dependency imposes a limit on our choices. I call this limit the *requirement of social interaction*.

In society, the efficacy of a paradigm as a means of survival depends, in large measure, upon its ability to induce others to behave in certain ways. More specifically, the paradigms we adopt must support actions whose outcomes are consistent with the expectations implicit or explicit in the paradigms in the first place. This condition will be met only if the behavior of other people with whom we interact is what we expect. In other words, the viability of a paradigm hinges upon whether or not the other parties fulfill their anticipated roles. The expected actions, in turn, will be forthcoming only if our actions prompt the proper responses from others according to their own paradigm choices, and so on *ad infinitum*. For any stable and ongoing relationship, the expectations implied by the paradigms each individual has chosen for the situation (which now includes all the other individuals in the society) must somehow be made mutually consistent. The absence of this sort of consistency would cause much uncertainty, personal suffering, chaos, and poverty.

Paradigm-seeking individuals, therefore, would endeavor to find *individually* a set of paradigms so that their lives become more manageable. The process of searching for paradigms is a spontaneous process. There is no constitutional convention. There is no guarantee that the process of groping will reach a successful conclusion. But only if a group arrives at a set of paradigms that work, that is, that meet the requirement of social interaction, its members will be able to manage a prosperous living among them.

To clarify this claim, imagine that a man and a woman who follow dramatically different paradigms find themselves stranded on an otherwise deserted island, as in Lina Wertmuller's *Swept Away*.[17] Given their divergent

---

16. This serves our purpose, as unsatisfactory as it may first appear. Ortega y Gasset (1957, 11–15) complained that after reading all the writings of Comte, Durkheim, and Weber, he was still unable to determine what society was.

17. In this fine movie, the man is a disgruntled sailor with communist leanings, while the woman's worldview is consistent with her happy status as the wife of the wealthy capitalist who had originally employed the sailor on his yacht.

expectations, this odd couple will find it difficult to coexist until both sets of paradigms have been adjusted to fulfill mutual expectations. Call this adjustment "a workable system of interaction" or "conventional order."

Rather than supposing that individuals in society simultaneously adopt practices that fulfill one another's expectations, we shall adopt an evolutionary perspective to examine the process by which just such a convention might emerge. The evolution proceeds as follows. Individuals can adopt whatever paradigms they like, as long as they meet the requirement of social interaction, because, unless we are supported by other people, that is, unless we can elicit other people's cooperation, we shall lead lives unsatisfactorily brutish and brief. Others' cooperation, however, need not be the result of any *conscious* efforts to be helpful. The requirement of social interaction specifies only that the adopted paradigms elicit collaboration from others. Intention is not the issue here. More often than not, our behavior produces unanticipated consequences, and not all of mistakes are personally or socially costly.[18] Eventually, the paradigms that facilitate cooperation will tend to dominate. The followers of those that meet the requirement of social interaction will grow in number through survival and imitation, while adherents to paradigms that fail in this sense will decline through abandonment and attrition.

The evolutionary process through which individuals collectively generate conventions is bounded at both ends: by the means employed by lower forms of life at one extreme, and by the meditated approach of the ideal scientist at the other. As creatures with well-developed craniums, we have an ability to reason like scientists. But, as practical beings, we share with lower animals the urgency of action, which imparts a certain inflexibility to our behavior and tends to make the criterion of paradigm choice that of value rather than truth.

In our search for paradigms, we take an experimental approach (proposition 3). In a social context, in which "the requirement of social interaction" compels us to seek the approval of others (proposition 6), the experimental approach is translated into two kinds of mental experimentation, namely, the method of imagined spectators (corollary 6a) and empathy (corollary 6b). That is, we tend to adopt such paradigms that we expect them to be approved by the significant others or our conscience. And we tend to judge others' actions as we would judge our own and respond accordingly. The awareness that others cannot completely empathize with us, given the insufficiency of their information, tends to put an additional damper on our choice of paradigms.[19] These orientations tend to facilitate the generation of sets of para-

---

18. It is not uncommon to be right for the wrong reasons. Christopher Columbus "discovered" the New World by embarking on a venture to India deemed practical only because he had grossly underestimated its distance from Europe.

19. Smith 1976b.

digms that form the basis of mutually consistent expectations in many areas where individuals frequently interact. The main difference between the scientists, or philosophers, and us as beings that must undertake constant action to sustain life, is that we often cannot afford the luxury of suspended judgment for long.

In a closed and stable environment, the evolutionary process may result in a state where the majority have their own paradigms adjusted to elicit the necessary cooperation of others in many recurrent situations. Individuals in such a state can therefore expect considerable regularity in other people's behavior, and the problem of dealing with uncertainty has, in good measure, been resolved by the generation of *social paradigms*.[20] This is indeed what is meant by the *conventional solution*, and we may call social relations regulated by the conventions the *regime of convention*.[21]

The paradigmatic approach is quite distinct from two other common models of convention: representative man and functionalism. The representative man approach extrapolates individual attributes to groups. Many economists, for example, extend characteristics of the profit-maximizing "representative" firm to industries, even though the fallacy of composition warns us that it is logically possible for individual and group behavior to exhibit substantial divergence. The functionalist approach, on the other hand, simply explains that conventions and social norms exist because they help to maintain the social system. But in the absence of an adequate explanation for how the maintenance requirement induces people to fulfill their roles in the system, this explanation is insufficient, even circular.[22]

Applying the representative man approach in the current context, by extending the individual behavioral implications already developed in chapters 2 and 3, to the behavior of society as a whole, would capture some important parallels but also miss some significant differences. Only by keeping firmly in mind how diverse individuals generate and maintain conventions can we keep our sights on the differences between the behavioral characteristics of an individual and the tendencies of the collectivity of individuals. By this approach only, can we view individuals as agents both of the perpetuation of the *status quo* and of change in the system. In contrast, the representative man approach fails to address composition and diversity, while the functionalist school begs the question of causation.

---

20. Hayek's concept of the evolution of spontaneous order is quite similar; see Vanberg 1986; Sugden 1989.

21. Especially in its stability, the paradigmatic approach's "regime of convention" bears some similarity to neoclassical economics' "equilibrium state" and, even more, to the Schumpeterian "circular flow." The differences are notable as well, however: as we shall see in chap. 5, the regime of convention is a dynamic concept that bears the seed of its own destruction.

22. See Ullman-Margalit 1977, 176–80; Elster 1983, 49–68; Vanberg 1986, 83–85.

I shall now demonstrate the validity of proposition 7, that the paradigm-seeking individuals in society tend to generate conventional "solutions" to meet the requirement of interaction. First, I shall divide the context of interaction into two types: the Coordination game and the Prisoner's Dilemma (PD hereafter).[23] These two games will be considered as the archetypes of social interaction.

## Games of Coordination

A social situation may be characterized as a Coordination game when participants face a number of alternative courses of action and may obtain mutually beneficial outcomes only when their actions are coordinated; in every other outcome, everyone will suffer.[24] One illustration involves deciding on which side of the road to drive. Let us suppose that there are two drivers and they can drive on either side of the road. Without traffic coordination, collisions can occur frequently and driving would be hazardous in the extreme. The situation could be presented as payoffs $(-1, -1)$ for drivers A and B in figure 1. If everyone drove on the same side of the road, no matter which, the payoffs would improve to $(1, 1)$. Consistency alone is important. People drive on the left side in England and Japan and on the right in the United States, to equally good effect.

Two individuals in a Coordination game may face more than two options. Assume that they are trying to meet each another without being able to communicate exactly where this meeting will be. Suppose that the payoffs for both of them showing up at the corner of Manhattan's 42d Street and Fifth Avenue ($F$), or at the World Trade Center ($W$), or at the Lincoln Center ($L$), are $(6, 6)$. In this case, it does not matter where they meet, be it $F$ or $W$ or $L$, as long as they are at the same place, that is, as long as they meet. If they show up at different locations, say A at $F$ and B at $W$, or A at $L$ and B at $W$, and so forth, then they all lose and the payoff is $(0, 0)$ (see fig. 2).

It is entirely possible, however, that A and B are not indifferent about where they meet (due to differences in tastes, commuting times, and so forth). For example, A may rank the meeting places $F$, $L$, and $W$ in the order of preference, while B ranks them $L$, $F$, and $W$, as shown in figure 3. In this example, meeting at $W$ is least preferred by both. But between $F$ and $L$, the

---

23. In the sections that follow, I am indebted and grateful to Viktor Vanberg for his suggestion that a more clear distinction between the two types of games is desirable. See also Vanberg and Buchanan 1988, 143–44. Ullman-Margalit (1977) identifies "inequality situations" as a third type of interaction; I do not find this game to be on the same level of generality and, therefore, stick to bifurcation.

24. See Ullman-Margalit 1977, 74–133; Vanberg 1986, 91–93.

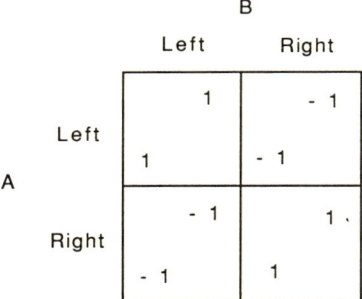

Fig. 1. 2 × 2 Coordination game

two are in conflict: A would rather meet at $F$, while B would rather meet at $L$. They still must coordinate their activities, since each would prefer "somewhere" over "nowhere" for their gathering: in other words, (6, 5), (4, 4), and (5, 6) are all better than (0, 0). Though it is more difficult to show the Coordination game situation with many people, the idea is sufficiently illustrated. And we can always take A as an individual and B as the rest of the community, for the purpose of illustration.

If individuals are faced with a coordinations problem, how will they behave? Suppose that there is no precedent. They will then move to become coordinated and predictable, but not necessarily with unanimous and explicit agreement. People could agree explicitly from the start to solve problems of coordination, thus saving the trouble of trial and error. But it may be difficult or costly to convince everyone of the benefits of coordination, or even of the nature of game they face.

In the absence of consensus or any prior examples, some people will experiment, while others will wait and see (proposition 6, vicarious experimentation). Of those adventurous souls who try different courses of action, some will succeed when their actions are met by chance with like-minded actions. Outcomes depend on many factors beyond the primary actors' control or even awareness. The successful outcome could be $(F, F)$ or $(L, L)$ or even $(W, W)$, as shown in figure 3. In any event, once some individuals attain success and prominence by certain practices,[25] others will take them as paradigms and imitate their actions (corollary 4a, imitation). As the number of people following one paradigm increases, it gains legitimacy in that its fol-

---

25. See Schelling 1960, 54–58; Sugden 1989, 89–90.

## 74  Paradigms and Conventions

|   | B |   |   |
|---|---|---|---|
|   | F | W | L |
| **A** F | 6 / 6 | 0 / 0 | 0 / 0 |
| W | 0 / 0 | 6 / 6 | 0 / 0 |
| L | 0 / 0 | 0 / 0 | 6 / 6 |

**Fig. 2. 2 × 3 Coordination game**

lowers tend to approve of others who follow the same paradigm, and disapprove those who do not (corollary 6b, empathy).

A brief consideration again of the rules of the road suffices to make the point. There is nothing in the abstract to favor right- over left-sided driving behavior, but once the majority drive on the right, then driving on the left is largely out of the question. The majority will express their strong disapproval of the minority who attempt to drive on the wrong side, willfully or by mistake. As driving behavior becomes more and more predictable—at least in this respect—it makes less and less sense even to contemplate driving on any side but the right. Even aside from utilitarian considerations, individuals would look for a paradigm that supports action expected to meet the approval of others (proposition 6, approval seeking). In this manner, the entire population comes to drive on the right.

Whether the stuff of real life or the construct of labs and ivory towers, those practices that emerge as dominant (the "solutions" to games of coordination) thus become conventional practices, or, simply, conventions, and can evolve over time.[26] Given the nature of the game, when a novel problem is recognized as one bettered by coordination, it can be solved (in principle) by a collective agreement or by the decree of an arbitrary selection among alternatives. *That* it is done matters more than *how* it is done; and it is in each individual's self-interest to adhere to conventions, even if their origins be fortuitous. The same cannot be said, alas, about games that resemble the Prisoner's Dilemma.

---

26. See Lewis 1969; Ullman-Margalit 1977.

|   |   | B |   |   |
|---|---|---|---|---|
|   |   | F | W | L |
| A | F | 6 / 5 | 0 / 0 | 0 / 0 |
|   | W | 0 / 0 | 4 / 4 | 0 / 0 |
|   | L | 0 / 0 | 0 / 0 | 5 / 6 |

**Fig. 3. A variant of the 2 × 3 Coordination game**

Prisoner's Dilemma Games

In many other situations of social production and distribution, although concerted and cooperative actions can greatly benefit society as a whole, if a conflict of interest exists over the distribution of gains and the shouldering of losses, the players can become quite divisive. Agreements can break down if everyone relentlessly pursues self-interest, and the result will be no cooperation and losses for all players.

The essence of such a situation is captured by the celebrated Prisoner's Dilemma (PD). Individuals A and B, suspected of being partners in a crime, are arrested, imprisoned, and placed, *incommunicado*, in separate cells. Unless at least one suspect confesses, the district attorney will lack sufficient evidence for conviction. To extract a confession, the district attorney notifies both suspects of the following: (1) if A confesses and B does not, A goes free and B gets sentenced for ten years; (2) if B confesses and A does not, B goes free and A gets ten years; (3) if both confess, both get reduced sentences of five years each; and (4) if neither confesses, both get one-year sentences on reduced charges. Figure 4 shows a summary of these possibilities.

If both A and B act based on utilitarian calculation, the dominant strategy will be confession, and the outcome, $(-5, -5)$, is clearly worse than the result when neither confesses, $(-1, -1)$. In this situation, rationality on an individual basis becomes irrationality collectively, hence the dilemma.

The PD game can be generalized to capture many other social situations and is especially useful in highlighting problems of free riding.[27] For ex-

---

27. See Hardin 1982.

76    Paradigms and Conventions

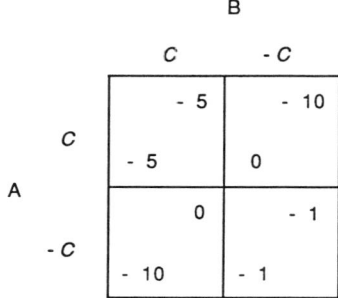

**Fig. 4. Prisoner's Dilemma game**

ample, imagine a work place. Suppose that there is a range of productive and managerial effort that workers and managers can exert. Order these ranges, $e_1 > e_2 \ldots e_n$ and $t_1 > t_2 > \ldots t_n$, so that $e_1$ is the most a worker can do and $e_n$, the least, similarly $t_1$ is the most the management can do for workers and $t_n$, the least.[28] What would be the result? If we suppose that the factory is staffed by rational utility maximizers, then the dominant strategy is for workers and management both to do the least they can get away with. Both cooperate as little as possible. Consequently, productivity will be lower and the proverbial pie from which they could claim their slices will be smaller. This outcome is a classic PD "solution" for calculating individuals, as shown in figure 5.

Reviewing the variations of PD games captures some of the salient features of interactions in the process of social production and reproduction, namely, the conflict between the benefit of exercising one's liberty and the benefit of cooperation. Since traditional formulations of the PD game can lead to significant paradox, it can also inspire us to extend our inquiries into the very nature of this economic cornerstone, rationality.

Are the outcomes we typically observe from real-life PD situations individually rational but socially the worst possible? No. The world may rarely be a Panglossian paradise, but the ultimate of Hobbesian savagery is uncommon as well. What, then, saves us from the nadir of social degeneration?

A number of considerations have been added to the PD game to shift and ameliorate the solution. Some proposals involve axiomatic exercises based on unrealistic assumptions about human nature.[29] Others have evoked ethics and

---

28. See Leibenstein 1984.
29. See Luce and Raiffa 1957 for discussions of Nash equilibria and Howard 1971 on "metastrategies."

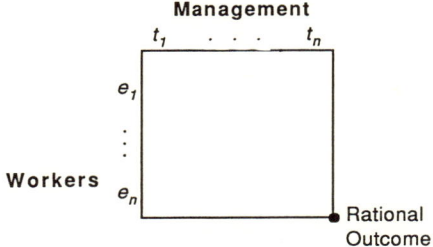

Fig. 5. A variant of the Prisoner's Dilemma game

morality, but these present problems as well.[30] To insure a favorable outcome, PD games must be transformed into situations that preclude opportunistic behavior as a viable alternative, not necessarily for each and every individual, but at least for the social majority.

For example, if we return to our original illustration of the two incarcerated suspects accused of a crime, the additional structure of their being members of organized crime can transform their payoff possibilities from those represented in figure 4 to those represented in figure 6. A's confession in the face of B's silence may still buy A's freedom—but not for long now. The specter of "cement shoes" haunts the new situation and makes squealing look downright unattractive to A. A's fears of being silent while B squeals, on the other hand, are slightly dampened by the prospect of outside revenge for B and clan and outside solicitation for the friends and family of A. Joint confession now results not only in being jointly imprisoned for a shorter period of time but also in being jointly disowned by the crime family, and if these forces are strong enough, the outcome is likely to be symmetric silence and very short sentences indeed. With added structure, the game is no longer PD, but cooperative in nature.

Thomas Hobbes proposed a similar way to improve on the appalling state of nature he envisioned, where the full excise of individual freedom, nay, bellicosity, in the pursuit of gain, safety, and glory, results in a state of "Warre . . . of every man, against every man . . . [with] no place for Industry; because the fruit thereof is uncertain"[31] This outcome of unbridled individualism provides ample incentive to come up with alternatives. Hobbes's vision is the Leviathan, to which people in society surrender their natural right to use violence.[32] This added structure transforms the initial solution into one

---

30. See Sen 1974, 54–67.
31. Hobbes 1968, 185–86.
32. Ullman-Margalit 1977, 62–73.

78    Paradigms and Conventions

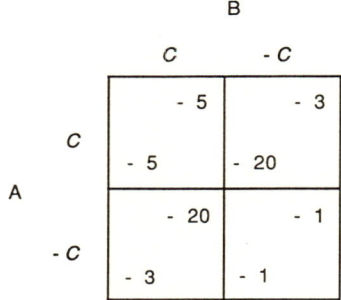

**Fig. 6. Prisoner's Dilemma game modified by crime family membership**

where individuals have good reason to behave peaceably. They can now be less fearful of being violated by others, who will be punished by the Leviathan, the state, for breaching the covenant.[33]

John Maynard Keynes's proposal for government intervention in capital markets can also be viewed as a solution to PD situations. According to Keynes, the marginal efficiency of capital "is fixed . . . by the market valuation as determined by mass psychology."[34] When pessimism reigns, the situation may be aggravated by a sharp increase in liquidity preference. The ensuing fall in the propensity to consume and widespread disinvestment tend to result in depression and unemployment. Individual liquidity preferences exacerbate the problem in this situation, and the outcome is collectively undesirable. Keynes concludes that "in conditions of *laissez-faire* the avoidance of wide fluctuations in employment may . . . prove impossible, . . . *the duty of ordering the current volume of investment cannot safely be left in private hands.*" [35] Thus, his recommendations for government intervention.

Until now, we have looked only at single games, and our framework has been implicitly static. The leashes of Leviathan, whether imposed by crime bosses, Hobbes, or Keynes, may transform PD games into cooperative situations, but the "solutions" have all been introduced from *outside* the system.

By what process are conventions, the "solutions," created to effect the change? A static framework is clearly not the context within which to examine transformation. Transformation involves interactions over time and experien-

---

33. The solution proposed by Alchian and Demsetz (1972) for firms to obviate the problem of shirking and free riding among peers is rather similar. They suggest direct supervision, with sufficient monitoring to make each individual responsible for his or her own production.
34. Keynes 1936, 170.
35. Keynes 1936, 320; italics added.

tial learning.[36] Now is the time to adopt an evolutionary perspective. In a dynamic framework of repeated games, "solutions" to PD situations in society are seen as emerging in the process of learning and connectedness.

### Repeated PD Games

Repeated PD games have the same structure of single PD games, but can be played over and over again. This one addition in setup yields a substantial difference in results. In a single PD game, noncooperation can be the dominant strategy for calculating individuals, but it can also result in a collectively undesirable outcome. If, instead, the PD game is played repeatedly among a number of participants, cooperation tends to emerge as the dominant behavioral pattern.

Consider, for example, the following experiment (undertaken by Robert Axelrod) involving two sets of round-robin tournaments.[37] The first tournament involved fourteen strategies, that is, predetermined rules of action, submitted by professional game theorists intent on winning after exactly two hundred moves. Each strategy was played both against all the submitted strategies and against a random "strategy." In this contest, the number of plays was known; unknown was the strategy of the opponent. For the second tournament, sixty-two people familiar with game theories and computer programming but otherwise of varied backgrounds submitted one strategy each. But in this round, the number of plays was left unspecified. To account for the fact that each play could, in principle, be the last, Axelrod discounted future payoffs.

In both tournaments, the tit-for-tat strategy emerged as the overall winner based on the present value of the cumulative payoffs. This strategy involves starting cooperatively, reciprocating cooperation with cooperation, retaliating promptly against noncooperation with noncooperation, and then quickly returning to cooperation. Every top performer, whether playing tit-for-tat or otherwise, was "nice" in the sense of never being the first to defect,[38] but most were quick to retaliate as well.[39] Cooperation was thus encouraged by both carrots and sticks.

Other experiments add support to Axelrod's findings. Asking people to play a PD game many times over, Rapoport and Chammah chose fifty plays as

---

36. This characteristic of social relations is conspicuously absent from traditional market analysis.
37. See Axelrod 1984.
38. Axelrod 1984, 33.
39. Axelrod 1984, 44. Indeed, Kuran (1990, 5) notes that experimentation in social psychology "demonstrates that the individual's propensity to conform declines markedly when he is led to believe that his dissent will not provoke criticism." See also Axelrod (1986, 1095–1111).

their experimental unit of analysis, characterizing each unit by the fraction of cooperation-cooperation sequences occurring within it. The purpose of the experiment was to determine whether or not there was a positive effect of interaction. If there were no such effect, one would have observed a normal distribution. But the experimental results showed a strong positive effect, leading Rapoport and Chammah to the following conclusion.

> The study of interaction effects indicates that these effects are very strong. They tend to make the *numbers of a pair behave like each other* . . . [and the tendencies] become progressively stronger as the session continues.[40]

The two main conclusions of the experimental studies are (1) that in the context of repeated interaction, individuals tend to "learn" to adopt practices that fulfill one another's expectations and (2) that a general disposition like tit-for-tat, to cooperate with others and to promptly punish noncooperators, is conducive to such social learning.

But what is it that drives individuals to learn to cooperate? Is it the desire to benefit from cooperation or the desire to please others? If we interpret the former as selfish and the latter as altruistic, then we lose the ability to interpret the experimental findings of Axelrod and Rapoport and Chammah.

## Paradigmatic Approach and Conventions

The paradigmatic approach suggests an altogether different interpretation. The approval-seeking individuals are driven by the desire to identify an appropriate paradigm (proposition 6). Thus do we sometimes adopt a paradigm that ends up displeasing others or that is not beneficial from the utilitarian point of view. We choose not from these vantage points but rather to please our imagined spectators (corollary 6a).

The most important implication of the experimental findings, that cooperation tends to emerge as the prevalent behavior among the most successful players and that they retaliate promptly against noncooperators, is *fully consistent* with the paradigmatic approach. We have already examined the tendency to approve or disapprove of others on the basis of our own paradigms; "cooperative behavior" in Axelrod's experiments translates rather straightforwardly into our "behavior following from mutually consistent expectations." Individuals reward, or reciprocate, cooperative behavior in both frameworks, and they discourage "opportunistic" or "inconsistent" actions. Cooperation from this point of view requires neither explicit agreement nor identity of

---

40. Rapoport and Chammah 1965, 63–65.

viewpoint. Individuals with disparate paradigms may act in a tolerably consistent manner within a narrow range of recurrent situations, acting more or less in concert *in spite of* themselves, as it were. In a similar vein, "opportunists" need be neither vile nor malign. They may simply have adopted paradigms that diverge and thus frustrate the expectations of certain others, who then find it easier to blame their frustrations on "evil perpetrators" than to rework their paradigms. A tit-for-tat feature, in brief, is inherent in the paradigmatic approach to uncertainty.[41]

As we follow our natural propensities both to guide our own actions in light of projected approval and disapproval (corollary 6a, imagined spectator), and to approve or disapprove of others according to the consistency of their actions with our expectations, (corollary 6b, empathy), each of us will come to possess paradigms that appear "cooperative." That is, we shall appear to act according to some shared rules of conduct, in much the same way as a group of people repeatedly playing PD games tend to establish cooperation as the dominant strategy, supported by tit-for-tat responses.[42] What is this, after all, but a reexamination of the line of argument already used to establish proposition 7 (conventional practices)?

Thus evolved, conventions tend to make the social environment less uncertain. By allowing us to expect regularities in the behavior of others, they relieve us (in some measure) from the predicament of having to act without knowing the consequences of our actions. As, literally, conventional solutions to PD situations in society, they prevent us from degenerating into a Hobbesian state of nature, a civil war, or a "rational" solution to a PD game. Convention, in brief, is what renders the paradox of the PD situation nonparadoxical in a world with repetition.

### Public versus Private Domain

Conventions are also public goods generated, willy-nilly, by paradigm-seeking individuals in PD situations and functioning to make social interaction tolerable or even profitable. As paradigms that individuals in society come to share, conventions can also be understood as "social paradigms." The use of language can greatly facilitate the process of generating social paradigms. But people need not communicate explicit information about their own paradigms. Nor need their paradigms be identical for conventions to exist. Individual paradigms can remain quite private, and quite unique. All that

---

41. For elaboration of this claim, see chap. 5.
42. Note in this context, Ross and Anderson's observation that people tend to "underestimate the potency of situational forces and constraints and to overestimate the role of individual dispositions" (Ross and Anderson 1982, 136).

convention requires is consistent actions in a narrow range of recurrent situations; individual thoughts are another matter altogether. People can behave in similar ways for quite dissimilar reasons. Each can have quite a different overall understanding of any given situation. In this case, individual actions governed by conventions are in the *public domain*, but there also exist *private domains* that are mutually incompatible.

Consider in this regard the two most famous disciples of Confucius, Mencius and Hsüntze. Mencius believed that people were inherently good, but had been corrupted in the process of socialization; education was necessary, in this case, to undo this damage. Hsüntze, on the contrary, posited that people were basically greedy and capricious, if not evil; education was necessary, in his view, to create a peaceful society. These two Confucian scholars thus came to the same recommendation from diametrically opposed starting points.

Imagine two individuals, A and B. In a given setting, A employs a paradigm whose explicit form is $Y_a = X^2 - 2X + 6$, while B's paradigm takes the form: $Y_b = X^2 - 2X + 6$, if $X < 1$ and $Y_b = -X^2 + 2X + 4$, if $X > 1$. As long as events unfold as usual (that is, in recurrent situations), so that $X < 1$ is the order of the day, A and B appear to be in complete agreement. In effect, they share a paradigm. But the differences in their perceptions of the world will be revealed as they face a novel situation, here represented by $X > 1$. That is, then another explanation of how discordant and mutually inconsistent actions can occur in response to a novel situation in what has previously appeared to be a stable regime of convention.

The paradigmatic approach can thus help us to avoid some mistaken ideas about conventions or norms as a solution for PD situations in society. For example, although we have seen that cooperation can emerge over time in experiments with repeated PD games, this possibility alone should not be viewed as a basis for optimism about human prospects as a whole. In a wider context, cooperative group outcomes need be neither moral nor rational—one thinks here of bribery and kickbacks, price fixing, and codes of honor among thieves as less than admirable acts of cooperation—and even when considered only in their own context, they may not be the best state of events imaginable. The paradigmatic approach makes it clear that social outcomes usually fall somewhere between the best and the worst.[43] The tendency to cooperate is the tendency to cooperate *around a given convention*. Moreover, as we have seen in corollary 3a (unpredictability) for individuals and shall state presently as

---

43. And this conclusion should make even the traditionalists smile: economists are always suspicious of all-or-nothing solutions—they smack of neglect of the margin.

proposition 8 for society, paradigms are, in considerable measure, fortuity and fortuity is rarely global optimality.[44]

**Ubiquity of Conventions**

Conventions are the social analogue of individual paradigms, and they are prevalent in any ongoing relationship. If family, school, or work groups are tight, their shared paradigms must be many. Conversely, a group that barely shares a paradigm must be loosely defined indeed. A community can, accordingly, be identified by the extent to which its members share paradigms.

Much as an individual has a panoply of paradigms, each useful for different occasions, so does society have a constellation of social paradigms, with varying degrees of normative implications,[45] and suitable for different groups of individuals and different sets of circumstances. Because of the importance of the identity of the interdependent actors to situational variation, different conventional practices come to be associated with distinct sets of partners; some are applicable in certain groups but not in others.[46] Hence, we see one set of norms among workers in a factory, a different set for them and their management, and yet another to articulate relationships with their families. What is polite in one culture may be rude in another; the acceptability and viability of a conventional practice is quite contextual and far from universal.

Consider more closely the conventions to which management may acquiesce concerning productivity in the work place. Elton Mayo comments on the Hawthorne studies as follows.

> In every department that continues to operate, the workers have— whether aware of it or not—formed themselves into a group with appropriate customs, duties, routines, even rituals; and management succeeds (or fails) in proportion as it is accepted without reservation by the group as authority and leader.[47]

---

44. In the next chapter, I show that even if the initial set of conventions represented a globally optimal solution, it will not remain optimal for long.

45. Some unconventional practices elicit only mild disapproval, while others evoke strong censure and even ostracism. Ullman-Margalit (1977, 114–20) observes that coordination norms and PD norms may acquire different degrees of sanctions to maintain them because the nature of interactions is also different in the two games. I differ from Ullman-Margalit in this observation only by using "conventional practices" instead of "norms."

46. Perhaps in some instances the group instead of the individual should therefore be the unit of analysis in economics and other branches of the social sciences.

47. Mayo 1971, 226–27.

Citing an example where U.S.-trained Chinese economists tried and failed to break traditional workplace norms by using an incentive scheme prescribed by neoclassical economic theory, Mayo judged economic theory harshly for ignoring conventions.

> In their behavior and their statements, economists indicate that they accept the rabble hypothesis (of economic man) and its corollary of financial incentive as the only effective human motive. They substitute a logical hypothesis of small practical value for the actual facts.[48]

Nor is conventional practice restricted to labor relations. Speaking from personal experience, Keynes observed that the pricing of equities depended upon conventional decisions on what should be factored into their value and what should be excluded from consideration.[49] In tracking the top economic forecasters' performances of late, Stephen McNees, vice president of the Federal Reserve Bank of Boston, concluded that they have erred greatly in calling every major recent turning point and erred alike.[50]

The view that conventions are pervasive in economic life is a venerable one going all the way back to Adam Smith, who observed that the social division of labor that creates so much good is less the product of rational calculation than the evolutionary outcome of human propensities.[51] Alfred Marshall remains firmly in the tradition of Adam Smith when he says that

> . . . the influence of custom . . . over the forms of production and the general economic arrangement of society has been underrated. . . . [Its] effects are not obvious, but they are cumulative.[52]

Joseph Schumpeter expresses a similar view, that production through social division of labor and distribution rests more on customs and traditions than on

---

48. Mayo 1971, 228.
49. Keynes 1936, 149–58. Business enterprises as a rule refer to *Industrial Balance Sheet Guidelines* for industry-specific balance sheet ratios on assets vs. debts, long-term vs. short-term debt, and so forth. These ratios are presumably regarded as some sort of convention or standard for different industries, and deviations may be viewed with alarm or disfavor by auditors and investors. Cross-country comparisons of corporate debt-equity ratios also indicate the importance of different national conventions in business practice: in the United States, corporate leverage over 50 percent would be considered risky, while leverage over 90 percent is common in Japan. I thank Hosein Kazemy for this point.
50. Stephen McNees, quoted in Linden (1991), 68.
51. Smith 1976a, 25.
52. Marshall 1961, 728.

explicit calculation, for which, in any event, our mental capacity is quite inadequate.[53] Viktor Vanberg goes even further.

> What we call a market is always a system of social interactions characterized by a specific *institutional framework*, that is, by *a set of rules* defining certain restrictions on the behavior of the market participants, whether these rules are *informal* . . . or *formal*.[54]

Conventions are pervasive indeed.

> *Proposition 8 (Fortuity).* Conventions evolve from a limited set of precedents whose origin is largely fortuitous.

This proposition follows rather straightforwardly from our arguments for the evolution of conventional practices in situations that resemble either coordination or PD games. In the former, where the existence of coordination is far more important than any precise form it may take, convention will be based on some earlier successful practices. Once a certain behavior is considered viable, it will be imitated and few will see any reason to act differently. Suppose, for example, that a less-developed country (LDC) has built a highway system and that, in the beginning, only a few natives, these being the wealthy and the powerful, are able to afford cars. These elite will undoubtedly drive their vehicles on the left side of the road, as the English do, because they studied at Oxford, Cambridge, and the like. As other people in this LDC become more prosperous and the nation becomes increasingly one of car owners, on what side will the new drivers drive? Only at their peril on the right. Once a precedent of this value is set, it tends to be maintained; logic may be neutral on the issue of side, but history speaks volumes.

The process of establishing convention is quite similar to a "Polya-urn Scheme," in which an urn containing one red and one blue ball is sampled not only with replacement but also so that every time one color is drawn, an extra ball of that same color is added to the urn. In the first drawing, the probability of red is only 50 percent, but if a red ball happens to be drawn, the probability rises to 66 percent for the second drawing; if red is drawn twice in a row, this probability increases to 75 percent for the third. According to Arthur (and others), if this process is continued indefinitely, the probability of selecting red converges to 100 percent.[55]

Consider now a situation where the manner, as well as the fact, of

---

53. Schumpeter 1934, 3–56.
54. Vanberg 1986, 75.
55. David 1985, 335.

coordination matters. Then, once a certain behavior happens to get established however fortuitously as convention, it will tend to be upheld even if the social outcome to which it gives rise is inferior to those supported by other practices. A clear-cut example of this tenacity or tyranny of the past is QWERTYUIOP, the arrangement of the letters of the alphabet on the top row of a typewriter or computer keyboard, known in shorthand as "QWERTY." Surely this is a convention. But why? According to Paul David, QWERTY came about because of the manner in which the early developers of the typewriter perfected the machine, at the then prevailing level of technology.[56] What may be somewhat surprising is that QWERTY persists in face of demonstrably superior keyboard arrangements, given today's technology. The Dvorak Simplified Keyboard (DSK), for example, is said to "[let] you type 20–40 percent faster."[57] Why does QWERTY persist? Because we start with heavy baggage of past and not from scratch. QWERTY had a headstart and had become the basis of convention for manufacturers, typists, and typing schools before new technology made DSK better. Only if we were to wipe out the past would DSK be adopted for its expected superiority in typing.[58]

Although conventions that emerge in PD situations have much stronger normative implications than those that arise in settings resembling games of coordination, the process of their evolution is much the same. From an initial set of circumstances, certain subgroups may be able to organize viable forms of cooperation that represent competing paradigms, or protoconventions. Through a fortuitous sequence of events, one practice may emerge as dominant, expanding the network of cooperation. But it is by no means globally optimal in all respects. Even if it started out as a superior practice initially, changing circumstances may have rendered some other practices potentially more appropriate. The next chapter will investigate this possibility in more detail.

---

56. David 1985, 332–37.
57. David 1985, 332.
58. Whether conventions are optimal solutions, as new institutionalists argue, will be examined in chap. 5.

CHAPTER 5

# Conventions and Social Institutions

So careful of the types she seems
So careless of the single life . . .

"So careful of the type?" but no,
from scarped cliff and querried stone
she cries, "A thousand types are gone . . ."

—Alfred Tennyson

This chapter continues the study of patterns in individual and social behavior. I show that, like individual paradigms, shared paradigms, that is, social conventions, promote stability—to such a degree that they also lead to institutional inertia and suboptimal social outcomes. Opportunities thus remain unexploited, ultimately creating a source of endogenous change and thereby playing an important role in the process of social development.

**Stability**

Conventions are solutions to problems of uncertainty. In this section I explore individual behavioral implications from the generation and existence of conventions.

*Proposition 9 (Conformity).* People tend to conform to conventions.

Conformity follows directly from proposition 7 (conventional practices). If conventions exist, they must be followed, by definition. Convention and conformity go hand in hand and groups can be identified by the set of conventions different majorities follow.[1]

Individual conformity to conventions develops in any of four ways:

---

1. In sociology, functionalists explain people's behavior by their conformity to certain norms (see chap. 4 for the circularity of this reasoning). Functionalism is noticeable in the recent trend toward modeling conformity as an argument in individual utility functions. For example, see Jones 1984.

88    Paradigms and Conventions

adoption of paradigms compatible with convention, imitation, utilitarian calculation, and "attrition." We shall consider each of these possibilities in turn.

People may behave conventionally because conformity accords with the individual paradigms they have identified and used to support successful actions. Over time, they thus meet the approval of their imagined spectators, the consciences they have developed while growing up. They are so convinced of the propriety of conventional behavior that they no longer consider the relative values of nonconforming modes of behavior. They have internalized the convention, as it were.

Newcomers to the community may find imitation a parsimonious form of decision making under all the uncertainty they face in their new setting, and they are more likely to imitate a general practice than one that is highly idiosyncratic. Imagine, for illustration, a Virginian suddenly and unexpectedly relocated in an Eskimo village. Some of his or her Southern ways are likely to be highly inappropriate to the culture and climate of the Arctic, and he or she will undoubtedly find it safer and quicker to do as the Eskimos do than to think out all options on his or her own.

We may also conform through utilitarian calculation. In this case, we choose to act like the others in our group in order to meet their approval and improve our lot even though we may privately believe that an alternative mode of behavior is more suitable or appropriate to the occasion. But this is an unstable situation. To act knowingly in an inappropriate fashion is to profess false faith. This is the sort of conformity that leads to mental disorder.[2]

In order to avoid the unstable, we tend either to change our behavior, given our views (paradigms), or to change our views, given our behavior. To escape an unstable situation, in other words, we tend to act according to the dictates of the imagined spectators, risking other people's disapproval. Otherwise, we become converts, that is, we revise our paradigms so that acting conventionally is fully consistent with our conscience.

Perhaps an intermediate step is possible in a situation where conformity to conventions conflicts with conscience. Instead of either risking the disapproval of others by acting according to our conscience or changing beliefs to make them consistent with actions that are socially condoned, we may buy peace of mind by providing provisional justifications, or excuses, for our conformity. Consider the following example.

The Sunni caliphs of the Umayyad dynasty, who began ruling the Arab empire from Damascus in the late seventeenth century, made it a test of

---

2. Kuran (1990, 9) observes: "[R]esearchers . . . have traced many specific anxieties, frustrations, obsessions, and phobias to the individual's suppression of his views and wants under the burden of getting along with others."

belief to insult the founders of Shi'ism. Seeing that failure to pass the test often brought death, the Shi'is adopted the *taqiya* doctrine, which made it permissible for a Shi'i to conceal his religious orientation under danger, as long as he preserved it in his own heart and mind. The justification for *taqiya* was taken to be a verse in Qur'an that states: "Whether ye conceal what is in your hearts or reveal it, Allah knows it."[3]

This type of behavior is often conformity in appearance only, however. Consider this second example.

Around the time of the Christian reconquest [of Spain], the Church launched a campaign of persecution against the country's non-Christian communities. It thus became increasingly unsafe to live in Spain as a practicing Jew or Muslim. Many Jews responded by fleeing abroad. But hundreds of thousands chose instead to accept baptism, resting their action on a provision in Judaic law that allows dissimulation in times of persecution. . . . In those days, religious conversion was understood to imply a change not just in faith but also of lifestyle. . . . Outwardly, therefore, the Marranos [converted Jews] began to live as Christians. In the privacy of their homes, however, they continued to practice their ancestral rites, waiting for the day when they could revert to Judaism.[4]

Timur Kuran argues that such "preference falsification" is quite common. It is also responsible, he suggests, for both the apparent stability of oppressive regimes in Eastern Europe and their sudden overthrow.[5]

The last pattern of developing obeisance to convention involves conformity by attrition. Nonconformists, that is, those who have identified the "wrong" paradigms, fail to flourish and multiply. Lacking cooperation or perhaps even being actively persecuted for their nonconformity by the majority, they may not even survive. The appearance of conformity has, therefore, some elements of the artifact of attrition or exit.

*Proposition 10 (Conventional Justice).* Our perceptions of justice are conditioned by conventions.

Conventions have normative implications. When we act conventionally, we often act with the belief that this action is appropriate and just, as judged by the imaginary spectators, and we tend to judge the actions of those who do not conform, who instead thwart our designs and expectations, as inappro-

---

3. Kuran 1990, 20.
4. Kuran 1990, 20–21.
5. Kuran 1991b.

priate and unfair. The system of justice, in this framework, can be viewed as a "superstructure" of the regime of convention.

Indeed, our very perceptions of equity depend upon roles and relationships implicitly defined by the customary practice of the community in its regime of convention. In David Hume's words, "artificial convention" establishes "the rules of justice" that underlie our notions of fairness.[6] Hume says that

> we have no real or universal motive for observing laws of equity, but the very equity and merit of that observance. . . . The sense of justice and injustice is not derived from nature, but arises artificially, tho' necessarily from . . . human conventions.[7]

Not all of us are comfortable with the concept of "conventional" justice, however. Some of us may prefer to think of justice as an ideal so high as to be quite beyond the realm of the arbitrary. Although most everyone seems to concur (in principle) that a distribution according to merit is just, few can come to an agreement on just what merit is. Regardless of our definitions, our daily affairs nonetheless proceed apace, and the majority of us behave as conventions dictate. That is, in the process of carrying on, we usually resolve interpersonal conflicts by the rules implicit in conventions. These rules are the standards for settling disputes among the people in a community, and any practice that deviates from them will seem unfair. Another name for this implicit notion of justice that underlies our daily action is conventional justice.

Perhaps the idea that we can adopt an independent criterion and rationally appraise our conventions is an illusion. Conventions and their attendant notion of justice are the outcome of a process of social evolution. The conventions that create social order are supported by moral beliefs: we feel that we ought to keep to these conventions. But we can find no principle of justice to provide an independent basis for these beliefs. The belief that we ought to follow a convention is itself the product of the same process of evolution as the convention itself.[8]

A system of conventional justice that upholds conformity as just and punishes deviation as unjust is essential in maintaining the viability of the regime of convention in any context, particularly in situations that resemble PD games, where the temptation for expedient violation of the rules can be quite strong. Conventions, I have argued, solve PD games by means of shared

---

6. Hume 1965, 480.
7. Hume 1965, 483.
8. Sugden 1989, 87.

paradigms. Under the regime of convention, we carry on with our activities under the assumption that others will fulfill our expectations about them. Confidence in the future regularity of their actions and reactions is, in fact, what prevents us from looking for alternative courses of action that might otherwise be considered individually "rational." If the majority of people lose confidence in the viability of this regime, they will begin to indulge their imaginations in looking for a new paradigm and thereby precipitate the general breakdown of cooperation. By providing mutual restraint and forbearance based on mutually consistent expectations, convention thus prevents society from degenerating into a Hobbesian "state of nature."

When we act according to convention, therefore, we not only believe that we are right, in the sense of being correct, but also that we have the *right* to expect others to behave in accordance with our expectations. Indeed, as the eminent legal scholar Lon Fuller has observed,

> Customary law arises . . . out of situations of human interaction where each participant guides himself by an anticipation of what others will do and will expect him to do. . . . Its underlying principle is a reciprocity of expectations.[9]

The substantial degree of variation observed among different societies' concepts of justice also supports our claim that justice is based not on some neutral, objective, and universal ground but rather on conventions in all their inherent peculiarity and idiosyncrasy. Conventions, recall, derive from largely fortuitous origins (proposition 8).

The implications of a system of conventional justice are important for many group situations that form the fodder of traditional economic inquiry. The majority of economic activities, be they matters of workplace norms and productivity, wage determination, or income distribution, are based on the understanding among the parties involved that enduring interactions are more or less equitable. Much of our behavior is, therefore, conditioned by our conventional notion of justice.[10] Economists' conventional practice of neglecting the issue of equity and expounding the virtues of "positive" economics may therefore be quite misleading. It may implicitly condone the sanctity of existing relationships and conventions, even when the likelihood that they are the best set possible is about as small as the likelihood of their being the worst. Perhaps this implicit support for the *status quo* is responsible for the fact that economists are generally considered "conservative" by most noneconomists in academia.

---

9. Fuller 1968, 116.
10. Schumpeter 1934, 9–10.

*Corollary 10a (Status Quo 1).* We tend to uphold the status quo as fair.

This corollary follows easily from proposition 10. Conventions or norms coordinate, in a predictable way, social interactions in the process of social production. A regime of convention therefore assumes a particular set of interdependent relationships among members, and these relationships constitute the *status quo*. People conform to conventions with the understanding that the *status quo* in social relations will be sustained. This they will uphold as fair, deeming any challenge unjust, insofar as their notion of justice is conventional. The *status quo*, after all, results from dominant practice, and to judge it unfair is to judge the majority unfair. Such a condemnation cannot be made, because, in a regime of convention, each individual in the majority thinks that conforming is proper.

*Proposition 11 (Deviance).* Not everyone will, however, conform; there are always deviants.

This proposition might, at first, glance appear to contradict proposition 9 (conformity). But a careful consideration of the concept of convention should convince us of its validity. Actually, we should be far more surprised to find total and complete obeisance to conventions than to observe divergent undercurrents manifested as occasional ripples or deviations. After all, conventions are far from such conscious products as deliberately designed constitutions. Rather, conventions are designations for discernible patterns of behavior that are evolutionary outcomes of disparate individuals' independently motivated behavior. It is highly improbable that so many minds become alike.

To see that this is the case, consider the fact that the sphere of conventions, a public realm that people create to better coordinate and cooperate among themselves, is not all encompassing. It coexists with a significant sphere of privacy within which individuals can be quite idiosyncratic without interference from the neighborhood. Consider language, a prime example of conventions. There is no inherent reason why a horse must be called a horse, or why we should say what we say the way we do, apart from the reason that other people use the English language that way and we wish to be understood by others. But nothing prevents us from calling a horse a *mahl* and making cryptic sentences, as long as we keep them to ourselves, or to our home. Each individual, each family, or each subgroup may have peculiar expressions that are not accepted by the community at large.

S. Ryan Johansson, who calls conventions "cultural software" because of the likeness she perceives to the computer softwares, argues that, even in primitive societies, people's actions and thoughts cannot be made uniform.

> [T]he goal of cultural software is to impose some minimal amount of standardization on human information processing. It never succeeds in getting every human being to think and act alike . . . even in the smallest and least technologically advanced societies.[11]

Moreover, conventions refer to practices, not thoughts. They describe outer states and observed patterns of common behavior rather than inner states and unobserved perspectives. Much of the conformance we do see could be rather superficial. Individuals may find it proper to conform for different reasons. As we have seen previously, they may conform because of their imagined spectators' bidding, by imitation, because at the moment they know of no better option, or by calculation, in spite of their beliefs, in a form of preference falsification. Divergent undercurrents beneath placid conformism provide the source of deviance.[12] Upon exposure to more effective practice, many imitators are willing to switch behavior at a moment's notice. If some conformists, by calculation, find themselves unable to bear the psychic costs of duplicity, they become true to themselves and deviate openly from social conventions.

Nor is the existence of deviants in a regime of conventions surprising from the dynamic perspective that alone is consistent with the evolutionary approach adopted in this study. Society in this framework may be stable, but it is far from stagnant. Community populations change in composition as some members exit through death or emigration, while others enter through birth or immigration. The constant inflow of people provides an important source of deviation. Although the majority of new members will tend over time to buy into existing conventions, their purchase will be neither immediate nor perfect. Proficiency in following convention requires practice and conditioning in specific contexts. Since conventions are largely implicit, some of the newcomers are bound to make mistakes. For example, slavery was widely accepted until the end of the eighteenth century. Even Christian theology justified it, despite contradictions with the "divine law of human brotherhood."[13]

---

11. Johansson (1989, 16) uses the term *cultural software* to designate what I call conventions. But her computer analogy implies a top-down approach. For example, she argues that individuals' thoughts and actions cannot be made uniform because they may have imperfect copies of the "Master copy." This reasoning sounds almost Platonic. I tend, instead, to take a bottom-up approach, as it were, using the individual as the ultimate unit of analysis.

12. See the section on Public versus Private Domain in chap. 4.

13. Fogel 1989, 201.

When Samuel Sewell, a Puritan from Massachusetts, published an antislavery tract in 1700, he was accordingly

> viewed by most of [his] contemporaries not as [a prophet], but as [a man] of questionable integrity, if not sanity, who for inexplicable reasons had set out to controvert both the Scripture and natural order.[14]

The majority of contemporary theologians and the faithful regarded Sewell as gravely in error. Only when enough people came to view slavery as Sewell and other liberal thinkers did it become socially unacceptable. Diversity in individual paradigms, in brief, is to cultural evolution what genetic mutation is to biological evolution. Deviants can become beneficial, if disturbing, agents of social change.[15]

*Proposition 12 (Ostracism).* Deviants tend to be ostracized.

Conventions are a useful way to reduce uncertainty and promote coordination and cooperation only if individuals predictably follow them and confidently believe that everyone else will as well. By definition, deviations frustrate not only the reliability of the conformists' actions but also their sense of propriety and justice. Conformists will, accordingly, go out of their way to punish and even banish deviants. Hence, ostracism.

This explanation of ostracism may also go the distance in explaining the prevalence of xenophobia. The very presence of foreigners creates unexpected behavior and responses. "Their" paradigms are different from "ours," and the added uncertainty means trouble—the very sort of trouble conventions enable us to prevent.

Not all communities are equally intolerant of deviants or foreigners. The circumstances under which a community may be more tolerant of them are: (1) when deviants are not taken seriously, that is, are seen not as threatening, but rather as objects of ridicule or amazement,[16] (2) when one deviant reminds people in the community of another deviant or foreigner who brought good tidings in the past, (3) when a significant number of deviants are already tolerated (in this case, conventions cannot be not firmly established), and (4) when there is a tradition of protecting the minority. The fact remains that, except under extenuating circumstances, deviants tend to be ostracized.

---

14. Fogel 1989, 204
15. See Margolis 1987, 33–34.
16. This can be terribly damaging to the deviants. It is often worse to be dismissed as unserious than to be criticized. Scholars, for example, would rather be read and criticized than ignored as buffoons.

*Proposition 13 (Stability).* Conventions tend to be stable.

As a means of coping with uncertainty, conventions should be stable. Whatever their nature or genesis, once firmly established or accepted by the majority in the community, they should have the character of stable equilibria, in the sense that they can withstand disturbances. This assertion rests on the twin pillars of Conformism and Ostracism (propositions 9 and 12). By definition, a regime of convention is populated by individuals who share paradigms, that is, who conform to conventions.

Those who practice other paradigms will certainly not prosper, and perhaps not even survive,[17] because conventional actors will not permit deviants the cooperation they require. The regime demands ostracism to preclude the survival, increase, and imitation of deviation. Recall that "cooperate, but retaliate swiftly" was the winning strategy of repeated PD games. These games also indicate that the tendency to cooperate becomes stronger as the reward for unconventional behavior becomes smaller.[18]

Even if deviants manage to eke out a meager existence, they will not increase substantially in number. Few imitate the unsuccessful. If sufficiently many share a new paradigm that makes cooperation more effective than the given convention, they can perhaps replace it.[19] But in this case, the convention by definition is not firmly established, or perhaps exists in appearance only, as when the majority conform only by calculation. The question in this instance concerns not the threatened stability of an established convention, but the competition among paradigms to win that position and that stability.

If the regime of convention is stable in the face of intermittent deviation, it will be stable over time as well. Traditions and customs are simply conventions that have survived the test of time.

*Corollary 13a (Inertia).* Conventions persist through inertia.

The inertia of conventions is a direct implication of their stability. This stability brings not only the benefit of reduced uncertainty in social interaction, but also the cost of inflexibility. Perfect flexibility, or continuous and instantaneous adjustment to the vicissitudes of life, is incompatible with

---

17. Except, as argued subsequently, in times of social upheaval.
18. Rapoport and Chammah 1960; see also Axelrod 1984. Repeated PD games can also indicate that, once a convention is firmly entrenched, deviants cannot easily succeed, in which case the deviant must then cooperate, perish, or exit, as Hirschman (1981) might say.
19. See my subsequent discussion for some of the conditions under which this replacement is possible.

stable conventions as a means of dealing with uncertainty. A regime of convention therefore leads to a certain amount of inadaptability.[20]

Conventional inertia is the social analogue to the inflexibility in individual behavior (corollary 1e) also implied by the paradigmatic approach. Conventions, after all, are but the paradigms individuals have come to share in the process of dealing with uncertainty in a social context. If anything, the regime of conventions should exhibit even greater inflexibility than individuals, since independently acting individuals, who might be amenable to change, may provide mutual checks, preventing one another from moving. The stability of conventions is a crucial element of the social dynamics to which we now turn.

To facilitate our discussion of social dynamics, I shall first introduce two terms, *apparent reason* and *real reason*. A real reason is an understanding that moves an individual to take an action aimed at achieving a stated goal, while an apparent reason is an understanding that moves an individual to take an action aimed at achieving something else—like the approval of others.

*Corollary 13b (Apparent Reason).* As long as apparent reasons remain, conventions will persist even after their real reasons have disappeared.

Customs and traditions are conventions that persist over time. The many customs and traditions we continue to see with no apparent rhyme or reason are signs that certain conventional practices tend to be upheld even after the conditions in response to which their establishment made eminent good sense are long gone.

If the circumstances people face are different than those of their forefathers, there may be real reasons to change the conventions. But each individual in the community seeks the approval of others in his or her paradigm choice. In a regime of convention, it is the conventional practices that are expected to meet the approval of others. Because even the imagined spectators of the majority tend to approve of the conventional, they have apparent reasons to follow the conventional even when times have changed, and those who quickly act upon (new) real reasons will be ostracized as radicals.[21]

---

20. Indeed, Matthews (1984, 99) conjectures that the distinctive feature of an evolutionary process "might be better thought of as the hypothesis of inertia." This approach is quite consonant to the one I have been taking here, but is raised by Matthews only to be abandoned in favor of an approach that emphasizes competitive selection and draws on findings in biology. Schumpeter (1934, 8–9) seems to have something similar in mind when he anchors his theory of economic development on Wieser's Principle of Continuity: "Everyone will cling as tightly as possible to habitual economic methods."

21. Mokyr (1990, 219) reports an example of how the Chinese in the eighteenth century preferred their own ways, even after they had been shown and persuaded that European technologies were superior.

Therefore, conventions tend to persist even where there are (real) reasons to replace them with another set of practices. Conventions that people generate to better coordinate and cooperate their activities in a specific circumstance may thus become hindrances when the circumstance changes.

Hans Vaihinger observes in a similar vein that, although ideas have been invented as the means of dealing with the end problems of survival, they tend to assume a life of their own. Pursued as ends, they are likely to become dysfunctional over time, and Vaihinger finds this tendency compelling enough to call it the *Law of the Preponderance of the Means over the End*.[22]

Caroll Quigley identifies a similar law for history. "All social instruments tend to become institutions,"[23] he says, defining "instruments" as social organizations that arise to meet human needs, and "institutions" as social organizations that take on a life and purpose of their own, distinct from original intentions, and thus become ineffective. Over time, the original purpose of the organization becomes no more than secondary for those within it, while their primary ambition becomes preserving and perfecting the conventions and maintaining the *status quo*. As they work to protect their vested interests, members resist even changes that could be helpful in new situations, and, in their competition for larger shares in distribution, they lose sight of the real goals of the operation as a whole.[24] Quigley provides some interesting examples from military history.

> The Roman army, which had conquered most of the known world by means of the legion, was unable, and probably unwilling, to transform itself into a force of heavily armed cavalry when this became necessary in the late fourth century of our era. As a result, the Roman army . . . was wiped from the earth by the charging horsemen of Germanic barbarians, beginning with the dreadful defeat at Adrianople in 378.
>
> In the centuries from A.D. 700 to 1200, cavalry in the form of the medieval knight became as established in military tactics as the Roman infantry had ever been. . . . The supremacy of the medieval knight was still unquestioned in the early decades of the fourteenth century. The defeat to French chivalry at the hands of bourgeois infantry before Courtrai in 1302 was dismissed by the losers as an inexplicable and

---

22. Vaihinger 1965, xxx.
23. Quigley 1979, 114, 101.
24. The tendency to resist even positive change will prove most relevant for the next corollary. Losing sight of the primary organizational goal is surprising from a systems perspective, but fully consistent with our approach of taking individuals as the unit of analysis. See Olson 1982 and 1988 for elaboration of how the concern for distribution tends to divert attention from the primary goals of an organization.

unrepeatable accident. . . . The inability of the French knights to analyze their defeat is one of the best examples we have of the reactions of an institutionalized force to weapons innovation. Of the numerous blinders on their eyes, the most significant perhaps was their inability to conceive that men of low birth could kill men of noble blood from a distance. A similar inability, in the same period, made it impossible for the noble cavalry of Burgundy and of the Hapsburgs to analyze their defeats at the hands of Swiss pikemen.

The advent of gunpowder and the intensification of firepower made cavalry obsolescent in the early nineteenth century and obsolete before the end of that century, yet by 1900 cavalrymen were still dominant in many armies and enormous resources were devoted to an army that was, by that time, largely worthless. As early as the Crimean War (1854–56) the poet Tennyson saw that it was a blunder to send cavalry charging against gunfire. . . . In the analysis of [the role of cavalry] in 1935, the military historian Liddell Hart wrote: French, Germans, Russians, and Austrians had unexampled masses of cavalry ready at the outbreak of war. But in the opening phase they caused more trouble to their own sides than to the enemy. From 1915 on, their effect was trivial, except as a strain on their own country's supplies.[25]

In brief, the Roman legion in A.D. 378, the French knights in 1302, and the European cavalry in 1913 owed their existence more to apparent than to real reasons. The observations by Quigley and Vaihinger are fully consistent with our corollary that conventions persist, even when their real reasons disappear, as long as apparent reasons remain.

*Corollary 13c (*Status Quo 2*)*. The *status quo* in relationships of production and distribution tends to be upheld as rational and just even after the real justifications for doing so have disappeared.

Because they believe that "social welfare" can be improved by altering the relationships of production and reproduction as the social conditions of production themselves change, reformers and revolutionaries typically denounce the *status quo* as "irrational." The very fact that these few feel compelled to speak up and try to persuade the multitudes is proof that the majority often views the situation very differently—so differently that notwithstanding the sometimes gifted oratory of those in pursuit of change, most of us tend to uphold and adhere to "life as usual."

Perhaps the fact that the insight afforded by this corollary seems as

---

25. Quigley 1979, 103–7.

neglected as it is clear-cut provides ironic but further evidence of its validity. Social phenomena should not be interpreted strictly under the assumption of individual optimization and the efficacy of material incentives. The mechanistic approach to society in general is quite hazardous.

Consider, for example, the "relative deprivation theory," which asserts that happiness depends upon relative, not absolute, position. If one were both to subscribe to this position and adopt a mechanistic approach to behavior, he or she would then expect a great deal of discontent among members of the lower strata at early states of economic development, when inequality in income distribution becomes more pronounced. But as de Tocqueville,[26] Hirschman,[27] and others have noted, this sort of problem surfaces much later, when inequality in income distribution is made less pronounced, and from different and unexpected quarters, from the middle class, who benefited most from development. As Kuran observes, "There are countless oppressed, impoverished, and mismanaged nations that have not risen to overthrow their governments."[28]

In a similar vein, Olson asserts that the common economic belief that people always seize the opportunity to capture gains from new coalitions is an "analytical fallacy" that stems from forgetting that "a need for a pressure group does not ensure its formation."[29] In basing his critique of the traditional understanding of rationalism on an analysis of society's failure to produce "public goods" in sufficient quantity as a consequence of the narrow and consistent rationalism of all the individual maximizers involved, Olson provides valuable insight.[30] But how does he explain the existence of public goods of any kind, in any quantity, at any time? In the paradigmatic approach, conventions are the supreme sort of public good. Social improvement, the public good of changing conventions, sometimes fails to be provided not because the social actors are maximizers seeking free rides, but rather because they get locked into the existing set of conventions. Traditional behavior can thus outlive its real reasons for existence, and the existing social relationships tend to be upheld as rational and just long after their economic rationale has come and gone.

*Proposition 14 (Unexploited Opportunities).* Rational action to realize the potential for material gain is not always forthcoming. In a regime of convention, unexploited opportunities may always exist.

---

26. See de Tocqueville 1955.
27. See Hirschman 1981.
28. Kuran 1990, 23.
29. Olson 1965, chap. 5.
30. See chap. 4 for an illustration of the nature of public goods within the context of PD games.

Consider the following definitions. The *potential for material* gain is a state of knowledge that could permit greater production or better coordination beyond the level of achievement under the current regime of convention, *rational action* is an action or combination of actions that transforms people's practices to exhaust the possibility of material gain, and *opportunity* is the gap between the potential and the actual, that is, the room for improvement by assembling discrete and scattered information.

With these admittedly rather casual definitions, assume, for the sake of argument, that the conventions in period 1 are such that the social coordination and cooperation have exhausted all opportunities. Now suppose that an exogenous shock of rather substantial proportion—a natural disaster or an explosion in population, say—occurs in period 2. No longer are the conventions of period 1 likely to yield optimal results. Will rational action be forthcoming? Will the conventions change to permit better cooperation? Not necessarily, because the reformers who initiate changes in conventions are likely to meet social ostracism rather than applause and approbation.

Stable conventions adapt even more poorly to improvements in the state of knowledge than they do to other shocks to the system. The majority continue to adhere to the existing conventions. They ignore opportunities almost at hand and tend to punish the nonconformists, even when these deviants are simply trying to take advantage of opportunities the majority ignore because of their conventional blinders, and might in the process have introduced and implemented superior practices. The opportunity for material gain is therefore likely to remain unexploited in a stable regime of convention. I do not deny the possibility that people can improve their lives within the context of existing conventions. What economists call "learning by doing" falls into this category.[31] But this type of improvement tends to be made at the cost of ignoring another kind of improvement that could be had if people adopted another set of conventions. Herbert Simon calls these two sorts of improvements "hill climbing" and "hill jumping," respectively. In a stable regime of conventions, people are likely to ignore the possibility of improvement by hill jumping, since it represents abandoning the existing regime and adopting a new one.

The existence of unexploited opportunities (proposition 14) is thus in direct conflict with the "neoclassical spirit" that Arrow defines as follows.

> [T]he true neoclassical spirit . . . [insists] that when a market could be created, it will be. . . . If an opportunity for a Pareto improvement exists, then there will be an effort to achieve it through some social device or another.[32]

---

31. Young 1991, 372.
32. Arrow 1974c, 7–8.

Within the neoclassical framework of competitive equilibrium, no opportunity remains unexploited. But in the absence of opportunities that lure people to deviate from conventional practices and to undertake innovative activities, how can we account for the process of social change? What prevents this state of exhausted opportunities from also becoming a state of personal exhaustion and a stability akin to stagnation? Only when we acknowledge the existence of unexploited opportunities, that is, of ignorance and mistakes, can we begin to appreciate the dynamism of social process. The impetus for social dynamism is given by individuals intending to exploit the opportunities others ignore. The stability of conventions (proposition 13) implies that such enterprising individuals do not always succeed, leaving many opportunities unexploited.

*Corollary 14a (Suboptimality).* The social outcome of conventional practices is unlikely to be optimal.

Opportunities remain untapped because people conform to current conventions rather than adopting new practices. The existence of unexploited opportunities means that the social outcome cannot be described as optimal.

The validity of this corollary can be illustrated within the context of a PD game in $2 \times n$ dimensions (see fig. 7). Consider two individuals (or parties), X and Y. X faces a variety of possible actions, arrayed on the vertical axis and ranked from top to bottom in order of their ability to produce cooperative outcomes. Y faces a similar variety of actions on the horizontal axis. Assume, for simplicity, that at any given moment a community displays *one* unique set of social practices concerning production, distribution, consumption, and so forth. In the following example, the best and worst solutions are $B$ and $W$, respectively. Conventional practice, $C$, with its origins in the precedents of viable practice, is likely to be somewhere between $B$ and $W$ (proposition 8, fortuity). It would be miraculous indeed if the first denizens of this society focused on exactly the right solution from so large a set of potentially viable ones. People who follow the paradigmatic approach are likely to believe, like de Tocqueville,

> that what we call necessary institutions are no more than institutions to which we have grown accustomed, and that *in matters of social convention the field of possibilities is much more extensive than men living in their various societies are ready to imagine.*[33]

Once $C$ is established as convention, it tends to persist (proposition 13, stability). Some individuals repress their new ideas for fear of ostracism,

---

33. de Tocqueville, quoted in Merton 1968b, 190; italics added.

102    Paradigms and Conventions

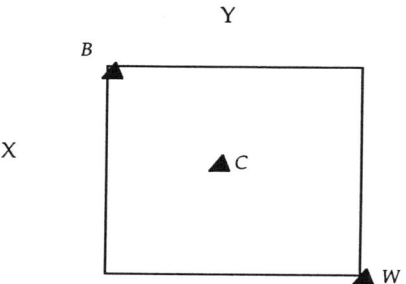

**Fig. 7. Suboptimality of conventions**

because audacity in the form of nonconformance is likely to meet the punishment meted out to most disturbing deviants.

Fine-tuning (or Simon's hill climbing or Arrow's "learning-by-doing") does, however, create movement toward what is locally optimal. But even if it were possible for successive generations to overcome their fears of ostracism from time to time and to improve upon $C$, piecemeal tinkering within the context of a given set of conventions is unlikely to yield the globally best $B$. Human actions are influenced to such an extent by past experiences that their "new" solution actually carries much baggage from the past. Starting from $C$ and starting from scratch yield different results even when everything else is the same.

For a moment, however, let us assume that the initial solution is the optimal solution. That is, the regime of convention begins at $B$, where the payoff matrix is represented by $BJWI$ in figure 8. Society is likely to stay at or near $B$ even as resource growth and *learning over time* expand the opportunity set, increasing potential output to $B'J'WI'$ and generating a new optimum, $B'$. Times change, but conventions tend to remain the same (proposition 13, stability). New material conditions (or improvements in knowledge) do not necessarily provoke altered behavior to take advantage of newly created opportunities, and what once was best may no longer suit the times so very well. Convention is therefore unlikely to be optimal over time, even if it started out as the best solution possible.[34]

Vicissitudes of life make frequent revision in individual and social prac-

---

34. See Olson 1988, 58–59. Olson supports my prediction that long-stable societies tend to become less efficient. While I base this view on the failure to take advantage of new information at odds with old paradigms, Olson relies instead on the observation that "long stable societies will have accumulated many of these special interest groups. . . . A society dense with these coalitions concerned with distributional struggle instead of production is like a china shop with wrestlers battling over its contents and breaking more than they carry away."

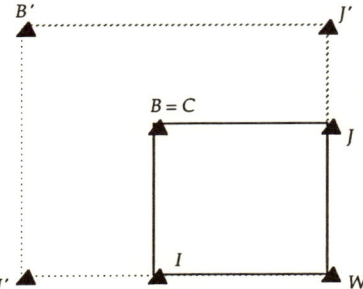

**Fig. 8. A variant of the suboptimality of conventions**

tices necessary to keep them the very best possible. But constant revision of expectations and behavior is consistent neither with the assumptions of the paradigmatic approach nor with the nature of convention itself. Social paradigms, that is, conventions, have been devised to reduce uncertainty, and do so only to the degree that they are stable. Hence, the very factor that makes them beneficial generally precludes their global optimality over time. Conventions, like paradigms, are both enabling and limiting. Suboptimality is the price we pay for the conventional resolution of uncertainty.

Consider Quigley's observation that the agrarian system of ancient Rome was

> an inefficient method of producing food even in respect of the existing technical knowledge, but to reform it would have involved abolition of slavery and division of the large estates. The reformers who wanted to do this were assassinated by the daggers of the landlords, some on the floor of the senate itself.[35]

The agrarian system of Rome remained, in a word, suboptimal. James Buchanan would agree with us: "The institutions . . . that survive and prosper need not be those which are 'best.'"[36]

That conventional practices tend to be imperfect (corollary 14a, suboptimality), directly contradicts the neoclassical proposition that social outcomes are generally efficient. Its affinity to Leibenstein's X-efficiency, which also raises fundamental questions about both production functions and the neoclassical paradigm of maximization, is close. How do we explain productivity studies that find a failure of some managers to minimize costs even

---

35. Quigley 1979, 117–18.
36. Buchanan 1975, x.

when given the necessary information?[37] Leibenstein's solution was "inert areas." But such neoclassical economists as Stigler have been quick either to dismiss Leibenstein's findings as aberrations or evidence of simple statistical clumsiness,[38] or to reconcile "inert areas" with maximization by considering mental exertion itself a costly enterprise.[39]

The paradigmatic approach suggests, on the contrary, that X-inefficiency is a predictable, not aberrational, consequence of conventions and that firms, like other groups, rarely operate with maximum efficiency. Firms are organizations with close group interaction over time. As we saw in chapter 4, in such a setting the groups are likely to generate and conform to conventions. We can therefore expect business firms, like other communities, to exhibit inertia (corollary 13a) and fail to exhaust all opportunities over time (proposition 14, suboptimality). Decision makers in firms *do* have the discretionary power to reorganize that many traditional authorities lack. But the influence of firm conventions and "corporate cultures" implies that they are neither so free nor so rational as neoclassical economic theory would suggest. Decision makers are thus liable to err, whether they are Fortune 500 CEO's or fishermen by the sea. These mistakes, far from being calculated risks (or the result of "trembling hands"), are often the systematic sort that derive from a certain mind-set, or paradigm (corollary 1g, possibility of systematic error). The employees most likely to be promoted to posts of decision making are those who seem most successful according to the firm's established standards, that is, the conventions prevalent in the firm. Corporate decision makers are therefore perhaps least likely to deviate from the very conventions that have been the benchmarks of their success. Moreover, if decision makers are open-minded enough to recognize an innovative idea, the success of its execution will depend upon how much cooperation can be garnered from subordinates, suppliers, and consumers, and these groups are themselves accustomed and loyal to existing conventions. The *status quo*, in brief, is likely to be very thoroughly entrenched, especially in firms with good track records where the corporate culture is very tight. Stability and inertia, in sum, will characterize this group as well as other social entities.[40]

Consider, for example, a firm whose production method has proved viable for workers and customers alike. As far as management is concerned, this is the way to do business, and the firm is committed to this successful convention. Time brings change, however, and suppose now that individual workers, engineers, or outside advisors suggest an innovation, that is, a new

---

37. See Leibenstein 1966; also see chap. 1.
38. See Stigler 1976.
39. See chap.1.
40. As I am going over the final draft of this book, I cannot help feeling how well the crisis at General Motors, which lost $4.5 billion last year in their North American operation, seems to be explained by my argument here.

technology with improved efficiency or quality. It takes a lot to overthrow a convention. Management must be convinced not only of the probity of the new action but also of the strong possibility of convincing employees and consumers to change their ways and support it. The *status quo* is likely to reign longer than it "should." The flip side of inertia is, therefore, suboptimality or X-inefficiency.

Social practices parallel individual behavior to some degree. The paradigmatic approach to problems enables individuals to deal with uncertainty by focusing their attention and helping them to make and keep commitments; but these responses to uncertainty also make biases and mistakes possible, not just for the moment but over substantial stretches of time. The stability of conventional practices also makes suboptimal social practices possible. Even when individuals are clearly aware of the follies of existing conventions, mutual checks may discourage change.[41] Shared paradigms therefore tend to be even more inflexible than individual paradigms.

Even strong loyalty must eventually yield to persistent forces of change, however. Institutional inertia may hold these forces at bay for a while, but, as the gap between actual and potential social outcomes widens, it will eventually play an important role in the process of social change, and to this topic I shall now turn.

### The Process of Social Change

Change presupposes room for change, the source for which may be either exogenous or endogenous. Either *deus ex machina* can shock the system, or a process in its interior can reach critical mass, as it were.

Traditional economics often examines how economic systems respond to the former. The presumptively somewhat passive and mechanistic response of the economy then conveys the impression of precise predictability. But this is misleading because the timing and manner of social change, in fact, remain largely unpredictable and uncertain.[42]

Neglected, but possible, meantime, is the study of the nature of social processes that permit the possibility of change through endogenous force. How is social change at all possible? While this question has the simulacrum of simplicity, the answer has been far from obvious to economists with a neoclassical (traditional) mind-set.

*Proposition 15 (Growing Opportunity).* The magnitude of unexploited opportunity, or the potential for material gain, tends to increase over time.

---

41. Kuran (1987) makes a similar point.
42. See Kuran 1991b, 124–25, for a similar viewpoint.

We have already established in proposition 14, that unexploited opportunities are likely to exist in a regime of convention. If everything always stays the same, these opportunities will remain unexploited. Something always changes, however, and that something is *knowledge*. In a regime of convention, disparate individuals carry on with their daily doings. The majority live happily in conformity with their shared paradigms. But some people are bound to *discover* (or think that they have discovered) a better way of doing things as they *learn* from experience and from mistakes they and other people make, that is, opportunities that other people ignore. Collectively, people learn over time.

And, as they learn, the potential for material gain increases—without immediate actualization because of institutional rigidities (corollary 13a, inertia). Deviants motivated to capture the opportunities through innovation, or deviations from the routine, are often punished (proposition 12, ostracism). And the majority in the community may conform to the existing conventions despite some discomfort in order to avoid the greater distress of ostracism (proposition 9, conformity). The magnitude of these unexploited opportunities therefore tends to grow with time, until people generate a new set of conventions that will permit the exploitation of some of the hitherto ignored opportunities.

In figure 9, *WIBJ* represents a PD situation, where $C$ is the initial, and more-or-less satisfactory conventional solution. As time passes and opportunities grow, the best solution shifts from $B$ to $B'$, and the gap between the actual and the potential widens, while the convention is stable (stagnant) at $C$. (Or, alternately, see fig. 10, based on the production possibility frontier.) The regime of convention thus becomes more and more out of tune with the growing state of knowledge and know-how in society, and the widening gap represents an increasingly attractive opportunity for those souls that are hardy. Tension between the stable regime and the unexploited potential intensifies over time, setting up an endogenous dynamic for dramatic change.

What is social change? If we regard the way people behave and relate to one another as the most significant feature of social life, then social change is the replacement of one set of conventions by another. An inquiry into the conditions of social change thus becomes an inquiry into the conditions under which one regime of convention is replaced by another.

When can this replacement occur? One necessary factor will be that a significant number of community members consider the existing convention increasingly inappropriate or unsatisfactory. This reaction will be sparked both by the frustration of many people in the community with the existing convention's repeated failure to yield expected results and by their beginning to see the outlines of alternative and superior ways to approach the vicissitudes of existence. Perhaps this perception arises as external conditions vary,

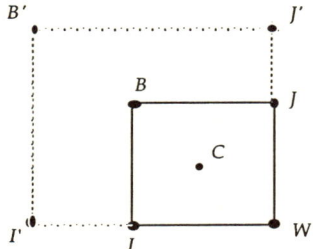
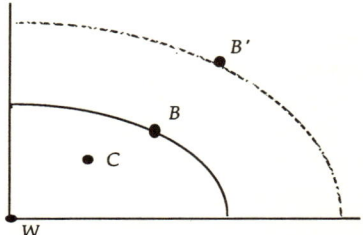

Fig. 9. Growing opportunity    Fig. 10. A variant of growing opportunity

or perhaps it results from such endogenous changes as increased knowledge or reassessed values or preferences. Whatever the reason, when a large number of people are dissatisfied with the current convention, they become more willing to search for an alternative and less apt to ostracize nonconformists, who no longer appear to be clear-cut violators of propriety.

Even under these conditions, however, the existing paradigm cannot be discarded until an alternative appears viable. This process is well documented in science,[43] and, as we have seen earlier, the most likely sources for substitution or replacement are nonconforming practices that appear to yield superior results.

The deviants that we always have with us (proposition 11, deviance) provide a pool of potentially viable examples, each of which can provide the basis for a new convention. Under more stable conditions, deviants are held in check by painful experiences, either personal and direct or vicarious and indirect, and their innovations often fail due to lack of fit or lack of cooperation. But there can be no change without deviation, and it therefore behooves us to examine the conditions under which some deviant practices become successful.

Somewhat arbitrarily, we may classify the factors that influence the fate of deviants as either those concerning the intrinsic goodness of the paradigms they identify or those involving the receptivity of other people, whose cooperation is necessary for success.[44] Both of these factors are closely related to the size of the unexploited gains.

*Proposition 16 (Discovery).* The probability of discovery tends to increase over time.

---

43. See Kuhn 1970.
44. See Kuran (1991b) for a convincing argument on how the distribution of receptivity to new paradigms influences the process of social change.

A regime of convention always has its deviants, individuals who believe they can fare better by behaving nonconventionally (proposition 11, deviance). While many of these deviants are simply social misfits, some represent genuine attempts to capture opportunities conformists often fail even to recognize (proposition 14, unexploited opportunities).

If the regime is stable, the majority of people in the community will not be receptive to new ideas (proposition 9, conformity). And if the regime is fairly young, the magnitude of unexploited opportunities may be so small that alternative practices represent minor improvements probably not worth the risk of upheaval. But over time, opportunities will increase as people learn from their own and others' experiences, and the gap between the possible and the actual will widen (proposition 15, growing opportunities). Other things being equal, the probability of some deviants *identifying* a paradigm that could be the basis of successful exploitation of ignored opportunities should increase with time as well. At issue here is the *discovery* of opportunities ignored by others; the claim here is that it is more and more difficult not to notice what is growing larger and more distinct over time. Whether or not the deviants can successfully actualize potentially superior paradigms is another question—one of innovation and social change.

Let us define *innovation* as successful deviance: the act of taking advantage of opportunities ignored by others because of their conventional blinders. Is a successful innovation more or less likely over time?

The probability of innovation depends upon the disparity between the actual and the potential. Unexploited opportunity is the target that, to repeat, becomes larger and larger and more and more noticeable over time. Given ability, the probability of hitting a target improves with its size. The probability of, and the rewards from, successful deviation will therefore increase with time.

Even when a convention is firmly established, nonconformists can affect the regime if they can muster a "critical mass" of their own. In other words, the deviants must cooperate sufficiently among themselves based on their own conventions to be able to enjoy a higher standard of living than possible under the dominant conventions.[45] But even when the deviants act independently, their behavior may have the cumulative effect of building tolerance among the conformists, so that the probability of forming this critical mass increases with the frequency of deviation. The conventional regime then becomes less and less viable as its twin pillars, conformity and ostracism, begin to crumble, eventually setting off a veritable stampede toward what Leibenstein has called the "latent PD game solution," and precipitating a crisis.[46]

---

45. Schelling 1978.
46. Leibenstein 1982b. This is his term for the "rational" solution I discussed in some detail in chap. 4.

"Crisis" describes a state of affairs in which conventions break down. People are then exposed to profound uncertainty, since customary behavior does not yield customary results under these circumstances. Despite their dissatisfaction, many may still adhere to conventions, because they know nothing better to do. They will respond, in part, by blaming others but also by searching for an alternative set of paradigms. Unfortunately, as individuals begin to experiment with new paradigms that might be successful but are not yet mutually compatible, the situation could become worse.

Without a crisis, however, there can be no social change of radical proportion. Growing opportunity is necessary but not sufficient to overthrow one set of conventions in favor of another. Conventional wisdom must also be questioned. People must abandon the means by which they have traditionally made possible social cooperation and coordination and search for new methods. In order to do so, most must be very troubled indeed, that is, they must be "in crisis." Crisis may be precipitated by a major shock to the system, or it may develop gradually by a fortuitous sequence of unrelated events that seem innocuous, one by one. In any case, a gap between the actual and the potential must become too glaring to ignore, and would-be reformers or innovators must propose to close it. They will succeed if and only if others are sufficiently disgruntled to follow suit.

A crisis is also a time of great opportunity. Almost everyone is looking for a new approach, and possibilities for structural change and social opportunity open wide. Those who can take advantage of this situation have a chance substantially and permanently to upgrade their status within a new regime of convention, thus making notable claim to the social surplus of the new order.

Consider, in this context, Joseph Schumpeter's role of the entrepreneur in his efforts to explain the process of economic development.[47] His first step is to establish a model of "circular flow," within which economic activities are fully rationalized and routinized, as they are in both the competitive equilibrium of neoclassical economics and the stationary state of J. B. Clark. In this sort of circular flow, there is no room for economic profit. Schumpeter argues that only those atavisms of chivalry, entrepreneurial innovations, can destroy the doldrums of routine capitalism. Dazzling innovative successes provoke imitation, in spite of initial resistance from established firms, and those who are slow to adapt face the danger of liquidation. This process of "creative destruction" continues until the situation stabilizes in a new and higher level of circular flow.[48]

The parallels between this model and the paradigmatic approach are striking. Schumpeter's "circular flow" resembles our "regime of convention,"

---

47. Schumpeter 1934.
48. Schumpeter 1950.

and his "entrepreneurial innovations" are quite like our "successful deviations."

The differences are also marked, however. For all his apparent radicalism, Schumpeter follows standard economic theory in taking the circular flow (or equilibrium) to be the natural state to which capitalistic systems tend. The majority of his actors, the economic agents, are mere average, law-abiding folk, whose activities and associations devolve unexceptionably into the circular flow. His entrepreneurs are a breed apart. Romantically credited with superior judgment and willpower, they resemble shades of Nietzschean heros, laws unto themselves. While Schumpeter posits two radically different kinds of people, I posit a unified view of human nature. No one in my approach is purely "rational" or "entrepreneurial." Every human action presumes a judgmental process that involves both aspects. The self-same human nature is responsible for generating conventions to facilitate coordination and cooperation, leaving opportunities unexploited, and then discovering and exploiting them. We need not introduce the entrepreneur from outside the system. Would-be entrepreneurs are always in the system, as deviants. The scope of their success depends on the magnitude of the ignored opportunities, which in turn depends on time and the degree to which conventions are stable. My process of change is truly *endogenous*.

We also have the framework in place to explore some of the reasons for the varying degrees of innovation under different social arrangements. Innovation is possible under any system—under no system are opportunities completely exhausted (proposition 14, unexploited opportunities). But not all systems are equal in encouraging innovation. Schumpeter's theory of entrepreneurship is incapable of addressing this issue. His entrepreneur is a breed apart, independent of variations in the system. Schumpeter is equally comfortable illustrating the role of the entrepreneur in such diverse situations as an "isolated manorial estate," an "isolated socialist society," and modern capitalism.[49] My theory can, however, provide an explanation for why the rate of innovation is higher in capitalism than in feudalism or socialism. As we shall see in chapter 7, by encouraging people to look for gainful activities, the existence of markets can quicken the evolutionary process that occurs even in feudalism.

Schumpeter errs not only in dividing human nature into two disparate camps but also in overstating the importance of individual activities on the entrepreneurial side. Many try, but very few succeed. Entrepreneurial success must contain a goodly element of luck, or at least circumstances, because admirable individual attributes, from whatever perspective, are not the exclu-

---

49. Schumpeter 1934, 138–45.

sive province of the successful. Indeed, based on this discussion of the process of innovation and social change, I can now propose another property of the paradigmatic approach, that the nature of social change is intermittent and downright chancy.

*Proposition 17 (Discontinuity).* Social change, the process of replacing one set of conventions with another, tends to occur intermittently and discontinuously.

Imagine the contrary. Suppose, for a moment, that social changes were constant, so that conventions were in constant flux. Such variability defies the very notion of "convention." Whatever still existed by this name could not well be the basis for expected regularity in other people's behavior. Interaction among individuals would become chaotic because, without some sort of constancy of shared paradigms, social coordination and cooperation are impossible.

Consider in this context Mao Tse-tung's advocacy of constant change in society, his clarion calls for "Permanent Revolution."[50] What happened during the Cultural Revolution, when radical Maoists tried to set off the "Permanent Revolution"? The task was impossible. The result was a prolonged crisis and, in the end, a new set of conventions that represented a cultural degeneration. The price is still being paid more than two decades later.

The concept of constant change in environment goes against the grain of human nature. Our actions presuppose judgment and decision making, which in turn rely upon a certain stability in the environment, including interpersonal relationships. Conventions are the evolutionary outcome of the interaction of disparate and interdependent individuals longing for certitude; their stability helps us routinize a goodly part of our daily action, coordinate our activities, and cooperate in social production.

At the same time, however, stability limits our adaptability. Most of us are almost slavishly obedient to conventions, owing to some combination of conviction of their propriety and fear of punishment for deviation. Institutional inertia thus tends to let gaps between the actual and the potential persist, even enlarge, over time, until a critical mass of dissenters overthrows the regime and replaces it with another. In this manner, social changes tend to occur choppily and in spurts, intermittently rather than smoothly or gently. Although change is sometimes continuous, it is still broken from time to time by episodes of sudden, quick, and discrete changes.

---

50. In this he echoes Leon Trotsky's earlier call for a "continuous revolution." See Hughes 1986, 14.

Because regimes of convention prevail wherever there is durable human interaction, the propositions of this chapter are widely applicable. In the chapters that follow, for example, I shall soon be applying these insights to the oft observed and oft neglected phenomenon of social status and envy. Perhaps the reader will be inspired to extend the range even further.

CHAPTER 6

# Status

> What people say behind your back is your standing in the community in which you live.
>
> —Anonymous

This chapter aims to better our understanding of the concern for status and its effect on individual behavior and social tendencies. In contradistinction to such scholars as James Duesenberry[1] and Robert Frank,[2] I shall distinguish sharply between status and envy. Only in chapter 7 shall I discuss the latter component of an individual's concern for relative standing.

*Definition (Status).* An individual's status is communal certification of his or her relative proficiency in conventions.

Duesenberry has observed that in the United States, where attaining a higher standard of living is the most widely accepted goal, our status is largely determined by where we stand in the income hierarchy. People with average incomes will have middling status, and those with above-average incomes will find that they have above-average status. This observation provides a good working definition of status in a materialistic society. But I wish to be more general.

Since status is based on a ranking according to a given criterion, it must be determined by the standards shared in a community. In the world of golf, for example, professional golfers have high status, while in the world of yoga, those yogi who can tolerate the severest bodily mortification will achieve this standing. Among business people, status may be determined by financial net worth. Among Vincentian or Franciscan friars, the metric will be charity toward the needy. In general, then, rank or status in a community must be judged by the prevalent conventions or shared paradigms of success.

The quality of an action is judged by conventions. A stable society is

---

1. Duesenberry 1949.
2. Frank 1985.

characterized by a high degree of conformance to conventions. Because individual members have selected and calibrated their paradigms in such a fashion that for a wide range of recurrent events most of us in the community can imagine ourselves acting in similar ways in similar circumstances, a typical behavior is likely to meet with group approval—else we would also disapprove of ourselves. Because everyone judges conforming actions favorably, conformists will obtain the "average rate of return." If society is stable, therefore, conformists, who are in the majority, meet community approval and are ranked average in the community, while nonconformists, in the minority, meet with disapproval and find themselves below average in the pecking order.

This is not to say, however, that all conformists will have the same status. In a stable regime of convention, those who act more or less conventionally will be accorded intermediate status, reflecting others' abilities to imagine themselves behaving similarly in similar situations. But individuals who are more proficient in their exercise of conventions and who are therefore judged outstanding according to these criteria, will gain higher rank in reflection of community *admiration* for excellence. Examples abound. Among economists, whose contemporary conventions favor mathematical power and elegance, the mathematical sophisticates command the highest status. In primitive times, when naked force was a useful talent, society accorded the highest rank to those of great physical prowess and daring. Whether the might is of mind or muscle, status is a communal phenomenon, resting squarely on the conventional criteria of propriety and excellence. Our status is our community's certification of our proficiency in conventions, and the higher our rank, the higher our proficiency; the lower our rank, the lower this skill—as perceived by community.[3]

*Proposition 18 (Status Seeking).* Individuals in society seek to attain higher status in their community.

This proposition follows easily from the definition of status and proposition 6 (approval seeking), which is itself but an expression of proposition 2 (paradigm seeking) in a social context. The reformulated story is as follows.

---

3. Because each community defines its own criteria of status based on its own conventions, individuals can find that they stand highly in some communities but not in others. Attempts to establish an objective criterion for society as a whole have varied in virtually everything but their ultimate failure. Individuals can belong simultaneously to a number of communities whose ranking criteria are not comparable. Creating a universal metric from subgroups, each of which has its own idiosyncratic measure of success, is quite impossible. Multiple criteria are therefore inevitable in a pluralistic society where each group has (and can maintain) its own set of conventions.

Faced with a novel situation, we seek to identify a paradigm that suggests a viable course of action. While we must feel sufficiently confident in the suitability of this paradigm to act upon it, the process of identification is still experimental and tentative, and our confidence would be greatly strengthened if the paradigm supported successful practice. In society, where the viability of an action depends largely on other people's cooperation, which in turn depends on their approval, it is in our interest to seek this approval by the "proper" choice of paradigm. Not only are we accorded respectable status, by definition, when our actions meet with community approval, but the attainment of status *cum* approval and all the trappings of success associated therewith increases our confidence in our paradigm choices. In society, we therefore seek status as a matter of practicality as well as vanity.

Status refers to relative standing in a community, and it is impossible for everyone be above average. If everyone in the community tries to raise his or her status, will the result be perpetual competition and chaos? On the contrary. Status seeking can actually work as a stabilizing force, as I shall show.

*Proposition 19 (Emulation).* People emulate those of higher status.

This proposition is merely a restatement of corollary 4a (imitation). Paradigm seekers imitate the successful examples of others whom they deem identical to themselves in all attributes relevant to the problem at hand. Individuals rank highly in society because their practices are considered outstanding, as judged by conventional criteria. Not only the trappings of their success but also the paradigms that presumably lie behind their successes, that is, their wisdom and insights, come also to be admired. As Philip Wicksteed observed,

> [t]he relatively wealthy and successful man, by unconsciously shewing what the things for which he most cares really are, directs the ambitions and moulds the aspirations of those who have less power of realizing their ideals than he has himself.[4]

Imitation is the highest form of flattery.

Although individuals of below-average status could conceivably experiment with unconventional practices and gain status as innovators, the likelihood of their success is quite small in a stable regime of convention. To adopt a new paradigm, visionaries must reject the option of conforming to and becoming more proficient in conventional practices. They must abandon a proven model in favor of one that is unproven, however good it may sound.

---

4. Wicksteed 1933, 702.

The larger the change involved, the more uncertain will be the probable outcome. Therefore, people are not likely to abandon practices to which they are accustomed and venture into new paradigms whose consequences are uncertain. Apprehension of other people's disapproval and the attendant loss of status also deters some people from taking every available chance to advance their status. Recall that cooperation as well as intrinsic merit is necessary for success and that members of a stable community tend to ostracize innovators, who upset their customary expectations. Because conformists will not diverge from their proven ways and cooperate with nonconformists until they are convinced of the felicity of new ways, which is, in turn, a function of their cooperation, the upshot is a catch-22 situation where success requires cooperation, which requires success. This is the predicament of those who seek a higher status by innovation.

When ordinary people try to enhance their status, they are therefore more likely to make this attempt within the confines of existing conventions. In imitating the successful, they will be concerned with acquiring the attributes of success as defined by conventional criteria. As Frank Knight observed,

> [The] motive of business is to such a large extent that of emulation. . . . Industry and trade is a competitive game, in which men engage in part from the same motives as in other games or sports. This is not a matter of want-satisfaction in any direct or economic sense; the "rewards" of successful participation in the game are not wanted for any satisfying power dependent on any quality which they possess as things, but simply as insignia of success in the game, like the ribbons, medals, and the like which are conferred in other sorts of contests.[5]

Emulate the successful! This injunction sounds easy to follow; it is not. The fundamental purpose of emulation is to replicate the success of other people. But which other people? Can their success be replicated? How commensurable are the qualities (and circumstances) of the successful and the emulator.

Should I, for example, imitate Michael Jordan because he makes several million dollars a year playing basketball and advertising sports products? Unfortunately, I just don't have the kind of talents that make Michael Jordon the success he is. Would he be a good role model if I were strong and agile? Perhaps. But each individual is a bundle of complex features, and even two seemingly similar individuals represent two distinct amalgams of characteristics. It is never altogether clear which qualities are responsible for success. While a tall and strong African-American lad would seem on the face of it to

---

5. Knight 1935, 46.

have a much better chance of success in emulating Michael Jordan than a short Asian kid with thick glasses, he too may lack a few of the crucial ingredients that set Michael Jordan apart from the pack. In that case, neither will make it in the world of basketball. And, as the Chinese saying goes, "If you miss the target, it does not matter whether you miss it by fifty steps or by one hundred."

When the members of a community are heterogeneous and the causes of success are not exactly known, emulating the successful carries no guarantee of joining their ranks. Patterning oneself after another involves a fair amount of guesswork and gambling as well as slavish imitation. With a limited number of paradigms in stock, we rely on metaphoric interpretation and reasoning to deal with an infinity of unique events. Hoping to gain status conventionally— either by joining a higher rank according to conventional criteria or by outsmarting someone within the established rules of the game—we try to become (or appear) more proficient in the use of our shared paradigms. The room for the discretionary—and the arbitrary—being virtually unlimited, divergent and conflicting interpretations and opinions can easily arise, especially when the situation at hand deviates from the norm in even the slightest degree.

The result may well be the creation of secondary conventions as yet related to no concrete results. In other words, the allegorical and metaphorical interpretation of conventions may engender "artificial" criteria of status, acquired by association with established status. *Derived status* is the name I shall give to social standing based on such artificial criteria.

Like status itself, derived status is a consequence of decision making under uncertainty. Unlike direct status, however, the derived version is based on what is already artificial, namely, conventions, and even higher orders of derivation are certainly conceivable. All too often, the basis of derived status is quite flimsy. Sometimes our attempts to rise in rank founder because we misidentify the attributes of success. For example, when a pretty secretary gets a raise or a promotion, her co-workers may try to "out pretty" instead of "out type" her, in the possibly mistaken view that appearance, not intelligence and energy, was the relevant factor. The often illusory aspect of derived status does not, however, make its pursuit irrational.[6] Those who base their actions on a system of derived status seem to be dead serious, with an elaborate logic of their own. As I pointed out in chapters 2 and 3, all inference, or paradigmatic choice, is characterized by a certain arbitrariness and unpredictability.

The routes to derived status are many. We can gain status in one area by

---

    6. Asch (1987, 390–91) discusses Koehler's example of a chimpanzee that moved a box to get the food on the ceiling after seeing another trained chimpanzee reaching the food by using the box. The trouble with the second chimpanzee was that he moved the box in wrong direction. We humans tend to do much better than chimpanzees. But there is no guarantee against foolish inference if the situation becomes relatively more complex.

virtue of having established status in another, because people of high status are shown deference and credited with superior wisdom that can be used in areas other than where they attained successes. Thus do rich and famous people appear in advertisements of products for which they can claim no special expertise—does Michael Jordan know as much about Coke, Wheaties, and Big Mac's as he knows about slam dunks and, maybe, Nikes? Probably not, but business firms seriously oriented to the bottom line willingly pay him millions of dollars on the premise, as assured by marketing experts, that consumers will listen to, and act on, his testimony.

Nor is deriving status in this fashion limited to frivolous goods. According to W. H. Hutt, the economics profession paid heed to the *The General Theory of Employment, Interest, and Money*, whose progeny is macroeconomics, not necessarily because of its intrinsic merit but because of the reputation and status John Maynard Keynes had established in his other pursuits.

> Mr. Keynes's attitude towards the Classical tradition, in his recent *General Theory of Employment, Interest and Money*, may easily prove to be the source of the most serious single blow that the authority of orthodox economics has yet suffered. . . . Mr. Keynes boldly belittles orthodoxy. . . . Others before Mr. Keynes have taken a similar line. . . . Now if Mr. Keynes had not already been in a position to catch the ear of an influential section of the public, there would have been no danger in his contribution. . . . But Mr. Keynes's reputation commands . . . *immediate* prominence for all his writings. . . . He is at present known to the world at large as an eminent economist. He writes from the University of Cambridge. He is Editor of the *Economic Journal*.[7]

We can also gain status by association with people of higher status. For example, through friendship with the rich and famous, we may gain social standing as well as material and spiritual advantage.

Acquiring some of the attributes of people our conventions deem socially prominent is yet another route to getting there ourselves. If wealthy people drive Cadillacs and poorer people drive Chevrolets, then a materialistic society will tend to associate the former with high status, and the latter with low. Many of the poorer people may therefore be tempted to drive Cadillacs for the prestige as well as the comfort. Who among us would turn down high status,

---

7. Hutt 1936, 245–46. Coats (1964, 106) considers Hutt's insight helpful in understanding the economics profession as a whole, and observes that "although liberal epistemological optimists generally assume that there is a necessary antithesis between authority and reason, authority necessarily plays an indispensable role in any intellectual discipline" (86). In this case, authority stems from status. See also Schumpeter 1954.

which means the admiration of others? But for a great many poor, buying a Cadillac, well beyond their means, would be an act of folly. Of course, limited means do not always prevent people from pursuing status. Adam Smith made the following observation.

> Many a poor man places his glory in being thought rich, without considering that the duties (if one may call such follies by so very venerable a name) which that reputation imposes upon him, must soon reduce him to beggary, and render his situation still more unlike that of those whom he admires and imitates, than it had been originally.[8]

The great majority of the folks whose means are modest, but whose prudence is not, are likely instead to try to own the "cheaper Cadillacs" that enterprising business firms are most eager to supply. These vehicles may begin as Chevrolets with extra chrome here and there, and therefore well within the means of prudent folks. But sooner or later, innovative firms are able to replicate most of the Cadillac's features, at much lower cost, and almost anyone is able to drive a Cadillac—or something like it. These days, for example, Suzuki offers a car with air conditioning, antilock brakes, air bags, and so on, features found only in some of the most expensive cars only a few years ago, for a little more than the price of a motorcycle.

If we were all to drive Cadillacs, or something indistinguishable from them, would we gain equal status? No. The rich are status seekers too. They would quickly respond by finding new and more expensive insignia of status.[9] People of high status are, in fact, trend setters, precisely because others imitate them. Indeed, much of our economic activity and the process of economic development can fruitfully be viewed as a reflection of the perpetual race for status. Absurd? Think on this: so many goods and services that were once the exclusive preserve of the very rich are now the common fare of the very poor. Two forces have generated this state of affairs—the incessant desire to emulate the successful and the eagerness with which entrepreneurs cater to this fancy.

Thorstein Veblen used the term *conspicuous consumption* to describe this tendency of people to emulate the life-styles of people with higher status.[10]

---

8. Smith 1976b, 64.

9. With the great material advances that characterize modern times, most gadgets are within easy reach of the common working folks. Even a garbage collector (excuse me: "sanitary engineer") in New York City may drive a Cadillac, for example, and it becomes quite difficult for even the moderately well-off to find ways to distinguish themselves. I have read that some city drivers of means now own old Chevrolets covered with dust. Why? Dust-covered cars are supposed to signal ownership of homes at the end of dirt roads—apparent luxuries in urban areas. Hobsbawm (1969) observes similar motivations in the origin of English middle-class dress codes.

10. See Veblen 1899.

The main source of conspicuous consumption, he says, lay in identifying status with the buying patterns of people with higher status. Thus do we try, even at great personal cost, both to associate with those we presume to be successful and to emulate their attributes and accumulate their possessions. According to Veblen, "pecuniary emulation" is the driving force of modern civilization, and along with "invidious comparison," he repeatedly used "conspicuous consumption" to explain—and discredit—the consumption and leisure patterns of the masses.[11]

The tendency to copy the successful and their trappings implies that the system of status has a profound influence on the allocation of resources. To the extent that individuals of high status are recognized examples of success, they will be considered superior either in the set of paradigms they employ or in their proficiency in the use of a set already shared by many. Much time and many goods will be allocated toward their emulation.[12]

The evermore specialized division of labor has probably increased this tendency. As we hone in on our own particular tasks, our direct knowledge of other activities diminishes, and our uncertainty about areas beyond our narrow expertise undoubtedly rises. If so, the concern for status (i.e., relative standing) will become more and more significant.

We are all engaged in a race for higher status, and we advance by means of emulating our heroes and heroines. In a stable community, their range tends to be limited, however, and the competition for status and distinction then falls largely within the confines of conventions. Given our budget constraints, the most we can usually do is attempt to gain a slight edge over people of similar status, rather than leap boldly into a whole new class and set of surroundings. Most of us meet this challenge head on, by "keeping up with the Joneses," and we often compete with maddening ferocity and tenacity over rather trivial matters. The sight is discouraging to many, and prominent among them is Philip Wicksteed, who suggested that we stop caring about how we may be compared with our neighbors.

---

11. Veblen's teacher at Yale University, Sumner (1979, 45), observed that selected classes, i.e., people of higher status, "have led the way in luxury, frivolity, and vice, as also in refinement, culture, and the art of living."

12. Those who realize that they are emulated by the masses can use this knowledge as a means of exacting rent, capitalizing, for example, on their function as recognized leaders. Thus was it discovered that, in 1982, Saloman Brothers had cornered a block of bonds just hours before that brokerage firm's highly respected economist, Henry Kaufman, predicted that interest rates would fall. His authority was such that bond prices shot up immediately after the announcement, and Saloman Brothers pocketed tens of millions of dollars in quick profit. David Ricardo, renowned for his investment acumen as well as his force in economic reasoning, was in a similarly influential position in the London stock market, and one wonders to what use he put his power.

[H]ow are we individually to "prepare for the Kingdom"? . . . By learning to feel that "keeping up with appearances" is a sorry substitute for grasping realities.[13]

But how can this sort of admonition stop people from seeking status, when, as I have shown, status seeking and emulation are an integral part of the decision-making process and "not keeping up with the Joneses," or diverging from conventional consumption standards, may result in other people misjudging our worth?

Some have argued that the competition for status, distinction, and relative advantage ("positional goods" in Fred Hirsch's parlance),[14] results in considerable waste and inefficiency. Contrary to the "Human Capital" theory that asserts that schooling enhances worker productivity, Michael Spence, for example, sees schooling primarily as a signaling device for workers (screening device for employers) that stands not for acquired training but rather as a surrogate for innate abilities.[15] In this view, employers favor a job applicant with more (or higher quality) schooling over another with less (or lower quality) schooling presumably because the differences in education reflect the differences in native endowment. But from the point of view of the parents who must decide how much schooling their children should have, more schooling represents an entry ticket to better paying jobs, regardless of the innate abilities of their children. Parents who wish their offspring a better chance in life will collectively end up overinvesting in education, rather in diplomas. Although this choice may be individually rational, it results in the socially inefficient allocation of scarce resources, according to Spence.

Robert Frank supports this line of argument fully and concludes that *laissez-faire* in schooling may easily result in "an undesired escalation of the total resources devoted to education."[16] Much of the competition in society that is driven by the desire to obtain relative advantage, he believes, is like the "hackle-raising mechanisms" of the canine species.[17] One dog may be able to enhance his chance of survival by raising his hackles, thus increasing his apparent size, detering his opponent, and reducing the probability of getting into a fight. But the success of this strategy over time has been its undoing. By now, most dogs can raise hackles; relative apparent size is thus unaltered, and

---

13. Wicksteed 1933, 701.
14. Hirsch 1976.
15. Spence 1973.
16. Frank 1985, 211.
17. Frank 1985, 132–33.

[a]s effective as the hackle-raising mechanism is from the standpoint of any individual dog . . . there is something inescapably futile about it when viewed from the perspective of the species as a whole.[18]

Instead of competing to gain relative advantages by raising hackles, canines could have acquired better sight, or hearing, and so on. As it is, they have come to raise hackles for nothing.[19] What a waste!

In like manner, when we compete to gain relative advantage, we may end up working too hard, neglecting safety, underinsuring, forsaking leisure, and consuming too much for our own good, Frank argues. He comes to the conclusion that

> both private firms and government might take the numerous steps they do to restrict the ways in which people allocate their time, their incomes, and even their lives among the various alternatives they face . . . [in order] to slow the positional treadmill.[20]

Frank's assertion that restricting competition can provide much advantage is, however, somewhat rash. Among other things, distinguishing nonproductive from productive competition is quite difficult.[21] Economic agents often attempt to gain relative advantage not by pushing others down but rather by innovation and extra work.[22] For example, consider Frank's own case of the "airfoil that now adorns the cab of virtually every large truck on the road."[23] The airfoil was a response to rising fuel costs in the 1970s, and the truck owners who adopted it early on enjoyed economic profit from their cost advantage over those who did not. Frank observes that, over time, most large trucks were adorned with airfoils and their owners garnered only an average rate of return. Fine. Should one conclude that the government ought to have banned airfoils, without which they would also have earned a normal rate of return, no more, no less? Of course not. Although there is no long-run profit

---

18. Frank 1985, 153.

19. I do not believe that Frank's observation is entirely sound, based on the following considerations: (1) perhaps most dogs can raise hackles because those that could not died out, and (2) even now, hackle raising may enhance dogs' survivability not *vis-à-vis* dogs, but rather *vis-à-vis* other species.

20. Frank 1985,153. Would taxation thus be a second-best solution to a labor-leisure choice distorted by competition for relative position?

21. This woefully prejudiced as well as bootless distinction is one whose roots are deep; see Smith 1976a.

22. People in society may agree to prohibit truly destructive competition, e.g., setting rival's factory on fire, spreading a false rumor that the rival's products are unfit for human consumption, and so on.

23. Frank 1991, 365.

for truck owners as a consequence of adopting airfoils, there is considerable conservation of energy—a scarce resource. Relative advantage may have been individual, and ultimately frustrated, motivation, but social gain was the result.[24]

Consider another example. In the 1960s, South Korea had an average level of education that was inordinately high for a country with its meager per capita income of some one hundred dollars per year. Even though a great proportion of college graduates ended up either unemployed or underemployed, everyone who could afford the expense, and even many who could not, aspired to acquire a college education. Indeed, it was not uncommon for farmers to incur heavy debts, and even to sell their farms, in order to finance their children's higher education or to buy their college diplomas. Had Robert Frank been in Korea at the time, perhaps he would have judged that this parental effort to purchase signals resulted in an overinvestment in education, and he would not have been alone in reaching this conclusion: many restrictions on education were proposed at the time. The received wisdom some twenty years later, however, is that this heavy private investment was largely responsible for South Korea's meteoric economic development.[25]

In sum, the verdict on the efficiency effect of the competition for status and relative advantage is not yet in. And under these circumstances, in condemning the search for relative advantage, how can we avoid condemning (the intrinsically rivalrous) competition as a whole? Indeed, in response to some economists' harsh judgment of advertisements as duplicative and wasteful, Israel Kirzner makes the following observation.

> To condemn duplicated (and apparently unnecessary) advertising effort on the part of two rivals . . . is to condemn the duplication that occurs generally during the competitive process. In calling such duplication wasteful one is presumably passing judgment from the perspective of assumed omniscience. In the absence of such omniscience, to criticize competitive duplication as wasteful is to criticize the very process through which the market assembles the entrepreneurial knowledge to perceive the occurrence of waste.[26]

What Kirzner says about advertising is surely applicable to all other measures of competition that entrepreneurs adopt to beat out their rivals.

Competition for status contributes to stability. Even in modern society, where we tend to believe in human equality as never before, differences in the

---

24. Elster 1989, 263, makes a similar point.
25. Bae 1992, 56–62; see also Barro 1991.
26. Kirzner 1973, 179.

resources we control force us to be primarily interested in maintaining our relative standing *vis-à-vis* our peers and those immediately above and below us in the pecking order. Those of moderate means who try to keep up with the consumption patterns of the higher-ups court ruin more often than upward mobility. In a stable society, this is probably no hidden result. When a community has a well-developed social hierarchy, its members are therefore likely to be most concerned with maintaining the *status quo*. When people compete, and they compete incessantly and intensely, they tend to compete for a trifling advantage over their rivals. And when everyone jealously guards relative position, the *status quo* tends to be preserved.

In that almost everyone in the system has an interest in maintaining current conventional practices, the *status quo* resembles an equilibrium state. In the short term, any rearrangement of status will probably look worse to the majority than what they are already accustomed to, even before they factor in the genuine uncertainty associated with altering social relationships. We all, in brief, have an interest in maintaining the *status quo*, whether our standing is high or low.

Low as well as high? Don't those at the very bottom of the ladder have the least apparent chance of success within a given convention? Are they not the "certified failures"? Are they then not likely to rise up against the *status quo*?

The answer is largely negative. To the extent that the lowly are imbued with convention, they must admit the legitimacy of their current status. If they put themselves in others' shoes, they would probably not accord themselves any improvement in rank. Suppose, for example, that I ran a one-hundred-meter dash against Bo Jackson, Carl Lewis, and Hirschel Walker. Although I am not certain who would be in first place, of one slot I *am* certain—the last would be mine! Had I been raised to believe that this sort of dashing were the manly way to go, and did I suspect no tampering in the competition, I would concede the outcome and accept my status among the lowly. I might not be overjoyed with the standing. But I probably should not suggest a dart-throwing or differential calculus contest instead. Then I would appear childish or churlish in my own eyes, as I viewed the spectacle from the perspective of others who shared the paradigm that one dashes to success. Most people in a stable community acquire this ability to see the world as others see it. We are thus much more likely to admire and imitate the winners than to change the rules of the game—although some few of the more enterprising of us will doubtless disappear to the laboratory in hopes of emerging with wonder drugs or canny contraptions with which we can win the race in which society has placed us. Far from being incompatible with stability, then, the concern for status is rather likely to be the stuff of its bastions.

CHAPTER 7

# Envy

> If you do anyone a favour, the whole neighborhood is up in arms; the clamour is like that of a rookery.
>
> —William Hazlitt

This chapter develops a novel approach to the topic of envy, seen now in the context of the paradigmatic approach to decision making under uncertainty. Although many economic theorists conflate the concepts of status and envy, I show that, at least within this approach, they are quite distinct. While status is a communal reflection of an individual's relative proficiency in the use of conventions, envy is one individual's pained response to another's relative gain in society. Not only the causes but also the consequences are radically different, as we shall see.

First consider Robert Nozick's definitions of competition and envy.[1] Suppose that there are two women, X and Y. Further suppose that a slender waist is a desirable attribute. If X prefers the state in which she has a slender waist and Y has one like a wine-barrel to the state in which neither is wasp-waisted, and is indifferent between the state in which both are wasp-waisted and one in which both are like wine-barrels, Nozick finds X to be *competitive*. (Or should we say that she is concerned with status?) X is *envious*, however, if she prefers the state in which neither X nor Y has a slender waist to the state in which Y has a slender waist and X does not, and if she also prefers the state in which she has a slender waist while Y does not to the state in which neither has a slender waist. In other words, the competitive individual seeks to obtain relative advantage by acquiring an attribute not available to others, while the envious individual seeks the same with the added twist that, if she cannot acquire the desired attribute, she seeks to deny it to others as well. Envy, in this sense, may be described as "ugly competition."

Indeed, envy is regarded in all civilized societies as one of the most ignoble of feelings. The envious feels sorrow at others' prosperity and rejoices

---

1. Nozick 1974, 239.

in their harm,[2] and few would openly admit that they are envious in this sense. "I envy you" in common parlance means, rather, "I admire you" or "I wish I were in your shoes." But, in John Rawls's view, "envy proper, in contrast with benign envy which we freely express, is a form of rancor that tends to harm both its objects and its subject."[3] Admission of envy in the proper sense of the term would amount to a confession of ignominy, and few of us are willing to do so.

Although Nozick's definition captures the ignominy of envy, it lacks social context and is therefore of little use in helping us make sense of the many social institutions that have risen in response to this emotion, whether their *raison d'être* be to pander or to contain. As Helmut Schoeck observes:

> The phenomenon described by the word *envy* is a fundamental psychological process which of necessity presupposes a social context: the coexistence of two or more individuals. Few concepts are so intrinsic a part of social reality yet at the same time so markedly neglected in the categories of behavioral science.[4]

We are now ready to place envy in the context of our desire to preserve the *status quo*.

*Definition (Envy).* Envy reflects the pained response of our awareness of others' relative gain; envious individuals are so determined to regain former parity that they are prepared to dispossess others.[5]

---

2. Consider, in this context, Aesop's fable of envy. Two Greeks lived in a town. One day, one Greek prayed to Zeus for a cow, and his wish was promptly granted. The next day, the other Greek prayed to Zeus for two cows, and was most happy to receive them. On the following day, the first Greek prayed to Zeus for three cows; on the fourth day, the second for four, and so on. Well, this incessant pestering finally made Zeus quite irate, and he summoned Apollo to deal with the situation. Apollo, being the god of wisdom, quickly understood the nature of the problem, and proposed the following to the Greeks: "I will grant whatever you wish, but I shall also double your wish and give it to the other." Without much hesitation, one Greek responded thusly: "Pray, O Apollo, pluck out one of my eyes!"

3. Rawls 1971, 533.

4. Schoeck 1987, 6. Aside from Schoeck, scarcely anyone has written on the subject of envy. Therefore, I rely somewhat heavily on his work. However, Schoeck and I are different in an important respect: Schoeck seems to think that envy is phylogenetic, an outgrowth of sibling jealousy; I view it more generally as a reflection of decision making in the face of uncertainty. In the final revision of the manuscript of this book, I came across Elster (1989, 252–63) who briefly discusses envy. But he uses the term *envy* to designate both envy and the concern for status.

5. Do note, in the spirit of avoiding later confusion, that this definition involves a pattern of behavior, not feelings. Behind each action we presume to find thoughts and feelings, but not all feelings are translated into *observable behavior*. It is this behavioral response to other people's affairs that is of interest here.

At the heart of envy is a sense of relative loss and the desire to restore parity. Even when our own consumption or wealth is unchanged, our happiness may decline as other people's possessions increase. Indeed, even an increase in our own consumption may make us less happy if others gain even more.

Consider two individuals, C and D, who work in the same office. If they have come to consider themselves equal in the criteria deemed relevant to their performance (qualifications, ability, appearance, hours put in, and so on), they will also come to expect equal pay. The parity may be perceived as the norm: a fair day's work for a fair day's pay. Suppose now that D gets a raise and C gets no raise at all (or it may be that C gets a raise, but D gets twice as much). C may demand a comparable increase in compensation. Or he or she may reduce his or her output as a justification for his or her lower wage. He or she may even sabotage D's performance to prove that D is not worth his or her raise. All these actions represent "envious" behavior on the part of C.

Envy in this sense is widespread. Consider, for example, Keynes's speculation that wage rigidity is rooted in workers' concern for relative wages: they will refuse to suffer wage cuts even if the alternative is layoffs (cuts to zero) unless workers they deem comparable accept similar cuts in other industries.[6] Never mind that the consequent wage rigidity may not be as significant to macroeconomics as Keynes claimed it was. The phenomena itself is undisputed, and woe betide the manager who disregards it. Employers who ignore employees' demands for comparability and try instead to restructure their compensation schemes will face lower productivity and higher turnover as the undesirable but predictable consequence of their workers feeling cheated and mistreated.[7]

The desire to maintain relative parity has a nontrivial effect not only on wage demands and productive efforts,[8] but also on consumption,[9] general motivation,[10] and a host of other human behaviors. Seemingly invariant across cultures, envy helps explain not only the sharply progressive income taxes and confiscatory death duties of modern civilizations, but also such customs among primitive people as the "muru raids" and "tabu" (from which the word *taboo* is derived) of the Maoris.[11]

---

6. Keynes 1936, 14.
7. Mayo 1945; Thurow 1975 and 1983.
8. See Mayo 1945; Homans 1953 and 1954; Adams and Rosenbaum 1962; Hammermesh 1975.
9. See Veblen 1899; Duesenberry 1949; Leibenstein 1976.
10. See Keynes 1936; Hyman and Singer 1968.
11. Schoeck 1987, 11.

*Proposition 20 (Envy).* Envy is a reaction to disturbances in social relationships in production and reproduction that have been perceived as equitable.

In isolation, envy can signify nothing but the vile temper of the individual in question. In the context of conventions, however, envy becomes communal[12]—a predictable consequence of changes in the *status quo*, which conventional justice tends to uphold as fitting and proper.

As we saw in chapters 4 and 5, the fact of decision making in the face of uncertainty forces people who interact closely over time to adopt individually paradigms that tolerably sustain expectations. In a stable community, conventions underlie the *status quo*. It is simply in our nature to regard what we do day in and day out as fitting and proper. It is, therefore, also in our nature to regard unconventional activity as unfitting and improper. Irregular activity violates the rules. By violating our "right" to expect conformance, it not only seems unfair but also forces upon us unexpected consequences and, therefore, costly adjustments in our own behavior. Such is the genesis of "conventional justice" (proposition 10) within the paradigmatic approach we have been developing, and thus does the system of conventional justice uphold the *status quo* just as much as the law upholds the behavior of the majority as legal or at least not illegal.[13]

Consider a translation of this proposition into mathematics. Suppose that the *status quo* in a regime of convention can be expressed as $Y = f(X)$, with $\partial y/\partial x > 0$, where $Y$ is remuneration and $X$ is an index of conventional merit (a composite of skill, qualification, effort, presentability, and so forth.) For individuals A and B, if $X_a = X_b$, then $Y_a = Y_b$ will be considered a just outcome, and any other outcomes, such as $Y_a > Y_b$, or $Y_a < Y_b$, will be decidedly unjust. Upholding the conventional equation of $Y = f(X)$, individual

---

12. This is not to say that envious people are community minded. The distinctions between "communal" and "community minded" are exemplified by the Sirionoian life style. The propensity of this Bolivian tribe to exhibit highly envious and individualistic behavior is extraordinary. Members tend to group in numbers of no more than fifteen or twenty, and to live highly isolated lives even within these small units. Schoeck (1987, 39) observes that "the individual generally eats alone and at night, because he does not wish to share his quarry with others. If he eats by day, a small crowd of people outside his immediate family gathers round him. They stare at him enviously. Although he hardly ever gives them anything, he is nevertheless disturbed. Even Allan Holmberg, an American anthropologist, while living with them, eventually adopted this practice of eating alone."

13. In discussing the alleged connection between envy and justice, Rawls (1971, 538) argues that "the conception of justice is chosen [in the original position] where by definition no one is moved by rancor and spite." Again, both the concept of justice and envy are discussed in a static framework.

A would be saddened and outraged to find $Y_b > Y_a$ when $X_a = X_b$. (And B may feel uneasy about the outcome as well, as we shall see subsequently.) This inequality in outcome, which would smack to A of unjust treatment, would make A suspect impropriety and unfairness in B—a phenomenon perhaps more disturbing to A's peace of mind than such externalities as loud music and pollution. A would demand the restoration of justice: that $Y_a = Y_b$ as long as $X_a = X_b$, even if $Y_b$ must be reduced rather than $Y_a$ increased to bring them back into equality. In our framework, the desire for restitution is therefore as much a part of envy as moral outrage at the violation of conventional justice and the disturbance of the *status quo*.

Rawls argues, on the contrary, that what we call envy is better labeled resentment.

> Envy is not a moral feeling. No moral principle need be cited in its explanation. It is sufficient to say that [when] the better situation of others catch our attention, . . . [the resultant] sense of hurt and loss arouses our rancor and hostility. . . . [R]esentment [on the other hand] is a moral feeling. If we resent our having less than others, it must be because we think that their being better off is the result of unjust institutions, or wrongful conduct on their part.[14]

Resentment in Rawlsian parlance is envy in ours. But the distinction Rawls draws between his envy and resentment is not without flaw. Because it rests largely on differences in inner frames of mind, this demarcation is highly subjective and therefore quite difficult to pin down. As Rawls himself notes, "The appeal to justice is often a mask for envy. What is said to be resentment may really be rancor."[15] What is said to be envy can also be resentment, were the true motivation only apparent, and sometimes even the individuals with these feelings cannot honestly articulate their own feelings. Resentful people often cannot articulate the principle of justice that has allegedly been violated because the factors involved are largely implicit and they lack the facility to state explicitly what is largely implicit.

Perhaps Rawls has a hidden political agenda in classifying resentment as a moral feeling and envy as an amoral feeling. Perhaps he means to divert the conservative criticism that he alleges tries to discredit liberalism. In his words, again,

> Many conservative writers have contended that the tendency to equality in modern social movement is the expression of envy. In this way they

---

14. Rawls 1971, 533.
15. Rawls 1971, 540.

seek to discredit this trend, attributing it to collectively harmful impulses.[16]

Since envy is widely regarded as one of the deadliest of sins, in this way conservatives put those who argue for social justice on the defensive. Rawls, therefore, means to put conservatives themselves in the hot seat by distinguishing between envy and resentment on moral grounds, giving the former the low, and the latter, the higher ground.[17]

In the context of my theory of conventions, Rawls's distinctions are particularly difficult to maintain. As he himself states,

> Envy is held to be pervasive in poor peasant societies . . . [where the] social system is regarded . . . as a conventionally established and unchangeable zero-sum game. Now actually, if this belief were widespread . . . *[what] is said to be envy may in fact be resentment* which might or might not prove to be justified.[18]

Hayek also observes that "social justice" and the concomitant duties and obligations (the demands for which manifest themselves as "envy") are necessary for the continued existence of closely knit groups in ancient times.[19] Surprising as it may sound, Rawls and Hayek are both in agreement with me on this issue. And it is difficult to resist appealing to authority, to justify my new approach's proposition that envy is but a reflection of conventional justice that people in a closely interacting group tend to generate.[20] Fortunately, there is justification enough elsewhere.

Let us, then, consider the logic behind my proposition that envy is an attempt to redress the violation of conventional justice. I shall explore two widespread observations, first, acts of revenge and retribution and, second, the feelings of guilt among the successful, both of which, on the surface, appear irrational. In this way, I shall try to make sense of the senseless by placing it in the context of the paradigmatic approach and clarifying its implications for individual and social tendencies.

---

16. Rawls 1971, 538.
17. Or does he? A reading of Hayek (1978) suggests that the object of what is perceived to be a conservative attack is not necessarily "envy" but the very concept of "social justice" itself. Hayek, who claims that he is not a conservative, argues that the concept of social justice, or distributive justice, is an atavism with no place in an "open society," where the forces of market competition should reign supreme.
18. Rawls 1971, 539; italics added.
19. The argument rests on the consideration that when productivity is very low, as in primitive societies, the forced sharing through envy, or social justice, may have the character of insurance, enhancing the chances of survival.
20. I shall argue subsequently that human beings never wholly graduate from this tendency in any form of society. The question is what form of its expression is tolerable.

Consider, first, the observation that envious individuals often seem to ignore utilitarian consideration when they act or react to others at what appears to be great personal cost. It is very difficult to understand why rational individuals would behave in this fashion unless we view envy as a reaction to violations in the system of conventional justice to which they are deeply committed. Nothing moves people like the feeling of being treated unjustly. Robert Axelrod supports this view when he observes that norms are stable only when credible threats to their violation exist, so that the majority of individuals must be willing to punish transgressors even when personal cost is greater than the personal benefit.[21]

Consider, second, the observation that individuals who come to command advantage over others often so fear the resultant envy that they try to minimize the significance of their own attainment or to compensate the disadvantaged in some fashion. Fear of envy here takes the form of certain uneasy or even guilty feelings, even when the successful have violated no moral or legal code en route to their triumphs. An example of this sort of uneasy understatement comes from Raymond Firth and his study of Polynesian communities.

> If a man catches only one or two fish while no one else has any success then he will give them to other members of the crew and not keep any. If he did retain his fish, allowing the others to go away empty-handed, then he runs the risk of slanderous talk. . . . [Giving away the fish one caught] is described directly as "the blocking of jealousy."[22]

Data in support of fending off envy also come from the keen eye of Paul Tournier, focused here on staff behavior in typical office settings.

> In an office, the great speed of one typist will constantly arouse in her slower fellow-workers a sense of guilt which will paralyze them still further in their work. . . . [If] she is at all sensitive, the rapid typist will come to feel guilt for being the involuntary cause of umbrage among others and will do many little services for them to win their forgiveness.[23]

In analyzing this pattern, Helmut Schoeck believes that the speedy typist arouses in her slower fellow workers not guilt and paralysis, but *envy*; nor is her response one of guilt, but rather of *fear of envy*. Again, it is difficult to understand why a rational individual who has violated no law or moral code

---

21. See Axelrod 1986.
22. Raymond Firth, quoted in Schoeck 1987, 38.
23. Paul Tournier, quoted in Schoeck 1987, 309–10.

should feel uneasy about attaining an advantage over others *until* we recognize the strength of the human capacity to be envious, especially in a closely interacting group setting. Those who fear envy are *empathetic* enough (corollary 6b) to see that they would behave in a similar fashion in similarly disadvantaged circumstances.

Envy in the sense proposed here may also explain the ancient Greek practice of ostracism that exiled any "unpopular" people for a decade.[24] In my view, envy and ostracism are of a piece. Both presume the propriety of conventions and the *status quo* they support. Both are reactions to individuals who bring unexpected changes to the regime of convention. Among the many interpretations of ostracism in antiquity is Danish sociologist Svend Ranulf's belief that the basic root of ostracism is envy.[25]

> *Proposition 21 (Peers 2).* Envy is most strongly exhibited among people regarded as belonging to the same community, and, within that community, among people regarded as similar in standing; it is less likely among individuals regarded as members of different classes or different communities.

This proposition follows immediately from combining my discussion of envy immediately preceding with corollary 5a (peers 1), discussed in chapter 3. Simply stated, we are more likely to envy those to whom we constantly compare ourselves and to whom we feel more or less equal, and less likely to envy those to whom, in our own eyes at least, we are scarcely comparable. Workers are more envious when their co-workers receive wages than when this bounty befalls their managers. And they are more envious when their company executives receive bonuses than when people in unrelated fields strike it rich. For similar reasons, university professors watch the salaries of their colleagues in the same department more than those in other departments, and the salaries of their colleagues in the same school more than those in other universities. In short, the stronger the sense of group, the stronger the sense of envy.

Using the conventional language of contemporary economics, with $w$ denoting wage and $MP$ denoting marginal product, economist Robert Frank observes that the derivative $\partial w/\partial MP$ is both less than unity and a negative function of the strength of the interaction among workers.[26] In other words,

---

24. Schoeck 1987, 247.
25. Others include justifiable fears of demagoguery, oligarchy, and tyranny and increased humanitarian feelings among the Athenians, coupled with the view that ostracism was the least harsh of the probable punishments. See Schoeck 1987, 248; Elster 1989, 254.
26. Frank 1985, 64–86.

relatively more productive workers thus receive less than their productivity would warrant, while relatively less productive workers receive more, and this divergence between marginal product and marginal remuneration is more likely among a tightly knit group than with one of looser weave. Frank's interpretation of his finding is that more productive workers both gain status for themselves and are responsible for its loss among the less productive. If everyone were paid according to his or her individual productivity, the less productive would therefore suffer uncompensated damages, that is, the loss of status and the more productive obtain gains (in status) at no cost. Bribes then become necessary to prevent these workers from making good on threats to leave the group and form another comprised solely of workers of like productivity. The more productive may also decide to leave the group and receive full compensation for their productivity in a group of like achievers, but their higher pay would come at the cost of the loss of whatever benefits they derive from their status as top dogs. Those who remain in a group where they are paid less than their marginal product have thus demonstrated their willingness to pay the "implicit price of status," as Frank calls it.

In these sorts of group dynamics, I tend to view the hand of envy rather than that of status. Interacting in close proximity, workers are likely to regard one another as more comparable and to expect more comparable salaries as their equitable reward. If internal wage structures tend to appear more egalitarian than individual productivities would suggest, the explanation, I suggest, lies less in the more productive workers' purchase of status than in their appeasement of the envious. Why else would wages be more uniform in closely knit work units? The more productive must fear that the less productive and envious will disrupt the productive process, even to their own detriment. Both envy among the below-average workers and fear of envy among the above-average workers are exceedingly keen in a group of closely interacting individuals.

*Proposition 22 (Envy Barriers).* Envy poses barriers to innovation and progress.

The process of innovation and progress, as I argued in proposition 16 (discovery), consists of taking advantage of unexploited opportunities—opportunities that grow over time (proposition 15, growing opportunity) yet remain unnoticed, or noticed but ignored, by the majority of conformists (proposition 14). Once enterprising individuals achieve outstanding success by exploiting these possibilities through innovative—and therefore unconventional—practices, they may become role models (proposition 19, emulation). In due course, the innovative practices will become routine and conventional. Thus does society change and progress.

But before entrepreneurial success becomes a *fait accompli* and innovative practices become the object of admiration and emulation, the innovators become the object of envy. Innovation is difficult. We all tend to conform to conventions (proposition 9, conformity) and to look askance at the nonconforming and the unconventional (proposition 12, ostracism). These tendencies alone handicap the innovative, whose success often hinges on cooperation. If, even under this hobble, the deviants obtain any degree of relative advantage over the conformists, the conformists, whose world, after all, is framed by the conventions to which they pay full heed, fail to understand how this state of affairs came to be, tend to suspect unfair practice, and react to bring about restitution. In a word, they are envious (proposition 20), and they try to eliminate the apparent inequity even at great personal cost. Envy thus tends to stunt innovations that would prove successful in a more hospitable environment and acts as a barrier to progress.

But the deleterious effect of envy on innovation and progress does not stop here. Individuals who envy others are also capable of imagining the envy of others (corollary 6b, empathy). Steeped in prevalent conventions, they may thus fear the envy that accompanies the relative advantage they themselves cannot fully rationalize. Consider here Schoeck's observation.

> A situation of happiness, of assured health, of imminent success is described to someone who is then asked to imagine himself in that situation. Having done this, he is asked: "What is the first thing you'd do?" The answer is nearly always: "I'd touch wood, or make this or that sign." On being further pressed, and asked to think back as to why he would have done this, he is likely, for the first time in his life, to discover his fear of envy of some anonymous other, which he has thus sought to assuage.[27]

In a society with much acting out of envy and little interaction with the outside, this fear of envy may lead to a substantial self-inhibition against innovation.[28] Even when an individual in this sort of community comes across a promising new practice by accident, he or she will tend to ignore it, minimize its significance, and squander rather than nurture the opportunity. No doubt, by discouraging nonconventional practice, envy contributes to the stability of social relationships in production and reproduction, but it may also cause this stability to degenerate into stagnation. Schoeck again aptly makes the following observations.

---

27. Schoeck 1987, 154.
28. Elster 1989, 261–62, makes a similar point.

Institutionalized envy . . . or the ubiquitous fear of it, means that there is little possibility of individual economic advancement and no contact with the outside world through which community might hope to progress. No one dares to show anything that might lead people to think he was better off. Innovation is unlikely. Agricultural methods remain traditional and primitive, to the detriment of the whole village, because every deviation from previous practice comes up against the limitations set by envy.[29]

The social sciences have put forward numerous theories on the assumption that the normal man seeks a maximum in production and in property. All men today, including those of the so-called developing countries, ostensibly desire the greatest possible progress. These theories, however, overlook the fact that *in a great many situations the object of human activity is a diminution*; that regularly recurring modes of human behavior have as their object the lessening of assets.[30]

The Haitian experience of G. E. Simpson, again in the words of Schoeck, is apparently no isolated example.

A peasant will seek to disguise his true economic position by purchasing several smaller fields rather than one large piece of land. For the same reason he will not wear good clothes. He does this intentionally to protect himself against the envious black magic of his neighbors.[31]

How nice it would be to have a world free of envy. If not for envy and the inhibitions it creates, if not for envy barriers, in other words, would not innovation and progress be the order of the day? Sometimes we harken back to a past when people shared equally and lived lives free of envy. But this idyllic portrait of the Golden Age, for example, of primitive communism, remains largely myth. It is the stuff of modern dreams, not the reflection of daily doings millennia ago. If the study of modern primitives has any lesson, it is that great equality is purchased at great cost—social and economic stagnation. *Utopia* is "no place."

The envy-free life is impossible. Those who find the causes of envy in inequality may believe that it could be eliminated by making distribution equal. But is perfect equality possible and would it eliminate envy? My answer is firmly negative. Let us suppose, for the sake of argument, that our

---

29. Schoeck 1987, 58.
30. Schoeck 1987, 59.
31. Schoeck 1987, 58.

initial condition is one of perfect equality and, therefore, no envy.[32] Over time, people will become differentiated. Their talents are different, and they tend to discover different opportunities based on their stations in the social division of labor. Not all discoveries will be of equal value. Opportunities discovered by some will be valued more highly than others, and those who discover the more valued opportunities will reap disproportionate gain. "Nature abhors uniformity." It is unlikely that everything will either remain the same or change at a uniform rate. Depending upon the prevalent conditions, some people's gains will be viewed as unfair and they will be envied.[33] Perfect equality in the original state, even if initially possible, will not endure over time as a state that is envy-free, or "fair" as Hal Varian calls it. Therefore, even if all transactions are voluntary, the changes will have altered the *status quo*, the majority commitment to which alone makes social life possible.

An envy-free state is impossible because *envy reflects our desire to secure the world as we know it*. If we did not jealously guard our rights, no system of rules, including the rule of law, could be maintained. Again we turn to Schoeck, who argues that "too much" envy is unfortunate, but that without the relatively costless police functions that the human potential for envy provides, social stability would be impossible.

> Social co-existence, and especially coordination, requires reasonably efficient social control. . . . No motive that we have been able to discover, however, ensures conformity more certainly than fear of arousing envy in others and the sanctions it entails. To the degree, therefore, that man has developed the capacity for mutual control out of suspected envy in others, large social groups with division of labor for their members have become socially possible. . . . Hence man, as an envious being, and by reasoning of his capacity of envy, becomes truly human.[34]

Is humanity, then, forever condemned to live in backwardness by virtue of the envy barrier? Many people are unable to overcome this impediment and

---

32. Varian (1975) argues that if the initial distribution of resources is perfectly equal, then the competitive outcome is fair, in the sense of being envy free. Nozick (1974, 232–38) observes that, in modern political discourse, the desirability of equality as an ideal is assumed instead of justified.

33. Varian (1975) or Nozick (1974), whose "entitlement theory" Varian adopts, might object that if both the initial condition and the process through which it is altered are deemed fair, then the final outcome must also be considered equitable. But I argue that, even if they are not party to the transaction, members in a community ruled by conventions as makeshift efforts to deal with uncertainty may feel that they have the right to interfere in outcomes made possible by deviants who move into uncharted territory. See also Kirzner 1979, 200–224.

34. Schoeck 1987, 421–22.

are therefore condemned to eke out their living at standards barely above subsistence levels (where equality—among the surviving—is the greatest). But many others have been able to lower the envy barrier, build civilizations, and prosper. The height of the envy barrier, as well as its existence, apparently matters a great deal. Let us now turn to the factors that affect the intensity of the envy feeling and the height of the envy barrier.

The more the social production process is viewed as a zero-sum game, the higher the envy barrier. If the social pie is seen as fixed in size, one individual's gain in distribution is another person's loss. This perception is most likely to occur when society is stagnant, as has been the case among primitive people today or in ancient times. Confucian literati registered the following complaint in the court of Emperor Chao of the Han dynasty in 81 B.C.

> Profit . . . does not fall from Heaven, nor does it spring forth from the Earth; it is derived entirely from the people. . . . For Heaven and Earth do not become full at the same time: so much more is this the case with human activities! Profit in one place involves diminution elsewhere just as *yin* and *yang* do not radiate at the same time and day and night alternate in length.[35]

The perception of the zero-sum nature of the production game is not, however, limited to the primitive and the ancient. The view that exchange and trade in the market cannot be mutually beneficial, and that one party gains only at the expense of the other, for example, is known as the Montaigne dogma after the sixteenth-century French essayist.[36] In our time, at the beginning of the Reagan years, Lester Thurow published a book, *The Zero Sum Society*.[37] This argument frequently resurfaces in the form of hatred against business as a whole and merchants in particular.[38] It is reflected today in the epithets used by African-Americans boycotters of Korean grocers: "blood suckers" and "exploiters." It is also reflected in the demands of the form: "close the shops" or "hand over the store to one of us."

As I was completing the final draft of the book, major riots had broken out in Los Angeles. There were dozens of deaths, around two thousands injured, and property damages valued at around a billion dollars. Until the

---
35. Huan 1967, 41–42.
36. Shapiro 1985, 33. The term *Montaigne dogma* derives from the title of Montaigne's essay, "That One Man's Profit Is Another's Loss" (Montaigne 1979, 48–49).
37. Thurow 1980, 11–15, 194–200.
38. Hughes (1986, 403) observes that the period from 1870 to 1914, when the United States enjoyed enormous economic growth, is known paradoxically as one of monopoly domination and attendant abuses.

U.S. Army units restored calm, Korean-Americans were among the main targets of the rioters and looters. Some eight hundred of their shops and stores had been looted and set afire.[39] Many black leaders and others observed that the riots had been caused by an unjust verdict in the "Rodney King case," where the court acquitted four white policemen of wrongdoing in the beating of a black motorist. But what do Korean-Americans have to do with the injustice of the case? The real reason is that "in the South-Central area, . . . Korean shops have become the object of resentment even as they provide what is often the only retail service to residents."[40] Lawrence Aubry, a member of the Los Angeles County Human Relations Commission, seems to have come very close to identifying envy as the real cause of the hatred and violence toward Koreans when he is reported to have said: "Many blacks in Los Angeles have remained poor as, one after another, immigrant groups [such as Jews and Koreans] have arrived and climbed past them to prosperity."[41]

On the other hand, the more the social production process is regarded as positive instead of zero sum in nature, so that one person's gain does not necessarily mean another's loss, but may mean that others gain as well, the lower the envy barrier.

If goods are "positional" in the Hirschian sense, so that even a change that gives everyone more gives some more envy than goods, and if relative standing itself is an object of desire, there is no getting around the Montaigne dogma, however. Thurow concurs that "every increase in the relative income of one group is decrease in the relative income of another group. The gains are exactly counterbalanced by an equal set of losses."[42]

The envy barrier also tends to be higher, the more equal people in society believe the distribution should be. Recently, in Mlawa, Poland, a mob of drunken Poles ransacked luxurious homes of prosperous Gypsies. Mlawa's Gypsies, mostly gold and car traders, emerged as a comfortable middle class in the reformed Poland and a weekly newspaper, *Polityka,* described their wealth as "provocative." Zdzislaw Swimorski, the police chief of Mlawa, made the following observation.

> Whoever rises above the average level—we are spoon-fed under communists—is automatically pulled back, torn down, until he suffers, too. . . . If you live in Poland and you somehow got rich over the years, you are going to inspire jealousy and resentment.[43]

---

39. Reinhold 1992.
40. Mydans 1992.
41. Mydans 1992.
42. Thurow 1980, 189–90.
43. *New York Times*, July 25, 1991.

Egalitarians tend to regard any deviation from perfect equality as unjust. Envy in a society where egalitarians constitute the majority is likely to be intense, because what is demanded is not so much equality before the law as equality in opportunity or even in outcome.[44] Despite all the complaints about the shortage of capital or entrepreneurial skills, I believe that the envy barrier will prove to be the most significant obstacle to the economic development of the former socialist countries in Eastern Europe and the USSR.

There are plenty of believers in perfect equality among my peers, as well. On the day of the stock market crash in 1987, I found a few of my colleagues at the small liberal art college where I used to teach in euphoria. I asked them what the occasion was. The answer was that "the stock market crashed and the filthy rich must have lost a bundle." I was astonished by the answer since I knew that these senior professors had nothing but pensions to fund their approaching retirement, and these accounts were invested mostly in stocks. Such is the spirit of envy.

Another factor raising the envy barrier is precision in the perceived social production process. Suppose, for example, that this process can be pinned down as $Y = AX$, where $Y$ is the distribution of desired goods and $X$ is the individual attributes seen as factors of production, then everyone will expect $Y = AX_1$ for $X_1$, $Y = AX_2$, for $X_2$, and so on, with no random factor whatsoever. Suppose, now, that there are two individuals with $X_1$. Both expect $AX_1$ as outcomes. If one receives $AX_1 - j$ and the other $AX_1 + k$, where $j, k > 0$, then the former may feel envy, and the latter may fear envious behavior. Only a redistribution may restore the equality they expected between them.

The less definite the social production process is perceived to be, the lower the envy barrier as well. Suppose that the social production process is no longer widely regarded to take the precise form, $Y = AX$, but now adds a random term, $e$, for accidents, luck, and what have you, so that $Y = AX + e$. In this community, two individuals with $X_1$ will no longer necessarily expect the same outcome all the time. Luck plays an important, nay crucial, role in lowering the envy barrier.

Man can come to terms with the evident inequality of the individual human lot, without succumbing to envy that is destructive of both him-

---

44. Kuran (1991a, 244–46) observes that "Americans have always agreed on the desirability of equality. But they have attached different meanings to the concept, and over the years the dominant interpretation has undergone a series of transformations. . . . [T]he United States [has] come in barely two centuries from widespread acceptance of individual inequality to a situation where celebrated professors debate whether footnotes in scholarly texts should be rationed by skin color." Kuran refers here to a 1984 article in the *University of Pennsylvania Law Review* that fired a salvo at scholars for their "racism" in failing to cite a sufficient number of minority scholars in their research.

self and others, only if he can put the responsibility on some impersonal power—blind chance or fortune which neither he himself nor the man favoured is able to monopolize. "Today it's the other man who is lucky—tomorrow it may be I."[45]

As long as they maintain average parity over time, they can tolerate unequal outcomes better than those whose outlook is more definite.

As I discussed in chapter 3, Albert Hirschman offers a similar line of argument by suggesting, in his "tunnel effect" hypothesis, that belief in the possibility of similar blessings somewhere down the road may delay the envious reactions otherwise provoked by the good fortune of others.[46] In this way, he explains why, contrary to the relative deprivation hypothesis, the lower strata of society tend not to revolt in the early states of economic development when changes in the income distribution are so heavily tilted toward the upper classes, but rather only after development is well under way. Conjuring up images of drivers stuck in a massive traffic jam in a one-way, two-lane tunnel, Hirschman observes that as one lane starts to move, the average driver will stay put, expecting his own lane to move in due course. Similarly, the poor, whose incomes stagnate initially, will sympathize or even identify with those whose means increased, thus infering "initial gratification" from improvements at the top (corollary 6b, empathy), not because they delight in others' well-being but because they expect to enjoy the same good fortune at some inconsiderable remove. But this tunnel, or sympathy, effect will dominate the lane-shifting or envy effect only temporarily. After a long and vain wait in their own line, even the most polite drivers will eventually cut into the moving lane, and envy will ultimately dominate sympathy if the poor lose hope of economic enfranchisement.

The envy barrier may be raised if, over time, the belief becomes widespread that the system holds inherent bias in favor of the haves and against the have-nots, (i.e., if one lane always moves faster than the other, in Hirschman's imagery). Robert Merton has labeled this sort of belief, "Matthew's law."

> For to everyone who has will more be given, and he will have abundance; but from him who has not, even what he has will be taken away. (Matthew 25:29).[47]

This view of how the real world works is not uncommon. Consider the words of Frank Knight, that champion of the unfettered economic process,

---

45. Schoeck 1987, 285.
46. Hirschman 1981, 39–58.
47. Merton 1968a.

who reasoned that the protest of "the propertyless and ill-paid masses" springs in good measure from the sense they have of playing in "an unfair contest," where all the cards are stacked against them.[48] Certainly, this perception leads people to advocate redistribution to the point where no one has any material advantage over others.[49]

Conversely, the longer the perspective, the lower the envy barrier. Throughout history, no race, no nation, no clan, no family, no species has enjoyed glory and prosperity for ever and ever. People can rise from obscurity to power and domination, for awhile—isn't the saying "from shirtsleeves to shirtsleeves in four generations" a testimony to the cumulative effect of hubris and debauchery? If the have-nots believe that with hard work, a stint of good luck, and time they can supplant the current haves, then they will respond with the most intense of competition, not envy.

Although the suppression of envy by the concept of luck may not be a permanent solution, the more widely accepted this concept of luck ($e$ in the preceding production function), the lower the envy barrier and the higher the tolerance for inequality. After all, the word *happiness*, or well-being, has its origin in the Old English *hap*, meaning accident or luck. Earlier people must have tried to lessen others' envy by calling an extraordinary success a fortuity or fluke. From the fact that English-speaking people have come to have no hesitation in describing themselves as happy, that is, no hesitation in counting their luck, we can infer that their envy barrier had been significantly lowered, thus allowing for progress.[50] Note, however, that words can mean many things, and they can also change and raise envy barriers. As happiness has come to mean well-being or something desirable, its demands have become universal—as if everyone could be lucky, all at once.[51]

Changes in institutional arrangements may therefore prove a steadier, more assured way to reduce envy barriers over time.[52] The more secure and clearly defined the private property rights, the lower the envy barrier. Private property rights provide, as it were, a protective cover for entrepreneurs.

In a regime of convention, the majority behave conventionally and predictably. But there is no economic profit—out of ordinary advantage—in doing what is expected, so the majority will earn the customary return, no more and no less, day in and day out.

If someone believes that he can gain over and above the customary

---

48. Knight 1935, 60–64.

49. Confiscatory taxes are political expressions of the most acute form of envy.

50. The word for happiness in Chinese, *hsing fu*, has a similar origin and its literal meaning is good luck. The word is commonly used for happiness or well-being not only in China, but in Korea and Japan as well.

51. Schoeck 1987, 286.

52. This institutional arrangement may, exclusively or in combination, have evolved spontaneously, been adopted by agreement, or been imposed from above.

expectations, he must *see* what others do not. That is, he must discover a way of doing things (a paradigm), which, he is convinced, will lead to superior results. Such a person who discovers opportunities that others fail to notice because of their conventional blinders, and who audaciously exploits them as others do not because of their conventional inhibitions, is the *entrepreneur*.

The entrepreneur, as we have seen, arouses suspicion among conformists. He (or she) breaks from the pack. He claims to know more than we do, perhaps not in words, but in actions that speak louder than words. He has the conviction that he can expose our ignorance, parochialism, and undue inhibitions. The majority in the community regard the would-be entrepreneur as flippant, brash, disloyal to time-honored institutions, opportunistic, and worse. We respond to his failures with vindictive indignation: "I told you so!" or "I knew it!" We might even take pity at the indignity of his plight if he fails.

The success of the entrepreneur, on the other hand, throws the masses into confusion. The masses who work as diligently as ever according to conventions cannot understand why the demand for their products is disappearing, making them poorer, while the entrepreneur is swarmed by customers, making him rich. How could he have earned more than is expected of someone like him? Not by accident, if the success persists. Then the explanation must lie either in his having possessed superior wisdom (paradigms) or in having exercised "evil tricks" and gained unfairly. The former line of reasoning supports emulation, not envy. But the weight of tradition and our reluctance to admit our own shortcomings often lead us to conclude the latter, that conventional justice was violated. At this point, people in the community will feel slighted and unjustly dealt with by the shady character, and they will demand restitution. The entrepreneur has become the object of envy.

The entrepreneur may attempt to deal with this envy by appeasement. But if he wishes to continue in his entrepreneurial activities, he must also procure protection by other means. Because raising a private army or hiring itinerant mercenaries will be beyond the means of all but the most successful of entrepreneurs, many opportunities will be left unexploited if entrepreneurs have to secure their own protection. Bribing someone like a king, who already maintains such a force, is a cheaper and therefore more common route to the same end. Once the practice of buying protection and the strategy of "letting them keep theirs in order for me to keep mine" become sufficiently widespread, safeguarding one person's gain from another person's envy is a matter of routine, and the institution of private property rights has been born.[53]

---

53. Thus it would appear that, while fanning the fires of envy, such socialist slogans as "Property is [the basis of] theft!" and "The private ownership of the means of production is the basis of human exploitation and alienation!" offer considerable insight into the origin of the institution of property rights as a means of suppressing the envy barrier.

Once the protective cover of private property rights proves tolerably effective, the fear of envy will diminish. Emboldened entrepreneurs will be more inclined to pursue gains by exploiting the opportunities they discover. The envy barrier is then lowered, opening the floodgate of innovation and entrepreneurial activity and encouraging economic development.

*Definition (Market).* The market is a social institution in which individuals, including entrepreneurs, are allowed to act freely under the protective cover of private property rights as long as no coercion is involved. The market process thus allows separate individuals to work out their fancies and frustrations, convictions and concerns, in short, to exercise freedom, shielded somewhat from the threat of envy.

In the market, the deal $X$ that Ms. C desires to make with Mr. D will be concluded only if D is also interested. Ms. C will therefore do everything in her power to spark D's interest in $X$. Once the transaction is completed, so is the relationship between C and D. If, in retrospect, D did not pursue his gains as far as possible, for whatever inhibitions or conventional considerations, that is too bad.[54] Ms. C will still have the right to keep her gains, with little fear of envy. Property rights prevent envy from undermining the market in the name of conventional justice. The task of protection, that is, the enforcement of property rights in this case, is often delegated to the political authority, for a fee in the form of taxes.[55]

*Proposition 23 (Social Learning).* The market process is the process of social learning.

This follows from proposition 14 (unexploited opportunities) and the definition of the market immediately preceding. I argued in chapter 5 that a stable regime of conventions tends to leave possibilities for gain unexploited and, therefore, opens up a window of opportunity for the enterprising. These would-be entrepreneurs remain, however, somewhat restrained by barriers of envy (proposition 22, envy barrier)—until their potential gains are well protected by property rights in the market. The window is then wide open indeed.

How do entrepreneurs presume to gain? There are many ways. One approach may be the path of innovation: reducing the costs of producing old products by novel technological or organizational means or introducing new

---

54. Kirzner (1979, 200–224) advances the "finder-keeper" as the principle of justice.
55. One of the most important questions in political economy is under what conditions political authorities will be most likely to perform the tasks entrusted to them. The temptation is great for those in power to fleece the entrepreneurs and share the spoils with the envious masses.

products or services that satisfy latent demand.[56] Another may be simply betting against the crowd, who fail to notice opportunities because they adhere so tightly to conventional wisdom.[57] "Greenmailing" is an example of such a bet, where the managers and the majority of the stockholders go about their routine business, and, in the meantime, an audacious few seize the opportunity by acquiring—or threatening to acquire—control over the firm. Whether innovating or arbitraging in nature, the essence of gain-seeking activity is being unconventional. It consists in exploiting opportunities that the conventional tends to ignore. The entrepreneur, in short, always does things differently and sometimes does them better.

Although entrepreneurs rarely survive ostracism and envy within conventional regimes, such inhibition is largely irrelevant in the marketplace, with its lower barriers of envy. In the market (which may be a superset to many communities with their own peculiar sets of conventions), everyone is free to pursue individual gain without fear of sanctions extending beyond the particular transaction involved. Everyone is, therefore, in some measure encouraged to deviate from relationships under established conventions that ignore developing opportunities.

Individual orientation toward gain also adds to the probability that more potential opportunities will be actualized in a market-oriented society than in a tradition-bound setting. More will perceive and more will set out to capture what has yet to be exploited.

Of course, many will fail—consider the countless small businesses that go bankrupt each year. But sooner or later, some will succeed and in spite of intense competition the probability of success is much greater in the market than under any other institutional form. As more and more people experiment with different paradigms, the probability of success increases, and the very fact of so many opportunity seekers reduces their risk of censure (being tagged the pejorative "opportunistic"). Once a gain is realized, perhaps with an element of luck, it is protected from envy by the institution of private property. People are not only encouraged but institutionally insured in their pursuit of opportunities left unexploited by the conventional blinders.

Entrepreneurial success will be met by emulation, and soon innovation

---

56. See Schumpeter 1934.
57. Kirzner 1973. Kirzner argues that his theory of entrepreneurship is radically different from that of Schumpeter (1934). Not only is his entrepreneur equilibrating, not disequilibrating, for example, but his theory is also more general, encompassing both Schumpeterian innovation and more mundane market activities. While I am quite sympathetic to Kirzner's view, his distinction seems overdrawn. With a clarification of terminologies and a more clear statement of ends to which the concepts are to be useful, probably the two theories can coexist peacefully. For example, I do not know how Kirzner's theory can explain the stylized fact of the "swarm-like appearance of innovations" that Schumpeter sees as the bases of business cycles.

becomes convention. Establishing an innovation follows a sequence quite like that involving the extension of agriculture. First, a method of extensive cultivation is applied to newly discovered virgin soil. Others imitate the innovation, or follow the discovery. The "soil" is soon exhausted and production shifts from extensive to intensive cultivation as people try to make marginal improvements.[58] The innovation is now rationalized. Propagation is complete as the innovation becomes routine.

The areas of potential routinization include production methods, labor-management relations, sources of input supplies, and targeted customers. Innovative practices that disrupt routines in each of these areas are likely themselves to settle into routine. In due course, new practices become conventional, not necessarily because they tend to degenerate over time but rather because they tend to become so accepted that followers conform to them automatically. Acquiring another set of conventional blinders, they ignore new information that crops up over the years. Again, the potential gains grow, thus preparing the ground for the next round of innovations and changes.

The process by which we come to acquire paradigms to deal with novel situations—or to improve our dealings with old situations—is called learning (corollary 2a). The market allows entrepreneurial learning, or the discovery of opportunities and innovations, to become commonplace knowledge in society. We shall call this process one of "social learning." People learn from one another, though few are intent on teaching. The competitive urge to exploit opportunities ignored, or at least not yet captured, by others is a stronger incentive to keep our information up-to-date and handy than even the best-meaning of teachers can provide. The prospect of becoming extinct unless we learn the lesson can fix our attention more closely than the sternest of taskmasters. To some people, this market process of learning appears lamentably chaotic and undisciplined. They would rather see discipline and direction. I doubt they would like the result. The market process of social learning involves contributions from everywhere and everyone. A more "disciplined" process would require a plan, which is at best the product of a few brains in a few places. Han Feitzu's observation of some two millennia ago remains true today.

> As one man in physical strength cannot rival a multitude of people and in wisdom cannot comprehend everything, using one man's strength and wisdom cannot be compared with using the strength and wisdom of the whole.[59]

---

58. "Learning by doing" seems to describe this phase. See Young 1991, 372.
59. Han 1939, 2:259–60. See Choi 1989 for further discussion.

Hayek has clarified this insight for modern ears with his phrase "market as discovery procedure."[60]

Though the market process shares with other institutions the manner of its change, its pace is much quicker. By removing the impediments and inhibitions tradition attaches to opportunism, it encourages innovators and arbitrageurs to exploit opportunities as far as they are able. Surely here lies the explanation for the higher rates of innovation and rapid economic development observed under capitalism than under such traditional institutions as feudalism or socialism.[61]

*Proposition 24 (Tendency toward Optimum).* Market processes tend to move society closer to the optimum.

This follows easily from proposition 23 (social learning) and the definition of the market. Entrepreneurs wrack their brains to discover opportunities ignored by others, that is, to discover other people's ignorance and mistakes. As entrepreneurs discover opportunities, they try to take advantage of their discoveries, gradually eliminating mistakes and ignorance in the process. As the existence of unrealized potential in society represents a suboptimal state, the market that permits entrepreneurs to capture the opportunities as they are discovered must *tend* toward the optimal.

I thus find the neoclassical economists' description of the *market tendency* toward maximization as one that reflects fundamentally sound insight.[62] But I consider this insight distorted. Economists do not say that the market "tends" toward maximization: they say it is optimal. They probably say so to gain the analytical convenience of equilibrium. But by assuming the limiting case as the given case, economists lose sight of the very market process that makes maximization a sound insight in the first place. As hard as individual entrepreneurs endeavor to exhaust opportunities and enrich themselves, new opportunities will continually arise in their stead. People learn from their experiences. Change is constant, and the battle is never ending.

History has shown us that the market is a powerful process that has transformed the world in the span of several centuries. Adam Smith brought our attention to the significance of the market for economic growth and social change. Marx and Engels described its processes with their customary flair for the dramatic.

---

60. Hayek 1978; see also Hayek 1945.

61. Hughes (1986, 14) observes that the open, U.S. society has more nearly achieved the "continuous revolution" Leon Trotsky advocated for socialist communities.

62. See the introduction and chap. 1, where I argued that maximization is an unsound description of the principles underlying individual behavioral patterns. In chap. 5, I extended this discontent to maximization as a description of social tendencies as well.

The world market . . . has given an immense development to commerce, to navigation, to communication by land. . . . The bourgeoisie, historically, has played a most revolutionary part. . . . [B]y the rapid improvement of all instruments of production, by the immensely facilitated means of communication, [the bourgeoisie] draws all, even the most barbarian, nations into civilization. The cheap prices of its commodities are the artillery with which it batters down all Chinese walls, with which it forces the barbarians' intensely obstinate hatred of foreigners to capitulate. It compels all nations, on pain of extinction, to adopt the bourgeois mode of production. . . . In other words, it creates a world after its own image. The bourgeoisie, during its rule of scarce one hundred years, has created more massive and more colossal productive forces than all preceding generations together.[63]

Why, were it not for the word *bourgeoisie*, one might think this were Milton Friedman speaking.

We can see from this point of view that the story of modern economic and social development is but a process in which the market has successfully expanded and invaded the domain once exclusively ruled by conventions—that is, the feudal sphere. The market has been truly dynamic, its consequences, far-reaching, and this process of expansion continues before our very own eyes. What used to be almost exclusively nonmarket household production, for example, is evermore part of the market, on both the input and the output side of the equation.

How and why do markets expand? And what are the effects of this expansion? These are some of the basic questions about the nature of market processes that neoclassical economists who take the market as given do not and cannot ask. This is so whether the approach be one of "market failure" (using the *perfectly competitive market* as the standard for judging the observed outcomes in the market)[64] or "transaction costs" (assuming that, in the absence of transaction costs, the market outcome would be efficient)[65] or "new institutionalism" (studying the business organizations and other institutional arrangements with the perfectly competitive market as the benchmark).[66] None of these approaches allows one to inquire about the process by which the market expands, since a well-functioning market is assumed to exist in the first place. Only by taking a different approach, an approach of analyzing the market from the perspective of conventions as general social tendencies, can one begin to appreciate the multifaceted dynamism of the market processes.

---

63. Marx and Engels 1919, 37, 39–40.
64. Pigou 1932.
65. Coase 1960.
66. Williamson 1975.

# Conclusion

The Emperor is naked!

—Hans Christian Andersen

Starting with the necessity of making decisions under conditions of uncertainty as fact, the paradigmatic approach to decision making represents a radical departure from neoclassical economics, the dominant tradition in the field of economics. As such, it can shed light on such important observations as the concern for status, envy, X-efficiency, and entrepreneurship, all of which conventional economics leave, in some measure, perplexing, neglected, shunted to footnotes, or banished to the dangerously powerful "irrational." For all its rudimentary nature, I am proud to offer this alternative to, as well as criticism of, the orthodox approach.

Neoclassical economists have raised the status of economics almost to that of the natural sciences. The core theory of maximization provides a unifying paradigm that lends itself easily to the elegance of mathematical expression and the art of quantification. These are big pluses in our scientific age. Good work in economics, alone among the social sciences, is acknowledged and rewarded by the Nobel Prize. Flushed with success and increasingly imperialistic in attitude, economists have extended their approach to an ever wider and more varied range of problems.

Two developments have followed: higher expectations and stiffened resistance. As the neoclassical economic approach is applied to an ever wider range of problems, utility maximization has come to be regarded as a general theory of humanity and society (if not a general theory of the life process, itself). But economists sound less and less convincing as they bravely claim that all aspects of human action and social life, for example, childbearing, marriage, divorce, national boundaries, and so forth, can be best understood by viewing agents as counting dollars and cents to maximize wealth. Questions have quite naturally been raised about the applicability or fruitfulness of the neoclassical economic approach in such situations, and even economists have come to challenge the dominant neoclassical tradition from within.[1]

---

1. See for example, Simon 1957; Leibenstein 1966; Kirzner 1973; Heiner 1983a; Schelling 1984.

After studying some of the criticisms of neoclassical economics and responses from the mainstream, I conclude that there is actually a great deal of disagreement concerning the status of maximization in economics. This disagreement, however, remains relatively obscure. Worse, it has caused considerable methodological confusion.

Almost all self-described economists would nowadays agree that the core theory involves maximization (and equilibrium). But if you ask who is supposed to do the maximization in their scheme of things, you will surely get many different answers.

The first answer, that maximization is an empirical proposition about market competition, is quite a venerable one. Even from my contrary perspective, it is also sound. But it is incomplete. "As if" justification and the "representative man" approach do not really improve the theoretical justification of the maximization approach. Although, it is claimed, they "work," they also beg explanation of how the interactions of disparate individuals generate this market tendency. Without a handle on the competitive process, many economists come to view markets as static, allocative mechanisms rather than as dynamic processes, thus oddly often exorcising the very competition that is supposed to generate this maximizing tendency in the first place.

The second response, that maximization is a model of how individuals make their separate decisions, gives implicit recognition to the essential incompleteness of the first answer, and acknowledges the need for microfoundations to remedy this deficiency. This is a valuable insight, but a difficult one to capitalize on within the neoclassical framework of analysis. Maximization simply cannot be a model of individual decision making in the face of uncertainty. Surely, the idea of utility-maximizing consumers conjures up an image of rational decision makers. But securing the rationality of choices requires a heroic amount of assumptions that either ignore or take as given what is important in decision making under uncertainty. I have argued, in the introduction and chapter 1, however, that central to what has been assumed away is what really matters in decision making under uncertainty—our judgment of the situation in which we find ourselves, or the problem of inference. This result is understandable, to a degree, because modeling inferential processes in general is inherently difficult. But to ignore this most crucial feature of decision making under uncertainty and to emphasize, instead, the logic of choice is akin to arguing that the dog is wagged by the tail. In addition, when such an approach is applied to aggregate issues, the result is a state of methodological confusion that is the stuff of answer three.

This third response, that maximization is both a hypothesis about market competition and a model of individual decision making, has become, by a sizeable margin, the most popular position of today's workaday economists, who usually pay scant attention to basic methodological issues. Maximization has become a catchall explanation of the behavior not only of individuals and firms, but also of industries, national economies, and even international economies. In gathering all these entities up into one fine principle, most economists have neglected or assumed away the prodigious problem of aggregation.[2] They may buzz about "providing microfoundations" for this and that, but they fail to clarify the entity or agency to which they attribute maximization as the operating principle. They may sound sustained voluntaries to the grounding of macroeconomics on microbases, but they still trumpet a leitmotif of "the representative man"—itself a characterization of market tendencies.

In the end, I identify two factors as the source of the difficulties in neoclassical theory—the widely felt need to understand individual decision making and the untenability of maximization as its model. The former is consistent with the methodological individualism adopted in the book. But because we are not omniscient, maximization cannot be a model of individual decision making. We must somehow *make up our minds* about the situation before we can act. Only after we "understand" it, that is, after we decide what the situation is, we can speak of acting to maximize values according to whatever goals we may happen to have developed. Inference about given situations thus becomes the primary aspect, the logic of choice is only a secondary aspect, and maximization becomes, at best, an idealization of the logic of choice. Viewed in this light, any effort to design a general model of decision making, maximizing or otherwise, becomes part of the impossible attempt to design a general model of inference.

If modeling decision making in the face of uncertainty is untenable, are we of necessity fenced in and should we therefore despair? No. The paradigmatic approach provides an escape and hope of a new journey. The paradigmatic approach allows us to explore patterns of individual and social behavior in an orderly fashion without committing ourselves to the bootless enterprise of proposing specific models of decision making under uncertainty.

The paradigmatic approach describes the structure of decision making in a way most people can accept. There are two logically distinct components to this problem: first, people must arrive at an understanding of a given situation, and, second, they must act rationally on the basis of that understanding. Taking the latter, the logic of choice, as nonproblematic, I have honed in on the former, arguing that the first fact of my theory is that every human action

---

2. Serious economic theorists are certainly aware of, and concerned with, the problem of aggregation. Still, most important results in economic theory are obtained by assuming away such problems as externalities that make aggregation difficult (Takayama 1974, 170, 202, 227–28, 261–62). The compulsion they feel to ground theory on individual decision making, however, leads me to think that even the finest theorists operate on the assumption that maximizaton is the proper model of analysis.

presupposes an associated paradigm, the identification of which is the crux of decision making under uncertainty.

The paradigmatic approach should not come as a complete surprise to economists already accustomed to justifying their maximization assumption as an "as if" proposition. Not only do they insist that it need not be a realistic description of any single agent, or collectivity thereof, as long as agents as a whole behave "as if" they follow the principle, but they argue that the "as if" approach is common in other sciences as well. Just as the scientist adopts an "as if" approach, the layperson adopts a variety of as if's, that is, paradigms, in dealing with his or her daily problems. My paradigmatic approach, therefore, can be seen as *a generalized as if approach*. Acknowledging that each individual, whether scientist or surfer, takes such an approach, it focuses on studying the behavioral implications of decision making under uncertainty without bogging down in introspective or circumstantial particulars.

One clear implication of the paradigmatic approach is that when people are faced with uncertainty they will do everything in their power to render their situation comprehensible, that is, to identify a suitable paradigm. To emphasize the primacy of personal experience, this quest is called *paradigm seeking*. The bulk of the book consists of deriving the behavioral implications of paradigm seeking in various contexts. By placing hypothetical individuals in the progressively more complicated contexts of isolation, groups without interaction, and groups with interaction, we can derive certain behavioral implications, such as the prevalence or power of precedent, imitation, approval seeking, status seeking, selectivity, inflexibility, and systematic mistakes. Paradigm seeking, as a process of acquiring the ability to deal with a situation as one previously could not, is also a process of (self-) education. The behavioral implications of paradigm seeking, therefore, are nothing but the patterns of learning behavior.

As the context for paradigm-seeking individuals increases to the ultimate complexity of a society characterized by close interactions of individuals over time, we learn that its members tend to deal with uncertainty by sharing paradigms and generating conventions. Only as individuals in a community come to regulate their actions, by means of conventions, is social life possible. Our desire and concern for status, instead of being frivolous, is essential in generating and maintaining conventions.

But the very stability of the regime of convention, supported by conformism and ostracism, tends to generate inertia and unexploited opportunities that grow with time and thus create the potential for entrepreneurial activities and endogenous change. Entrepreneurs are those enterprising individuals who dare to be different and risk envy and ostracism to reap possible personal gain from the exploitation of opportunities ignored by or even unknown to others. Sometimes they succeed, and sometimes they fail. Entrepreneurs are emulated as they become successful through their unconventional actions, and, in

Conclusion     153

the process, the innovations soon become conventions themselves. Of the many factors relevant in determining enterpreneurial success, most notable is the role of property rights in enabling entrepreneurs to overcome envy barriers, making possible the market process of social learning.

In this manner, the paradigmatic approach becomes a framework of analysis that is at once coherent, interdisciplinary, and evolutionary. Its coherence is a natural by-product of having derived a set of propositions from very few axioms and then exploring their implications relentlessly. It becomes interdisciplinary and integrative by providing a unique perspective on the way in which human beings make judgments, the nature of social order, the tension between stability and change, the nature of entrepreneurship and the market process, and social reactions to capitalist processes, thus enabling us to appreciate the dynamism of the market, not in spite of social relations, but *because of* them. In contrast to the mechanistic and deterministic nature of neoclassical economics, the paradigmatic approach is also open-ended and evolutionary, emphasizing the human capacity to reason, imagine, and learn, generating conventions in the process of dealing with uncertainty and changing them predictably over time.

Indeed, convention is the key concept in the theoretical framework developed here. Not only is it a natural human and social tendency, given the predicament of decision making in the face of uncertainty, but it also helps explain a host of other phenomena, such as conformity and ostracism, stability and social order, the concern for status, and envy. Generated to deal with uncertainty, conventions enable people to deal with a wide range of coordination and cooperation problems as a matter of routine. At the same time, their stability implies a degree of inertia and less than perfect adaptability. As people learn individually from their own experiences, conventions become inhibiting, allowing new opportunities to grow unexploited. As time passes, and as people learn more and more from their own experiences, the magnitude of unexploited opportunities grow, setting the stage for social change. Social change is a process in which one set of conventions is replaced by another, brought about by innovators taking advantage of opportunities. Without conventions, which generate the endogenous process of change, we would be looking only for exogenous shocks as explanations of change; without conventions, the dynamism of the market itself cannot be fully grasped. All this from uncertainty, inference, and paradigms! The theory is, indeed, coherent, interdisciplinary, and evolutionary.

Much of this sounds like Schumpter. Indeed, the concept of convention is quite analogous to his concept of "circular flow," and the role of the entrepreneur is similar in both setups. There is a crucial difference, however. Schumpeter conjectures that human nature comes in two distinct forms—that of the economic man, who maintains the circular flow, and that of the entrepreneur, who disturbs it through innovation. We admit only one sort of person

—the individual who invariably seeks paradigms but who, in various contexts, can both conform to and break with conventions. Differences in circumstances, not character, explain differences in observable behavior.

The paradigm approach is better contrasted with the neoclassical economic approach. I focus on conventions generated by paradigm-seeking individuals, while neoclassical economists center their analysis on markets created by rational (maximizing) individuals with perfect information at their finger tips.

Efficient markets leave no opportunity unexploited, and adjust compeletely and immediately to external shocks so that prices are perfectly flexible. Certainly, the view that markets promote efficiency provides valuable insight. But it is also rather misleading to take an asymptotic state as one's presumptive truth. Somehow the very dynamism of the market (consisting of rivalry and combatlike actions) that is responsible for the tendency toward efficiency in the first place gets eliminated from the analysis.

Indeed, the presumptive truth of perfect markets in neoclassical economics drives its research in a peculiar direction, where the world we live in is compared unfavorably to the presumed. It puzzles neoclassical economists that there are inefficiencies and that the market does not work as well as it should, and they look for factors that might account for these deviations. For example, when unemployment is observed, economists may find that wage rigidity prevents the labor market from clearing. This explanation, in turn, may lead them to look further for both an explanation for the rigidity—for example, relative comparisons, asymmetric information, money illusion, and so forth—and a policy suggestion—for example, easy money.

In my approach, the presumptive truth is not perfect markets but convention. We find the social process better characterized by such associated concepts as uncertainty, habit, stability, inertia, inflexibility, mistakes, unexploited opportunities, entrepreneurial discoveries, and envy. In my approach, the market is not given, but is driven by entrepreneurs, a characterization that underlines the aspect of the market as a social learning process. What is puzzling, from my perspective, is not that there are inefficiencies or poor coordination, but that in modern societies there are so many actions that are intended to eliminate inefficiencies and capitalize on other people's mistakes. From this perspective, research will be driven to examine factors that permit more entrepreneurial activities and their implications for social relations.

This book offers new vistas. The work is not done, but it has begun. It is my hope that economists and others will respond with criticisms and suggestions for modifications, corrections, and extensions of the paradigmatic approach. Such a response would further support the theory's contention that our ability to expand our knowledge over time is splendidly and centrally human.

# Appendix

**Table of Propositions and Corollaries**

| Individual Behavior Patterns | Social Tendencies |
|---|---|
| Static | |
|   Paradigmatic approach (prop. 1) | Conventional practices (prop. 7) |
|     Indeterminacy (cor. 1a) | Fortuity (prop. 8) |
|     Selectivity (cor. 1b) | Conventional justice (prop. 10) |
|     Veracity (cor. 1c) |   Status quo 1 (cor. 10a) |
|     Commitment (cor. 1d) | Stability (prop. 13) |
|     Inflexibility (cor. 1e) |   Inertia (cor. 13a) |
|     Possibility of systematic mistakes (cor. 1f) |   Apparent cause (cor. 13b) |
|     Possibility of consistent error (cor. 1g) |   Status quo 2 (cor. 13c) |
|     Discontinuity (cor. 1h) | Envy barriers (prop. 22) |
|   Conformity (prop. 9) | |
|   Ostracism (prop. 12) | |
| Dynamic | |
|   Paradigm seeking (prop. 2) | Unexploited opportunity (prop. 14) |
|     Learning (cor. 2a) |   Suboptimality (cor. 14a) |
|   Experiment (prop. 3) | Growing opportunity (prop. 15) |
|     Unpredictability (cor. 3a) | Deviance (prop. 11) |
|     Precedents (cor. 3b) | Discovery (prop. 16) |
|     Local optimums (cor. 3c) | Discontinuity (prop. 17) |
|   Vicarious experimentation (prop. 4) | Social learning (prop. 23) |
|     Imitation (cor. 4a) | Tendency toward optimum (prop. 24) |
|     Precedents (cor. 4b) | |
|     Group bias (cor. 4c) | |
|   Interpersonal comparisons (prop. 5) | |
|     Peers 1 (cor. 5a) | |
|     Equality (cor. 5b) | |
|   Approval seeking (prop. 6) | |
|     Imagined spectators (cor. 6a) | |
|     Empathy (cor. 6b) | |
|   Status seeking (prop. 18) | |
|   Emulation (prop. 19) | |
|   Envy (prop. 20) | |
|   Peers 2 (prop. 21) | |

*Note:* Although the categories capture the thrust of my arguments with some sufficiency, the distinctions between individual behavioral patterns and social tendencies and between static and dynamic are not as keen as they might be.

# Bibliography

Adams, J. Stacy. 1965. "Inequality and Social Exchange." In *Advances in Experimental Social Psychology*, ed. Leonard Berkowitz, 2:267–99. New York: Academic Press.
Adams, J. Stacy, and William B. Rosenbaum. 1962. "The Relationship of Worker Productivity to Cognitive Dissonance about Wage Inequities." *Journal of Applied Psychology*. 46:161–64.
Adams, Walter, ed. 1977. *The Structure of American Industry*. 5th ed. New York: Macmillan.
Akerlof, George A. 1980. "A Theory of Social Custom, of Which Unemployment May Be One Consequence." *Quarterly Journal of Economics* 94:749–75.
———. 1981. "Jobs as Dam Sites." *Review of Economic Studies* 48:47–79.
———. 1982. "Labor Contracts as Partial Gift Exchange." *Quarterly Journal of Economics* 97:543–69.
———. 1984. "Gift Exchange and Efficiency-Wage Theory: Four Views." *American Economic Review: Papers and Proceedings* 74:79–83.
Alam, M. Shahid. 1983. "Inter-firm Productivity: Comment." *American Economic Review* 71:817–21.
Albert, Stuart. 1977. "Temporal Comparison Theory." *Psychological Review* 84:485–503.
Alchian, Armen. 1950. "Uncertainty, Evolution and Economic Theory." *Journal of Political Economy* 58:211–21
———. 1977. *Economic Forces at Work: Selected Work*. Indianapolis: Liberty Press.
Alchian, Armen, and Harold Demsetz. 1972. "Production, Information Cost, and Economic Efficiency," *American Economic Review* 62:777–95.
Alker, Hayward R. 1965. *Mathematics and Politics*. New York: Macmillan.
Andreski, Stanislaw. 1972. *Social Sciences as Sorcery*. New York: St. Martin's Press.
Aristotle. 1925. *Ethica Nichomachea*. Trans. W. D. Ross. Oxford: Clarendon Press.
———. 1932. *The Rhetoric of Aristotle*. Trans. Lane Cooper. Englewood Cliffs, N.J.: Prentice-Hall.
Aronson, Elliot. 1980. *The Social Animal*. 3d ed.. San Francisco: W. H. Freeman.
Arrow, Kenneth. 1972a. "Gifts and Exchange." *Philosophy and Public Affairs* 1:343–62.
———. 1972b. "Models of Job Discrimination." In *Racial Discrimination in Economic Life*, ed. A. H. Pascal, 83–102. Lexington, Mass.: D. C. Health.
———. 1974a. "General Economic Equilibrium: Purpose, Analytical Techniques, Collective Choice." *American Economic Review* 64:253–72.

———. 1974b. *The Limits of Organization.* New York: Norton.
———. 1974c. "Limited Knowledge and Economic Analysis." *American Economic Review* 64:1–10.
———. 1982. "Risk Perception in Psychology and Economics." *Economic Inquiry* 20:1–9.
Arrow, Kenneth, and Frank Hahn. 1971. *General Competitive Analysis.* San Francisco: Holden-Day.
Asch, Solomon E. 1987. *Social Psychology.* Oxford: Oxford University Press.
Atkinson, Anthony B. 1975a. *Economics of Inequality.* Oxford: Oxford University Press.
———, ed. 1975b. *The Personal Income Distribution.* Boulder, Colo.: Westview.
———. 1980. *Wealth, Income and Inequality.* New York: Oxford University Press.
Augustine. 1963. *The Confession of St. Augustine.* Trans. Rex Warner. New York: New American Library.
Axelrod, Robert. 1984. *The Evolution of Cooperation.* New York: Basic Books.
———. 1986. "An Evolutionary Approach to Norms." *American Political Science Review* 80:1095–1111.
Backman, Jerald G. 1983. "Premature Affluence: Do High School Students Earn Too Much?" *Economic Outlook USA,* Summer, 64–67.
Bae, Chong-Keun. 1992. "Education, Top Reason Behind Rapid Growth: Schooling for Economic Take-Off." *Koreana* 5:56–62.
Bagehot, Walter. 1917. *Lombard Street: A Description of Money Market.* London: John Murray.
Barro, Robert J. 1991. "Economic Growth in a Cross Section of Countries." *Quarterly Journal of Economics* 106:407–43.
Bartlett, Randall. 1989. *Economics and Power.* Cambridge: Cambridge University Press.
Bass, Bernard M., and Gerald V. Barrett. 1972. *Man, Work and Organization.* Chicago: University of Chicago Press.
Baumol, William J. 1965. *Welfare Economics and the Theory of the State.* London: London School of Economics.
Becker, Gary S. 1962. "Irrational Behavior and Economic Theory." *Journal of Political Economy* 70:1–13.
———. 1973. "Theory of Marriage: Part I." *Journal of Political Economy* 81:813–46.
———. 1975. *Human Capital.* 2d ed. Chicago: University of Chicago Press.
———. 1976. *The Economic Approach to Human Behavior.* Chicago: University of Chicago Press.
Bell, Daniel, and Irving Kristol, eds. 1981. *The Crisis in Economic Theory.* New York: Basic Books.
Binmore, Ken. 1987. "Modeling Rational Player: Part I", *Economics and Philosophy* 3:179–214.
———. 1988. "Modeling Rational Player: Part II." *Economics and Philosophy.* 4:9–55.
Bladen, Vincent W. 1974. *From Adam Smith to Maynard Keynes: The Heritage of Political Economy.* Toronto: University of Toronto Press.

Boland, Lawrence A. 1981. "On the Futility of Criticizing the Neoclassical Maximization Hypothesis." *American Economic Review* 71:1031–36.
———. 1983. "The Neoclassical Maximization Hypothesis: Reply." *American Economic Review* 83:820–30.
Bork, Robert H. 1978. *The Anti-trust Paradox: A Policy at War with Itself.* New York: Basic Books.
Boulding, Kenneth E. 1969. "Economics as a Moral Science." *American Economic Review* 59:1–12.
Boxill, Bernard R. 1980. "How Injustice Pays." *Philosophy and Public Affairs* 9:359–71.
Braibanti, Ralph, and Joseph J. Spengler, eds. 1961. *Tradition, Value, and Socio-Economic Development.* Durham, N.C.: Duke University Press.
Brams, Steven J. 1975. *Game Theory and Politics.* New York: Free Press.
Brennan, Geoffrey, and Loren Lomasky. 1985. "The Impartial Spectator Goes to Washington." *Economics and Philosophy* 1:189–211.
Buber, Martin. 1966. *The Way of Response* Ed. N. N. Glatzer. New York: Schocken Books.
Buchanan, James M. 1965. "An Economic Theory of Clubs." *Economica* 32:1–14.
———. 1975. *The Limit of Liberty: Between Anarchy and the Leviathan* Chicago: University of Chicago Press.
———. 1977. *Freedom in Constitutional Contract.* College Station: Texas A&M University Press.
———. 1979. *What Should Economists Do?* Indianapolis: Liberty Press.
Cain, Glen G. 1976. "The Challenge of Segmented Labor Market Theories to Orthodox Theory: A Survey." *Journal of Economic Literature* 14:1215–57.
Cain, Louis P., and P. J. Uselding, eds. 1973. *Business Enterprise and Economic Change.* Kent, Ohio: Kent State University Press.
Caldwell, Bruce J. 1983. "The Neoclassical Maximization Hypothesis: Comment." *American Economic Review* 73:824–27.
Carswell, John. 1960. *The South Sea Bubble.* London: Cresset Press.
Casson, Mark. 1982. *The Entrepreneur: An Economic Theory.* Totowa, N.J.: Barnes and Noble Books.
Chandler, Alfred P. 1971. *The Visible Hand: The Managerial Revolution in American Business.* Cambridge, Mass.: Harvard University Press.
Choi, Young Back. 1986. "Decision Making and Economic Behavior under Uncertainty." Ph.D. diss., University of Michigan.
———. 1989. "Political Economy of Han Feitzu." *History of Political Economy* 21:367–90.
———. 1990. "Adam Smith's View of Human Nature." *Review of Social Economy* 48:288–302.
Clague, Christopher. 1977. "Information Costs, Corporate Hierarchies, and Earnings Inequalities." *American Economic Review* 67:81–85.
Clark, John M. 1938. *Studies in the Economics of Overhead Costs.* Chicago: University of Chicago Press.
Coase, Ronald H. 1937. "The Nature of the Firm." *Economica,* n.s. 4:386–405.
———. 1960. "The Problem of Social Cost." *Journal of Law and Economics* 3:144–71.

Coats, A. William. 1964. "The Role of Authority in the Development of British Economics." *Journal of Law and Economics* 7:85–106.
Cohen, Michael D., and Robert Axelrod. "Coping with Complexity: The Adoptive Value of Changing Utility." *American Economic Review* 74:30–42.
Conlinsk, John. 1980. "Costly Optimizers versus Cheap Imitators." *Journal of Economic Behavior and Organization* 1:275–93.
Commons, John R. 1924. *The Legal Foundation of Capitalism*. New York: Macmillan.
———. 1934. *Institutional Economics*. New York: Macmillan.
———. 1970. *The Economics of Collective Action*. Ed. K. Parsons. Madison: University of Wisconsin Press.
Cooley, Thomas F., and S. F. LeRoy. 1981. "Identification and Estimation of Money Demand." *American Economic Review* 71:825–44.
Coppleston, Frederick. 1979. *On the History of Philosophy*. London: Search Press.
Cornwall, John. 1983. *The Condition for Economic Recovery: A Post-Keynesian Analysis*. Armonk, N.Y.: M. E. Sharpe.
Croce, Beneditto. 1913. *The Philosophy of Giambattista Vico*. Trans. R. G. Collingwood. London: Howard Latimer.
Cross, John G. 1983. *A Theory of Adaptive Economic Behavior*. Cambridge: Cambridge University Press.
Dacy, Douglas C., and Howard Kunreuther. 1969. *The Economics of Natural Disasters*. N.Y.: Free Press.
Danziger, S., and D. Wheeler. 1975. "The Economics of Crime: Punishment or Income Redistribution." *Review of Social Economy* 33:113–31.
David, Herbert A. 1963. *The Method of Paired Comparison*. London: Charles Griffin.
David, Paul A. 1985. "Clio and the Economics of QWERTY." *American Economic Review Proceedings* 75:332–37.
Davies, J. C. 1963. *Human Nature in Politics: The Dynamics of Political Behavior*. New York: Wiley.
Day, Richard H. 1967. "Profits, Learning, and Convergence of Satisficing to Marginalism." *Quarterly Journal of Economics* 82:302–11.
Dewey, John. 1933. *How We Think*. New York: Heath.
———. 1948. *Reconstruction in Philosophy*. Enlarged ed. Boston: Beacon Press.
———. 1960. *The Quest for Certainty*. New York: Putnam.
Dick, James C. 1975. "How to Justify A Distribution of Earnings." *Philosophy and Public Affairs* 4:248–72.
Doeringer, Peter B., and Michael J. Piore. 1972. *Internal Labor Market and Manpower Analysis*. Lexington, Mass.: D. C. Heath.
Dooley, Patrick K. 1974. *Pragmatism as Humanism: The Philosophy of William James*. Chicago: Nelson-Hall.
———. 1982. "Kuhn and Psychology." *Journal for the Theory of Social Behavior* 12:275–89.
Dumont, Louis. 1981. *Homo Hierarchicus: The Caste System and Its Implications*. Trans. Basia Gulati. Chicago: University of Chicago Press.
Dunlop, John T. 1950. *Wage Determination Under Trade Union*. New York: Kelly.
Drucker, Peter. 1971. *Men, Ideas and Politics*. New York: Harper and Row.

———. 1981. *Toward Next Economics*. New York: Harper and Row.
Duesenberry, James. 1949. *Income, Savings and the Theory of Consumer Behavior*. Cambridge, Mass.: Harvard University Press,
Dye, Ronald A. 1984. "Trouble with Tournaments." *Economic Inquiry* 22:147–49.
Dyer, Alan W. 1984. "The habit of Work: A Theoretical Explanation." *Journal of Economic Issues* 74:557–64.
Earl, Peter E. 1983. *The Economic Imagination: Toward a Behavioral Analysis of Choice*. Armonk, N.Y.: M. E. Sharp.
Edwards, Ward. 1982. "Conservatism in Human Information Processing." In *Judgment under Uncertainty: Heuristics and Biases*, ed. Daniel Kahneman, Amos Tversky, and Paul Slovic, 359–69. New York: Cambridge University Press.
Einhorn, Hillel J. 1982. "Learning from Experience and Suboptimal Rules in Decision Making." In *Judgment under Uncertainty: Heuristics and Biases*, ed. Daniel Kahneman, Amos Tversky, and Paul Slovic, 268–83. New York: Cambridge University Press.
Elliott, John E. 1983. "Schumpeter and the Theory of Capitalist Economic Development." *Journal of Economic Behavior and Organization* 4:277–308.
Elster, Jon. 1979. *Ulysses and the Sirens: Studies in Rationality and Irrationality*. Cambridge, Cambridge University Press.
———. 1983a. *Explaining Technical Change*. Cambridge: Cambridge University Press.
———. 1983b. *Sour Grapes: Studies in the Subversion of Rationality*. Cambridge: Cambridge University Press.
———. 1989. *The Cement of Society*. Cambridge: Cambridge University Press.
Etzioni, Amitai. 1988. *The Moral Dimension*. New York: Free Press.
Fang, Lizhi. 1991. "Form and Physics." *Partisan Review* 58:656–64.
Feldman, Allan M., and A. Kirman. 1974. "Fairness and Envy." *American Economic Review* 64:995–1005.
Feldstein, Martin, and S. Yitzaki. 1982. "Are High Income Individuals Better Stock Market Investors?" Harvard Discussion Paper 918.
Festinger, Leon. 1954. "A Theory of Social Comparison Process." *Human Relations* 7:117–40.
———. 1957. *A Theory of Cognitive Dissonance*. Evanston, Ill.: Peterson, Row.
———. 1962. "Cognitive Dissonance." *Scientific American* 212:93–102.
———. 1983. *The Human Legacy*. New York: Columbia University Press.
Field, Alexander James. 1984. "Microeconomics, Norms and Rationality." *Economic Development and Cultural Change* 32:683–711.
Fletcher, Gerth J. O. 1984. "Psychology and Common Sense." *American Psychologist* 39:203–13.
Fogel, Robert W. 1989. *Without Consent or Contract: The Rise and Fall of American Slavery*. New York: Norton.
Fombrun, Charles J. 1984. "Structure of Organizational Governance." *Human Relations* 37:207–23.
Foucault, Michel. 1973. *The Order of Things*. New York: Random House.
Frank, Robert H. 1984. "Are Workers Paid Their Marginal Product?" *American Economic Review* 74:549–71.

———. 1985. *Choosing the Right Pond*. New York: Oxford University Press.
———. 1989. *Passions Within Reason: The Strategic Role of the Emotions*. New York: Norton.
———. 1991. *Microeconomics and Behavior*. New York: McGraw-Hill.
Friedman, Milton. 1953. *Essays in Positive Economics*. Chicago: University of Chicago Press.
———. 1962. *Capitalism and Freedom*. Chicago: University of Chicago Press.
Fuller, Lon L. 1967. *Legal Fictions*. Stanford: Stanford University Press.
———. 1968. *Anatomy of the Law*. New York: New American Library.
———. 1969. *The Morality of Law*. Rev. ed. New Haven: Yale University Press.
Furubotn, Eirik G., and Svetozar Pejovich. 1972. "Property Rights and Economic Theory: A Survey of Recent Literature." *Journal of Economic Literature* 10:1137–62.
Galton, Francis. 1902. "The Most Suitable Proportion Between the Values of First and Second Prizes." *Biometrika* 1:385–90.
Garelick, Herbert M. 1971. *Modes of Irrationality*. The Hague: Martinus Nijhoff.
Garner, C. Alan. 1982. "Uncertainty, Human Judgment, and Economic Decisions." *Journal of Post Keynesian Economics* 4:413–24.
Gerard, Howard B., and E. S. Conolley, and Charles W. Greenbaum. 1962. "Attitudes Toward an Agent of Uncertain Reduction." *Journal of Personality* 30:485–95.
Goodin, Robert E. 1976. *The Politics of Rational Man*. London: Wiley.
Gordon, Robert A. 1976. "Rigor and Relevance in a Changing Institutional Setting." *American Economic Review* 66:1–14.
Green, Jerry R., and Nancy L. Stokey. 1983. "A Comparison of Tournament and Contract." *Journal of Political Economy* 92:349–64.
Grether, David M., and Charles R. Plott. 1979. "Economic Theory of Choice and the Preference Reversal Phenomenon." *American Economic Review* 69:623–38.
Grossman, Sanford J., and J. E. Stiglitz. 1980. "On the Impossibility of Informationally Efficient Markets." *American Economic Review* 70:393–408.
Guasch, Jose Luis. 1982. "Equilibrium Analysis of Wage-Productivity Gaps." *Review of Economic Studies* 49:485–97.
Guasch, Jose Luis, and Andrew Weiss. 1981. "Self-Selection in the Labor Market." *American Economic Review* 71:275–84.
Hagen, E. E. 1958. "Economic Justification of Protectionism." *Quarterly Journal of Economics* 73:496–514.
Hahn, Frank H. 1970. "Some Adjustment Problems." *Econometrica* 36:1–17.
———. 1981. *Three Lectures in Monetary Theory*. Oxford: Basil Blackwell.
Hamermesh, Daniel S. 1975. "Interdependence in the Labor Market." *Economica* 42:420–29.
Han, Feitzu. 1939. *Han Feitzu*. 2 vols. Trans. W. K. Liao. London: Probsthain.
Hands, D. Wade. 1987. "A Review of Charles Taylor's Philosophical Papers I and II." *Economics and Philosophy* 3:172–75.
Hardin, Russell. 1982. *Collective Action*. Baltimore: Johns Hopkins University Press.
Hausman, Daniel M., ed. 1984. *The Philosophy of Economics: An Anthology*. Cambridge: Cambridge University Press.

Hayakawa, Hiroaki, and Y. Venieris. 1977. "Consumer Interdependence Via Reference Group." *Journal of Political Economy* 85:599–615.
Hayek, Frederick A. 1945. "The Use of Knowledge in Society." *American Economic Review* 35:519–30.
———. 1967. *Studies in Philosophy, Politics, and Economics*. Chicago: University of Chicago Press.
———. 1968. "The Confusion of Language in Political Thought." In *IEA Occasional Paper*, 20. London: Institute of Economic Affairs.
———. 1973. *Law, Legislation and Liberty*. Chicago: University of Chicago Press.
———. 1978. *New Studies in Philosophy, Politics, Economics, and the History of Ideas*. Chicago: University of Chicago Press.
Heidenheimer, Arnold J. 1970. *Political Corruption: Readings in Comparative Analysis*. New York: Holt, Rinehart and Winston.
Heilbroner, Robert L. 1962. *The Making of Economic Society*. Englewood Cliffs, N.J.: Prentice-Hall.
———. 1984. "Economics and Political Economy: Marx, Keynes and Schumpeter." *Journal of Economic Issues* 18:681–95.
Heiner, Ronald A. 1983a. "The Origin of Predictable Behavior." *American Economic Review* 73:560–95.
———. 1983b "Uncertainty, Signal Detection Experiments, and Modeling Behavior." Brigham Young University. Photocopy.
Hess, Eckhard H. 1973. *Imprinting: Early Experience and the Development of Psychological Attachment*. New York: Van Nostrand.
Hey, John D. 1979. *Uncertainty in Microeconomics*. New York: New York University Press.
———. 1981. "Are Optimal Search Rules Reasonable? And Vice Versa?" *Journal of Economic Behavior and Organization* 2:47–70.
Hicks, John R. 1979. *Causality in Economics*. New York: Basic Books.
Hill, Thomas E., Jr. 1979. "Symbolic Protest and Calculated Silence." *Philosophy and Public Affairs* 9:83–102.
Hirsch, Fred. 1976. *Social Limits to Growth*. Cambridge, Mass.: Harvard University Press.
Hirschman, Albert O. 1945. *National Power and the Structure of Foreign Trade*. Berkeley: University of California Press.
———. 1977. *The Passions and the Interest*. Princeton: Princeton University Press.
———. 1981. *Essays in Trespassing: Economics to Politics and Beyond*. New York: Columbia University Press.
———. 1984. "Against Parsimony: Three Easy Ways of Complicating Some Categories of Economic Discourse." *American Economic Review: Papers and Proceedings* 74:89–96.
Hirshleifer, Jack. 1985. "Expanding Domain of Economics." *American Economic Review* 75:53–68.
Hirshleifer, Jack, and J. G. Riley. 1979. "The Analytics of Uncertainty and Information—An Expository Survey." *Journal of Economic Literature* 17:1375–1421.
Hobbes, Thomas. 1968. *Leviathan*. Ed. C. B. Macpherson. Harmondsworth: Penguin Books.

Hobsbawm, Eric J. 1969. *Industry and Empire*. Harmondsworth: Penguin Books.
———. 1979. *The Age of Capital: 1848–1875*. New York: New American Library.
Hodgson, Geoff. 1988. *Economics and Institutions: A Manifesto of a Modern Institutional Economics*. Philadelphia: University of Pennsylvania Press.
Holmstroem, Bengt. 1979. "Moral Hazard and Observability." *Business Journal of Economics* 10:74–91.
———. 1982. "Moral Hazard in Teams." *Business Journal of Economics* 13:324–40.
Homans, George C. 1953. "Status Among Clerical Workers." *Human Organization* 12:5–10.
———. 1954. "The Cash Posters." *American Sociological Review* 19:724–33.
———. 1983. "Steps to a Theory of Social Behavior." *Theory and Society* 12:1–46.
Hoselitz, Berthold F. 1960. *Sociological Aspects of Economic Growth*. Glencoe, Ill.: Free Press.
Howard, Nigel. 1971. *Paradoxes of Rationality*. Cambridge, Mass.: MIT Press.
Huan, K'uan. 1967. *Discourses on Salt and Iron*. Trans. E. M. Gale. Taipei: Ch'eng-Wen Publishing.
Hubin, D. Clayton. 1979. "The Scope of Justice." *Philosophy and Public Affairs* 9:3–24.
Hughes, Jonathan. 1986. *The Vital Few: The Entrepreneurs and American Economic Progress*. Expanded ed. New York: Oxford University Press.
Hume, David. 1965. *A Treatise on Human Nature*. Oxford: Clarendon Press.
Hunt, E. K. 1981. *Property and Prophets*. 4th ed. New York: Harper and Row.
Hutt, William H. 1936. *Economists and the Public: A Study of Competition and Opinion*. London: Jonathan Cape.
Hyman, Herbert H. 1968. "Psychology of Status." In *Readings in Reference Group Theory and Research*. ed. Herbert Hyman and Elinor Singer, 147–65. New York: Free Press.
Hyman Herbert, and Elinor Singer., eds. 1968. *Readings in Reference Group Theory and Research*. New York: Free Press.
Ichiishi, Tatsuro. 1983. *Game Theory for Economic Analysis*. New York: Academic Press.
James, William. 1948. *Essays in Pragmatism*. Ed. A. Castell. New York: Hafner Press.
———. 1956. *The Will to Believe*. New York: Dover Publications.
Jasso, Guillermina. 1983. "Fairness of Individual Rewards and Fairness of the Reward Distribution: Specifying the Inconsistency Between the Micro and Macro Principles of Justice." *Social Psychology Quarterly* 46:185–99.
Jeffrey, Richard C. 1965. *The Logic of Decision*. New York: McGraw-Hill.
Jennings, Dennis L., Teresa M. Amabile, and Lee Ross. 1982. "Informal Covariation Assessment: Data-based versus Theory-based Judgments." In *Judgment under Uncertainty: Heuristics and Biases*, ed. Daniel Kahneman, Amos Tversky, and Paul Slovic, 211–30. New York: Cambridge University Press.
Johansson, S. Ryan. 1988. "The Computer Paradigm and the Role of Cultural Information in Social System." *Historical Methods* 21:172–88.
Jones, Stephen R. 1984. *Economics of Conformism*. New York: Basil Blackwell.
Kahn, Arnold, Robin Nelson, William P. Gaeddert, and June J. Hearn. 1982. "The

Justice Process: Deciding upon Equity and Equality." *Social Psychology Quarterly* 45:3–8.

Kahneman, Daniel, and Amos Tversky. 1979. "Prospect Theory: An Analysis of Decision Under Risk." *Econometrica* 47:263–91.

———. 1982a. "Judgment under Uncertainty." In *Judgment under Uncertainty: Heuristics and Biases*, ed. Daniel Kahneman, Amos Tversky, and Paul Slovic, 3–20. New York: Cambridge University Press.

———. 1982b. "Availability: A Heuristic for Judging Frequency and Probability." In *Judgment under Uncertainty: Heuristics and Biases*, ed. Daniel Kahneman, Amos Tversky, and Paul Slovic, 163–78. New York: Cambridge University Press.

———. 1984. "Choices, Values, and Frames." *American Psychologist* 39:341–50.

Kahneman, Daniel, Amos Tversky, and Slovic, Paul, eds. 1982. *Judgment under Uncertainty: Heuristics and Biases*. New York: Cambridge University Press.

Kahneman, Daniel, Amos Tversky, J. L. Knetsch, and R. Thaler. 1986. "Fairness as a Constraint on Profit Seeking: Entitlement in the Market." *American Economic Review* 76:728–41.

Kelly, George. 1963. *A Theory of Personality*. New York: Norton.

Keynes, John Maynard. 1921. *A Treatise on Probability*. London: Macmillan.

———. 1936. *The General Theory of Employment, Interest, and Money*. New York: Harcourt, Brace.

———. 1936–37. "The General Theory of Employment." *Quarterly Journal of Economics* 101:209–23.

Kilby, Peter, ed. 1971. *Entrepreneurship and Economic Development*. New York: Free Press.

Kindleberger, Charles P. 1951. "Group Behavior and International Trade." *Journal of Political Economy* 59:30–46.

———. 1979. "The Aging Economy." *Weltwirtschaftliches Archiv* 114:407–21.

Kirzner, Israel M. 1973. *Competition and Entrepreneurship*. Chicago: University of Chicago Press.

———. 1979. *Perception, Opportunity, and Profit: Studies in the Theory of Entrepreneurs*. Chicago: University of Chicago Press.

———. 1980. "The Primacy of Entrepreneurial Discovery." In *The Prime Mover: The Entrepreneur in Capitalism and Socialism*, ed. Arthur Selden. London: Institute of Economic Affairs.

Klein, Burton H. 1984. *Prices, Wages and Business Cycles: A Dynamic Theory*. New York: Pergamon Press.

Knight, Frank H. 1921. *Risk, Uncertainty and Profit*. Boston: Houghton Mifflin.

———. 1935. *Ethics of Competition*. London: Allen Unwin.

———. 1946. "Immutable Law in Economics: Its Reality and Limitations." *American Economic Review: Papers and Proceedings* 36:93–111.

Kuhn, Thomas. 1970. *The Structure of Scientific Revolutions*. 2d ed. Chicago: University of Chicago Press.

———. 1977. *The Essential Tension: Selected Studies in Scientific Tradition and Change*. Chicago: University of Chicago Press.

Kuran, Timur. 1987. "Preference Falsification, Policy Continuity and Collective Conservatism." *Economic Journal* 97:642–65.

———. 1989. "Sparks and Prairie Fires: A Theory of Unanticipated Political Revolution." *Public Choice* 61:41–74.

———. 1990. "Private and Public Preferences." *Economics and Philosophy* 6:1–26.

———. 1991a. "Cognitive Limitations and Preference Evolution." *Journal of Institutional and Theoretical Economics* 147:241–73.

———. 1991b. "The East European Revolution of 1989: Is It Surprising That We Were Surprised?" *American Economic Review: Papers and Proceedings* 81:121–25.

Lakoff, George, and Mark Johnson. 1981. *Metaphors We Live By*. Chicago: University of Chicago Press.

Langlois, Richard N., ed. 1986. *Economics as a Process: Essays in the New Institutional Economics*. New York: Cambridge University Press.

Lasswell, Harold D. 1936. *Politics: Who Gets What, When and How*. New York: Whittlesey House.

Lawler, Edward E., III. 1976. *Pay and Organizational Effectiveness*. New York: McGraw-Hill.

Lazear, Edward, and S. Rosen. 1981. "Rank-Order Tournaments as Optimum Labor Contract." *Journal of Political Economy* 89:841–64.

Leamer, Edward E. 1983. "Let's Take the Con out of Econometrics." *American Economic Review* 73:31–43.

Leibenstein, Harvey. 1966. "Allocative Efficiency vs. X-Efficiency." *American Economic Review* 56:392–415.

———. 1976. *Beyond Economic Man*. Cambridge, Mass.: Harvard University Press.

———. 1982a. "The Japanese Management System: An X-Efficiency Game Theory Analysis." Harvard Discussion Paper no. 938.

———. 1982b. "The Prisoner's Dilemma in the Invisible Hand: An Analysis of Interfirm Productivity." *American Economic Review: Papers and Proceedings* 72:92–97.

———. 1983a. "Intrafirm Productivity: Reply." *American Economic Review* 72:822–23.

———. 1983b. "Property Rights and X-Efficiency: Comment." *American Economic Review* 72:831–42.

Leijonhufvud, Axel. 1981. *Information and Coordination*. New York: Oxford University Press.

Leontief, Wassily. 1971. "Theoretical Assumptions and Nonobserved Facts." *American Economic Review* 61:1–7.

Levin, Michael. 1982. "A Hobbesian Minimal State." *Philosophy and Public Affairs* 11:338–53.

Lessa, William A., and Evon Z. Vogt. 1979. *Reader in Comparative Religion: An Anthropological Approach*. New York: Harper and Row.

Lewis, David K. 1969. *Convention: A Philosophical Study*. Cambridge, Mass.: Harvard University Press.

Lewis, W. Arthur. 1955. *The Theory of Economic Growth*. Homewood, Ill.: Richard D. Irwin.

---. 1980. "Rising Prices: 1899–1913 and 1950–1979." *Scandinavian Journal of Economics* 82:425–36.
Linden, Dana W. 1991. "Dreary Days in the Dismal Science." *Forbes*, January 21, 68–71.
Loasby, Brian J. 1976. *Choice, Complexity and Ignorance: An Enquiry into Economic Theory and the Practice of Decision Making*. Cambridge: Cambridge University Press.
---. 1986. "Organization, Competition, and the Growth of Knowledge." In *Economics as a Process*, ed. R. N. Langlois, 41–57. New York: Cambridge University Press.
---. 1989. "Herbert Simon's Human Rationality." In *Research in the History of Economic Thought and Methodology*, ed. W. Samuels, 6:1–17.
Loomes, Graham, and Robert Sugden. 1983. "A Rationale for Preference Reversal." *American Economic Review* 73:428–32.
Lord, C., M. R. Lepper, and L. Ross. 1979. "Biased Assimilation and Attitude Polarization: The Effects of Prior Theories on Subsequently Considered Evidence." *Journal of Personality and Social Psychology* 37:2098–2110.
Louis, Meryl R., and Robert I. Sutton. 1991. "Switching Cognitive Gears: From Habits of Mind to Active Thinking." *Human Relations* 44:55–76.
Lucas, Robert E., Jr. 1981. *Studies in Business Cycle Theory*. Oxford: Oxford University Press.
---. 1985. "The Case of the Little Frog." *Wall Street Journal*, July 31.
Luce, R. Duncan, and Howard Raiffa. 1957. *Games and Decisions: Introduction and Critical Survey*. New York: Wiley.
Luksetich, William A., and Michael D. White. 1982. *Crime and Public Policy: An Economic Approach*. Boston: Little, Brown.
Lydall, Harold. 1968. *The Structure of Earnings*. Oxford: Clarendon Press.
---. 1979. *A Theory of Income Distribution*. Oxford: Clarendon Press.
McCall, John J. 1970. "Economics of Information and Job Search." *Quarterly Journal of Economics* 85:113–26.
McCloskey, Donald N. 1973. *Economic Maturity and Entrepreneurial Decline: British Iron and Steel 1870–1913*. Cambridge, Mass.: Harvard University Press.
---. 1983. "The Rhetoric of Economics." *Journal of Economic Literature* 61:481–517.
McNulty, Paul J. 1968. "Economic Theory and the Meaning of Competition." *Quarterly Journal of Economics* 83:639–56.
---. 1984. "On the Nature and the Theory of Economic Organization: The Role of the Firm Reconsidered." *History of Political Economy* 16:233–53.
McPherson, Michael. 1983. "Efficiency and Liberty in the Production Enterprise: Recent Work in the Economics of Work Organization." *Philosophy and Public Affairs* 12:354–68.
Maddock, Rodney, and Michael Carter. 1982. "A Child's Guide to Rational Expectations." *Journal of Economic Literature* 20:39–51.
Maital, Shlomo. 1982. *Minds, Markets, and Money: Psychological Foundations of Economic Behavior*. New York: Basic Books.

Maital, Shlomo, and S. L. Maital. 1984. *Economic Games People Play*. New York: Basic Books.

March, James G. 1978. "Bounded Rationality, Ambiguity and the Engineering Choice." *Business Journal of Economics* 9:587–608.

Marger, Martin N. 1981. *Elites and Masses: An Introduction to Political Sociology*. New York: D. Van Nostrand.

Margolis, Howard. 1987. *Patterns, Thinking and Cognition: A Theory of Judgment*. Chicago: University of Chicago Press.

Markus, Hazel, and R. B. Zajonc. 1985. "The Cognitive Perspective in Social Psychology." In *Handbook of Social Psychology*, 3rd ed., ed. G. Lindzey and E. Aronson, 1:137–230. New York: Random House.

Marshall, Alfred. 1961. *Principles of Political Economy*. 9th ed. London: Macmillan.

Marx, Karl, and F. Engles. 1919. *Manifesto of the Communist Party*. New York: International Publishers.

Matthews, R. C. O. 1984. "Darwinism and Economic Change." *Oxford Economic Papers: Supplement* 36:91–117.

———. 1986. "The Economics of Institutions and the Sources of Growth." *Economic Journal* 96:903–18.

Mayo, Elton. 1933. *Human Problems of an Industrial Civilization*. New York: Macmillan.

———. 1945. *The Social Problems of an Industrial Civilization*. Cambridge, Mass.: Harvard University Press.

———. 1971. "Howthorne and Western Electrical Company." In *Organizational Theory*, ed. D. S. Pugh, 215–29. New York: Penguin Books.

Medoff, James L., and Katharine G. Abraham. 1980. "Experience, Performance, and Earnings." *Quarterly Journal of Economics* 95:703–36.

Merton, Robert K. 1968a. "The Matthew Effect in Science: The Reward and Communication Systems of Science Are Considered." *Science* 159:56–63.

———. 1968b. *Social Theory and Social Structure*. New York: Free Press.

Mitchell, Wesley C. 1969. *Types of Economic Theory: From Mercantilism to Institutionalism*. 2 vols. Ed. J. Dorfman. New York: Augustus M. Kelley.

Mokyr, Joel. 1990. *The Lever of Riches: Technological Creativity and Economic Progress*. New York: Oxford University Press.

Montaigne, Michel de. 1979. *Essays*. Trans. J. M. Cohen. New York: Penguin Books.

Morgenstern, Oscar. 1972. "Thirteen Critical Points in Contemporary Economic Theory: An Interpretation." *Journal of Economic Literature* 10:805–16.

Muth, John F. 1961. "Rational Expectations and the Theory of Price Movements." *Econometrica* 29:315–35.

Mydans, Seth. 1992. "A Target of Rioters, Koreatown Bitter, Armed and Determined." *New York Times*, May 3.

Nath, S. K. 1973. *A Perspective on Welfare Economics*. London: Macmillan Press.

Nelson, Richard R. 1973. "Neoclassical vs. Evolutionary Theory of Growth." Institute of Public Policy Discussion Paper no. 46. University of Michigan.

Nelson, Richard R., and Sidney G. Winter. 1982. *An Evolutionary Theory of Economic Change*. Cambridge, Mass.: Harvard University Press.

Nisbet, Richard, Eugene Borgida, Rick Crandell, and Harvey Reed. 1982. "Popular Inductions: Information Is Not Necessarily Informative." In *Judgment under Uncertainty: Heuristics and Biases*, ed. Daniel Kahneman, Amos Tversky, and Paul Slovic, 101–16. New York: Cambridge University Press.

Nisbett, Richard and L. Ross. 1980. *Human Inference: Strategies and Shortcomings of Social Judgment*. Englewood Cliffs, N.J.: Prentice-Hall.

North, Douglas C. 1984a. "Government and the Cost of Exchange in History." *Journal of Economic History* 44:255–64.

———. 1984b. Review of *The Rise and Decline of Nations*, by M. Olson. *Science* 175:163–64.

Nozick, Robert. 1974. *Anarchy, State and Utopia*. New York: Basic Books.

Olson, Mancur. 1965. *The Logic of Collective Action: Public Goods and the Theory of Groups*. Cambridge, Mass.: Harvard University Press.

———. 1982. *The Rise and Decline of Nations: Economic Growth, Stagflation and Social Rigidities*. New Haven: Yale University Press.

———. 1988. "The Productivity Slowdown, the Oil Shocks, and the Real Cycle." *Journal of Economic Perspectives* 2:43–69.

Ortega y Gasset, Jose. 1957. *Man and People*. Trans. W. R. Trask. New York: Norton.

Ortony, Andrew, ed. 1979. *Metaphor and Thought*. Cambridge: Cambridge University Press.

Ouchi, William G. 1981. *Theory Z: How American Business Can Meet the Japanese Challenge*. New York: Addison-Wesley.

Packard, Vance. 1958. *The Hidden Persuaders*. New York: Pocket Books.

———. 1959. *The Status Seeker*. New York: Pocket Books.

Papanicolaou, John, and George Psacharopoulos. 1979. "Socio-Economic Background, Schooling and Monetary Rewards in the U.K." *Economica* 46:435–39.

Parducci, Allen. 1968. "The Relativism of Absolute Judgment." *Scientific American* 218:84–90.

Pascal, Blaise. 1941. *The Works of Pascal (Pansees)*. New York: Random House.

Patinkin, Don. 1973. "Frank Knight as Teacher." *American Economic Review* 63:787–810.

Philips, Derek L. 1977. *Wittgenstein and Scientific Knowledge: A Sociological Perspective*. Totowa, N.J.: Rowman and Littlefield.

Pigou, Arthur. 1932. *Economics of Welfare*. 4th ed. London: Macmillan.

———. 1951. "Some Aspects of Welfare Economics." *American Economic Review* 41:287–302.

Plato. 1956. *Great Dialogues of Plato*. Trans. W. H. D. Rouse. New York: New American Library.

Polanyi, Karl. 1957. *The Great Transformation: The Political and Economic Origins of Our Time*. Boston: Beacon Press.

———. 1977. *The Livelihood of Man*. Ed. H. W. Pearson. New York: Academic Press.

Polanyi, Michael. 1962. *Personal Knowledge: Towards a Postcritical Philosophy*. Chicago: University of Chicago Press.

———. 1966. *The Tacit Dimension*. Garden City, N.Y.: Doubleday.

———. 1969. *Knowing and Being.* Chicago: University of Chicago Press.
Pollak, Richard A. 1976. "Interdependent Preferences." *American Economic Review* 66:309–20.
Popper, Karl. 1979. *Objective Knowledge: An Evolutionary Approach.* Rev. ed. Oxford: Clarendon Press.
Quigley, Carroll. 1979. *The Evolution of Civilization.* Indianapolis: Liberty Press.
Quine, Willard V. 1978. "A Postscript on Metaphor." *Critical Inquiry* 5:161–62.
Rapoport, Anatol. 1960. *Fights, Games, and Debates.* Ann Arbor: University of Michigan Press.
———. 1962. "The Use and Misuse of Game Theory." *Scientific American* 207:108–18.
———. 1967. "Escape from Paradox." *Scientific American* 217:50–56.
Rapoport, Anatol, and A. M. Chammah. 1965. *Prisoner's Dilemma: A Study in Conflict and Cooperation.* Ann Arbor: University of Michigan Press.
Rawls, John. 1971. *A Theory of Justice.* Cambridge, Mass.: Harvard University Press.
Ray, S. K. 1981. *Economics of the Black Market.* Boulder, Colo.: Westview Press.
Reinhold, Robert. 1992. "A City of Nightmares: A Terrible Chain of Events Reveals Los Angeles Without Its Makeup." *New York Times*, May 3.
Richardson, G. B. 1959. "Equilibrium, Expectations and Information." *Economic Journal* 69:223–37.
———. 1960. *Information and Investment.* Oxford: Oxford University Press.
Riley, J. G. 1975. "Competitive Signalling." *Journal of Economic Theory* 10:174–86.
Robertson, D. H. 1956. "What Does the Economist Economize?" In *Economic Commentaries*, 147–55. London: Staples Press.
Robbins, Lionel. 1946. *An Essay on the Nature and Significance of Economic Science.* 2d ed. London: Macmillan.
Roethlisberger, Fritz J., and William Dickson. 1939. *Management and Worker.* Cambridge, Mass.: Harvard University Press.
Rohwer, William D., Jr., Paul R. Ammon, and Phebe Cramer. 1974. *Understanding Intellectual Development: Three Approaches to Theory and Practice.* Hinsdale, Ill.: Dryden Press.
Roll, Eric. 1978. *The Uses and Abuses of Economics and Other Essays.* London: Faber and Faber.
Rorty, Richard. 1979. *Philosophy and the Mirror of Nature.* Princeton: Princeton University Press.
———. 1983. *Consequences of Pragmatism: Essays 1972–1980.* Lexington, Mass.: Lexington Books.
Rosen, Sherwin. 1981. "Economics of Superstars." *American Economic Review* 71:845–58.
Rosenthal, Robert, and Leonore F. Jacobson. 1968. "Teacher Expectations for the Disadvantaged." *Scientific American* 218:19–23.
Ross, Lee, and Craig A. Anderson. 1982. "Shortcomings in the Attribution Process: On the Origins and Maintenance of Erroneous Social Assessments." In *Judgment under Uncertainty: Heuristics and Biases*, ed. Daniel Kahneman, Amos Tversky, and Paul Slovic, 129–51. New York: Cambridge University Press.
Ross, Lee, M. R. Lepper, and M. Hubbard. 1975. "Perseverance in Self Perception

and Social Perception: Biased Attributional Processes in the Debriefing Paradigms." *Journal of Personal and Social Psychology* 32:880–92.
Rostow, W. W. 1980. *Why the Poor Get Richer and the Rich Slow Down: Essays in the Marshallian Long Period.* Austin: University of Texas Press.
Rousseau, Jean-Jacques. 1913. *The Social Contract and Discourses.* Trans. G. D. H. Cole. London: Everyman's Library.
Runciman, W. G. 1966. *Relative Deprivation and Social Justice.* Berkeley: University of California Press.
Sahlins, Marshall. 1972. *Stone Age Economics.* New York: Aldine.
———. 1978. *Culture and Practical Reason.* Chicago: University of Chicago Press.
Sahota, Gian S. 1978. "The Theories of Personal Income Distribution: A Survey." *Journal of Economic Literature* 16:1–55.
Samuels, Warren J., ed. 1982. *The Method of Economic Thought.* New Brunswick, N.J.: Transaction Books.
Samuelson, Paul A. 1965. *Foundations of Economic Analysis.* New York: Atheneum Press.
———. 1972. "Maximum Principles in Analytic Economics." *American Economic Review* 62:249–62.
Savage, Leonard J. 1954. *The Foundation of Statistics.* New York: Wiley.
Scharfstein, David S., and Jeremy C. Stein. 1990. "Herd Behavior and Investment." *American Economic Review* 80:465–79.
Schelling, Thomas C. 1960. *The Strategy of Conflict.* Cambridge, Mass.: Harvard University Press.
———. 1978. *Microeconomics and Macro-Behavior.* New York: Norton.
———. 1982. "Ethics, Law, and the Exercise of Self-Command." Harvard Discussion Paper no. 905.
———. 1984. "Self-Command in Practice, in Policy, and in a Theory of Rational Choice." *American Economic Review: Papers and Proceedings* 74:1–11.
Schere, Frederic M. 1980. *Industrial Market Structure and Economic Performance.* 2d ed. Chicago: Rand McNally.
Schoeck, Helmut. 1987. *Envy: A Theory of Social Behavior.* Indianapolis: Liberty Press.
Schoemaker, Paul J. H. 1980. *Experiments on Decision under Risk: The Expected Utility Hypothesis.* Boston: Martinus Nijhoff Publishing.
———. 1982. "Expected Utility Model: Its Variants, Purposes, Evidence and Limitations." *Journal of Economic Literature* 20:529–63.
Schotter, Andrew. 1981. *Economic Theories of Social Institutions.* Cambridge: Cambridge University Press.
Schumpeter, Joseph A. 1934. *The Theory of Economic Development.* Cambridge: Mass.: Harvard University Press.
———. 1950. *Capitalism, Socialism, and Democracy.* New York: Harper and Row.
———. 1954. *History of Economic Analysis.* New York: Oxford University Press.
———. 1964. *Business Cycles: A Theoretical, Historical and Statistical Analysis of the Capitalist Process.* Abridged by Rendings Fels. New York: McGraw-Hill.
Scitovsky, Tibor. 1978. "Market Power and Inflation." *Economica* 45:221–33.

———. 1976. *The Joyless Economy: An Inquiry into Human Satisfaction and Consumer Dissatisfaction*. New York: Oxford University Press.
Seers, Dudley. 1962. "Why Visiting Economists Fail." *Journal of Political Economy* 70:325–38.
Sen, Amartya K. 1974. "Choice, Ordering and Morality." In *Practical Reason*, ed. S. Koerner, 54–67. Oxford: Oxford University Press.
———. 1977. "Rational Fools: A Critique of the Behavioral Foundation of Economic Theory." *Philosophy and Public Affairs* 6:317–44.
Sen, Amartya K., and W. G. Runciman. 1965. "Games, Justice and the General Will." *Mind* 74:544–62.
Shackle, George L. S. 1966. *The Nature of Economic Thought: Selected Papers 1955–1964*. Cambridge: Cambridge University Press.
———. 1967. *The Years of High Theory*. Cambridge, Cambridge University Press.
———. 1972. *Epistemics and Economics*. Cambridge: Cambridge University Press.
Shapiro, Milton M. 1985. *Foundations of the Market-Price System*. Lanham, Md.: University Press of America.
Sheffrin, Steven M. 1983. *Rational Expectations*. Cambridge, Mass.: Harvard University Press.
Shih, Kuo-Heng. 1944. *China Enters the Machine Age*. Cambridge: Cambridge University Press.
Shils, Edward. 1981. *Tradition*. Chicago: University of Chicago Press.
Shoham, S. Giora. 1974. *Society and the Absurd*. New York: Springer Publishing.
Shonfield, Andrew. 1965. *Modern Capitalism*. Oxford: Oxford University Press.
Shubik, Martin, ed. 1964. *Game Theory and Related Approaches to Social Behavior*. New York: Wiley.
Simmons, Alan J. 1979. "The Principles of Fair Play." *Philosophy and Public Affairs* 8:307–37.
Simon, Herbert A. 1957. *Models of Man*. New York: Wiley.
———. 1978. "Rationality as Process and as Product of Thought." *American Economic Review Papers and Proceedings* 68:1–16.
———. 1982. *Models of Bounded Rationality: Behavioral Economics and Business Organization*. 2 vols. Cambridge, Mass.: MIT Press.
———. 1984. "On the Behavioral and Rational Foundation of Economic Dynamics." *Journal of Economic Behavior and Organization* 5:35–55.
Singer, Peter. 1973. "Altruism and Commerce: A Defense of Titmuss Against Arrow." *Philosophy and Public Affairs* 2:312–20.
Slote, Michael Anthony. 1966. "The Theory of Important Criteria." *Journal of Philosophy* 9:211–24.
Slovic, Paul, and Sarah Lichtenstein. 1983. "Preference Reversal: A Broader Perspective." *American Economic Review* 73:596–605.
Smith, Adam. 1976a. *An Inquiry into the Nature and Causes of the Wealth of Nations*. 2 vols. Ed. R. H. Campbell and A. S. Skinner. Indianapolis: Liberty Classic.
———. 1976b. *The Theory of Moral Sentiments*. Ed. D. D. Raphael and A. L. MacFie. Oxford: Oxford University Press.

Smith, John M. 1982. *Evolution and the Theory of Games*. Cambridge: Cambridge University Press.
Solow, Robert. 1980. "On the Theories of Unemployment." *American Economic Review* 70:1–11.
Sowell, Thomas. 1980. *Knowledge and Decisions*. New York: Basic Books.
———. 1981. *Ethnic America*. New York: Basic Books.
Spence, Michael. 1973. "Job Market Signalling." *Quarterly Journal of Economics* 87:355–74.
———. 1974. *Market Signalling*. Cambridge, Mass.: Harvard University Press.
Spengler, Joseph J. 1972. "Social Science and the Collectivization of *Hubris*." *Political Science Quarterly* 87:1–21.
Stark, Oded. 1982. "Rural-to-Urban Migration in LDC's: A Relative Deprivation Approach." Harvard Discussion Paper no. 924.
Steven, S. S. 1968. "Measurement, Statistics, and the Schemapiric View." *Science* 161:849–56.
Stigler, George J. 1958. "The Economics of Scale." *Journal of Law and Economics* 1:54–71.
———. 1961. "The Economics of Information." *Journal of Political Economy* 69:213–25.
———. 1962. "Information in the Labor Market." *Journal of Political Economy* 70:94–105.
———. 1976. "The Existence of X-Efficiency." *American Economic Review* 66:213–16.
———. 1982. *Economists as Preachers and Other Essays*. Chicago:University of Chicago Press.
———. 1983. "Nobel Lecture: The Process and Progress of Economics." *Journal of Political Economy* 91:529–45.
Stigler, George J., and G. S. Becker. 1977. "De Gustibus Non Est Disputandum." *American Economic Review* 67:76–90.
Strotz, R. H. 1955–56. "Myopia and Inconsistency in Dynamic Utility Maximization." *Review of Economic Studies* 23:165–80.
Sugden, Robert. 1989. "Spontaneous Order." *Journal of Economic Perspectives* 3:85–97.
Sumner, William Graham. 1979. *Folkways and Mores*. Ed. E. Sagarin. New York: Schocken Books.
Takayama, Akira. 1974. *Mathematical Economics*. Hinsdale, Ill.: Dryden Press.
Taylor, Marylee C. 1982. "Improved Conditions, Rising Expectations, and Dissatisfaction: A Test of the Past/Present Relative Deprivation Hypothesis." *Social Psychology Quarterly* 45:24–33.
Thompson, Earl A., and Roger L. Faith. 1981. "A Pure Theory of Strategic Behavior and Social Institutions." *American Economic Review* 71:366–80.
Thurow, Lester. 1980. *The Zero Sum Society: Distribution and the Possibilities for Economic Change*. New York: Basic Books.
———. 1975. *Generating Inequality*. New York: Basic Books.
———. 1983. *Dangerous Current: State of Economics*. New York: Random House.

Titmus, Richard M. 1971. *Gift Relationship: From Human Blood to Social Policy.* New York: Random House.

Tocqueville, Alexis de. 1955. *The Old Regime and The French Revolution.* Trans. Stuart Gilbert. New York: Anchor.

Toennies, Ferdinand. 1965. *Community and Association.* Ed. C. P. Loomis. London: Routledge and Kegan Paul.

Toulmin, Stephen. 1964. *The Use of Argument.* Cambridge: Cambridge University Press.

Tucker, Robert C., ed. 1972. *The Marx–Engels Reader.* New York: Norton.

Ullman-Margalit, Edna. 1977. *The Emergence of Norms.* New York: Columbia University Press.

Vaihinger, Hans. 1965. *The Philosophy of "As If": A System of the Theoretical, Practical and Religious Fictions of Mankind.* Trans C. K. Ogden. London: Routledge and Keagan Paul.

Vanberg, Viktor. 1986. "Spontaneous Market Order and Social Rules: A Critical Examination of F. A. Hayek's Theory of Cultural Revolution." *Economics and Philosophy* 2:75–100.

———. 1989. "Rational Choice, Rule Following and Institutions: An Evolutionary Perspective." George Mason University. Photocopy.

Vanberg, Viktor, and J. M. Buchanan. 1988. "Rational Choice and Moral Order." *Analyse und Kritik* 10:138–60.

Vannman, Reeve D., and Thomas F. Pettigrew. 1972. "Race and Relative Deprivation in the Urban United States." *Race* 13:461–86.

Varian, Hal. 1974. "Equity, Envy and Efficiency." *Journal of Economic Theory* 9:63–91.

———. 1975. "Distributive Justice, Welfare Economics and the Theory of Fairness." *Philosophy and Public Affairs* 4:223–47.

———. 1978. *Microeconomic Analysis.* New York: Norton.

Veblen, Thorstein. 1899. *The Theory of the Leisure Class: An Economic Theory of the Evolution of Institutions.* New York: Macmillan.

Viner, Jacob. 1948. "Wealth vs. Plenty as Objectives of Foreign Policy in the Seventeenth and Eighteenth Centuries." *World Politics.* 1:1–29.

Wachter, Michael L. 1970. "Cyclical Variation in the Interindustry Wage Structure." *American Economic Review* 60:75–84.

West, Edwin, and M. McKee. 1983. "De Gustibus Est Disputandum: A Phenomenon of 'Merit Wants' Revisited." *American Economic Review* 73:1110–21.

West, S. G., and R. A. Wicklund. 1980. *A Primer of Social Psychology Theories.* Monterey, Calif.: Brooks/Cole Publishing.

Wicksteed, Philip H. 1933. *The Common Sense of Political Economy.* 2 vols. London: Routledge and Kegan Paul.

Wildavsky, Aaron. 1964. *The Politics of Budget Process.* Boston: Little, Brown.

Williamson, Oliver. 1975. *Markets and Hierarchies: Analysis and Antitrust Implications.* New York: Free Press.

Williamson, Oliver, Michael Wachter, and Jeffrey E. Harris. 1975. "Understanding the Employment Relations" *Bell Journal of Economics* 6:250–80.

Winter, Sidney G. 1970. "Satisficing, Selection and Innovating Remnant." Institute of Public Policy Discussion Paper no. 18. University of Michigan.
Wittgenstein, Ludwig. 1969. *On Certainty.* Oxford: Basil Blackwell.
Wrong, Dennis H. 1961. "The Over-Socialized Conception of Man in Modern Sociology." *American Sociological Review* 12:183–93.
Young, Alwyn. 1991. "Learning by Doing and the Dynamic Effects of International Trade." *Quarterly Journal of Economics* 106:369–405.

# Name Index

Akerlof, George A., 4n, 14n
Alchian, Armen, 17n, 78
Anderson, 66, 81n
Andreski, Stanislaw, 1
Arrow, Kenneth, 19–21, 35n, 41n, 56, 100, 102
Arthur, Brian, 85
Asch, Solomon E., 54n, 55n, 117n
Aubry, Lawrence, 138
Augustine, 49n
Axelrod, Robert, 60, 79–80, 95n, 131

Bae, Chong-Keun, 123n
Bartlett, Randall, 68n
Becker, Gary S., 2n, 19n,
Binmore, Ken, 5n, 17n, 19n, 28–29, 32n, 43
Boland, Lawrence A., 17n, 28n
Booth, Wayne, 36
Buchanan, James M., 4, 17n, 19n, 21n, 72n, 103

Choi, Young Back, 34n, 67n, 145n
Clark, J. B., 19n, 109
Coats, A. William, 118n
Confucius, 82
Conlinsk, John, 58

David, Paul A., 85n, 86
Demsetz, Harold, 78n
Dewey, John, 30f
Duesenberry, James, 113, 127n

Earl, Peter E., 36n, 41n
Edwards, Ward, 28n

Einhorn, Hillel J., 30n, 35n, 36n, 38n, 46n
Einstein, Albert, 36
Elster, Jon, 20n, 71n, 123n, 126n, 132n

Fang, Lizhi, 39n, 50n
Feldman, Allan M., 4n
Festinger, Leon, 61n
Field, Alexander James, 68n
Fogel, Robert W., 93n, 94n
Frank, Robert H., 4n, 20n, 113, 121–23, 132–33
Friedman, Milton, 17, 147
Fuller, Lon L., 91

Garelick, Herbert M., 20n

Hamermesh, Daniel S., 4n, 127n
Han, Feitzu, 145
Hands, D. Wade, 1
Hardin, Russell, 75n
Hausman, Daniel M., 46n
Hayek, Frederick A., 8n, 24n, 71n, 130, 146
Heiner, Ronald A., 6, 22, 25–26, 41n, 46n, 149n
Hey, John D., 18–19
Hirsch, Fred, 121
Hirschman, Albert O., 62, 95n, 99, 140
Hirshleifer, Jack, 2n
Hobbes, Thomas, 77–78
Hobsbawm, Eric J., 119n
Homans, George C., 127n
Howard, Katherine, 68
Howard, Nigel, 76n

Huan, K'uan, 137n
Hubbard, 42, 57n
Hughes, Jonathan, 111n, 137n, 146n
Hume, David, 27–29, 32, 90
Hutt, William H., 22, 118
Hyman, Herbert H., 127n

James, William, 15n
Jennings, Dennis L., 30n
Jevons, William Stanley, 3
Johansson, S. Ryan, 63n, 92, 93n
Jones, Stephen R., 4n, 14n, 87n

Kahn, Arnold, 57, 58n
Kahneman, Daniel, 18–19, 29–30, 39n, 52
Kelly, George, 36
Keynes, John Maynard, 46n, 78, 84, 118, 127
Kirman, 4n
Kirzner, Israel M., 6, 8n, 22–26, 30, 43, 123, 136n, 143n, 144n, 149n
Knight, Frank H., 12, 16, 19n, 116, 140, 141n
Kuhn, Thomas, 7, 34–35, 38, 46n, 107n
Kuran, Timur, ix, 15n, 56, 66n, 79n, 88n, 89, 99, 107n, 139n

Langlois, Richard N., 26
Lao-tzu, 55
Leibenstein, Harvey, 2, 3, 5, 6n, 14n, 22–26, 68n, 76n, 103–5, 108, 127n, 149
Leontief, Wassily, 33n
Lepper, 41–42, 57n,
Lichtenstein, 18
Linden, Dana W., 84
Loasby, Brian J., 26n, 36
Lord, C., 41
Lucas, Robert E., 54
Luce, R. Duncan, 76n

McCloskey, Donald N., 36, 37n
McNees, Stephen, 84

Mao, Tse-tung, 111
Margolis, Howard, 7n, 13n, 32, 34n, 36n, 37n, 44n, 46n, 94n
Markus, Hazel, 6n, 33n
Marshall, Alfred, 3, 14, 84
Marx, Karl, 146, 147n
Matthews, R. C. O., 58n, 96n
Mayo, Elton, 14n, 83–84, 127n
Merton, Robert K., 101n, 140
Mises, L., 23
Mokyr, Joel, 96n
Montaigne, Michel de, 137n
Mydans, Seth, 138n

Nelson, Richard R., 32
Nisbet, Richard, 6n, 29n, 30n, 33n, 36n, 40–42, 52, 53n
Nozick, Robert, 125–26, 136n

Olson, Mancur, 97n, 99, 102n
Ortega y Gasset, Jose, 69n

Pascal, Blaise, 34
Plato, 23n
Polanyi, Michael, 36, 40
Popper, Karl, 7, 27–29, 35n, 37n, 40, 61n

Quigley, Carroll, 97–98, 103

Rapoport, Anatol, 79–80, 95n
Rawls, John, 126, 128n, 129–30
Reinhold, Robert, 138n
Roll, Eric, 33n
Ross, Lee, 6n, 29n, 33n, 36n, 40–42, 52, 53n, 57n, 66, 81n

Santayana, G., 56
Scharfstein, David S., 56
Schelling, Thomas C., 6, 20n, 22, 24, 73n, 108n, 149n
Schoeck, Helmut, 126, 127n, 128n, 131, 132, 134–36, 140n, 141n
Schoemaker, Paul J. H., 60n
Schumpeter, Joseph A., 17n, 42, 84, 91n, 96n, 109–10, 118n, 144n, 153

Selten, 43
Sen, Amartya K., 20n, 77n
Sewell, Samuel, 94
Shackle, George L. S., 6
Shapiro, Milton M., 137n
Shih, Kuo-Heng, 14n
Shoham, S. Giora, 62n
Simon, Herbert A., 6, 22, 25, 26, 32, 100, 102, 149n
Slovic, Paul, 18
Smith, Adam, 36, 63, 64, 65n, 66n, 67n, 70n, 84, 119, 146
Spence, Michael, 121
Stein, 56
Stigler, George J., 23–25, 104
Sugden, Robert, 43n, 71n, 73n, 90n
Sumner, William Graham, 120n

Takayama, Akira, 20n, 151n
Taylor, Charles, 1
Teigen, Ronald, 21n
Thurow, Lester, 127n, 137n, 138
Tocqueville, Alexis de, 99, 101

Trotsky, Leon, 111n, 146n
Tversky, Amos, 18, 19n, 29–30, 36n, 39n, 52

Ullman-Margalit, Edna, 71n, 72n, 74n, 77n, 83n

Vaihinger, Hans, 30n, 31n, 97–98
Vanberg, Viktor, viii, 46n, 71n, 72n, 85
Varian, Hal, 136
Veblen, Thorstein, 119–20, 127n

Walas, Leon, 3
West, S. G., 61n
Wicksteed, Philip H., 115, 120, 121n
Winter, Sidney G., 32
Wittgenstein, Ludwig, 38

Young, Alwyn, 100n, 145n

Zajonc, 6n, 33n

# Subject Index

*Accidia,* 62
Admiration, 114, 119, 134
Altruism, 21
Appeasement, 142
Approval seeking, 8, 63–65, 74, 80, 114, 152
As if, 7, 17, 150, 152
Atavism, 130n
Attrition, 88–89
Austrian, 24
Authority, 118

Bayesian approach to probability, 28–29
Beliefs, 17, 29
Benevolence, 2
Bounded rationality 6, 25

Cause and effect, 61–62
Circular flow, 71n, 109–10, 153
Cognition, 6
Cognitive dissonance, 39n, 62
Commitment, 34, 40–41, 43, 47, 105
Conformity (or conformism), 4, 87–89, 90, 92, 93, 95, 106, 108, 134, 152, 153
Congruence, 20
Conscience, 66, 88
Conservatism, 40
Convention(s), 5, 8, 9, 68–71, 74, 81–114, 116, 120, 125, 128, 130, 132, 134, 141, 144–45, 147, 152, 153, 154
  conventional blinder, 100, 108, 142, 144, 145
  conventional justice, 89–91, 128, 142, 143

Coordination game, 72–74, 85
Crisis, 8, 109, 111
Cultural Revolution, 111

Decision making, vii, viii, 1, 4–7, 9, 11, 15–17, 18, 26–32, 37–38, 45–47, 49, 53, 65–66, 88, 104, 111, 117, 121, 125, 128, 149–53
Deviance (or deviant), 92–94, 95, 107, 108
Dialogue, 48–49
Discontinuity, 44, 47, 111
Discovery, 107, 108, 133, 145, 146, 154
Diversity, 94
Doubt, 27, 46

Economic imperialism, 2
Economics of uncertainty, 1n
Education, 121–23
Empathy, 67, 70, 74, 134, 140
Emulation, 115, 116, 120, 121, 133, 134, 142, 144
Endogenous, 8, 87
Entitlement, 136
Entrepreneur (or entrepreneurship, or entrepreneurial), vii, 2, 5, 9, 23, 57n, 109–10, 119, 123, 134, 139, 142–46, 149, 152–54
  protective cover for, 141, 143
Envy, vii, 2n, 3, 62, 112, 113, 125–42, 143, 152, 153, 154
  defined, 126
  envy barrier, 9
  fear of, 131, 134, 143
  free of, 135

## Subject Index

Equality, 61, 139
Error(s), 2, 8, 23–24, 25, 42, 51
  systematic, 43–44, 53–54, 104
  Type I and Type II, 46–47
Evolutionary learning, viii
Expectation, 12, 19, 29, 53–54, 62, 65, 70, 71, 81, 90–91, 103
Experiment (or experimentation), 8, 50, 52, 53, 55, 109, 144
  mental, 50, 59, 65, 67, 70
  vicarious, 54–61, 67, 73
Externality, 2n, 20n

Fair (or fairness), 4, 90, 92, 136n
Feudalism, 110, 146
Finder-keeper, 143n
Flood insurance, 20, 56
Fortuity, 83, 85, 141
Framing, 18
Functionalism, 71, 87n

*Gestalt,* 44
Greenmailing, 144
Group(s), 8, 9, 54–62
  biase, 58
  heterogeneous, 58–62
  homogeneous, 55–58

Habit(s), 2, 5, 7, 32n, 51, 154
Hackle-raising, 121
Happiness, 141
Herd instinct, 56
*Homo economicus* (or economic man), 6, 20, 21, 153
Human capital, 121

Image, 15
Imagined spectators, 65–67, 70, 88, 96
  impartial, 66
Imitation, 5, 8, 55, 56, 58, 59, 70, 88, 93, 95, 109, 115, 117, 152
  rationalistic, 58
Indeterminacy, 8, 38
Induction, 27–28
Inert area, 5–6, 22–24

Inertia, 9, 87, 95–96, 104, 105, 106, 111, 152–54
Inference, 15, 27–30, 60n, 117n, 150, 151
Inflexibility, 41–44, 47, 52, 53, 70, 95, 96, 152, 154
Innovation, 6, 9, 57n, 104, 106, 108, 109–11, 116, 134, 135, 143–46, 153
Institutions, 2, 5
Interdependence, vii, 4, 14, 54, 55, 62, 63, 69
Interdependent utility, vii, 2, 3, 4, 21
Interpersonal comparison, 8, 59, 61
Invidious comparisons, vii, 3, 4, 15, 120
Irrationality (or irrational), 5, 6, 11, 19, 21–24, 98, 117, 149

Judgment, vii, 15, 29
Judgmental heuristics, 29–30
  primacy effect, 52
Justice, 89–92, 94, 128, 129, 130, 143

Law of gravity, 4
Learning, 23, 45, 47–49, 79, 102, 106, 145, 152
  by doing, 100, 145
  social, 143–46, 153, 154
Liquidity preference, 78
Logic of choice, 4–6, 11, 17, 28, 31, 150, 151
Los Angeles riots, 137–38
Luck, 110, 139, 141, 144

Malice, 2
Marginal Revolution, 3
Market(s), 2, 143, 144, 147, 154
  competition, 150
  failure, 147
  process, 3, 9, 24, 143, 146, 147, 153
Matthew's law, 140
Maximization, viii, 4, 5, 7n, 16, 17, 21, 23, 25–29, 57, 59, 103–4, 146, 149, 150–52
  expected utility, 17, 19, 21, 28, 29, 52

Metaphor, 38, 48
Methodology (or methodological), 3, 5, 34, 150
   methodological individualism, 151
Microfoundations, 5, 150–51
Mistake(s), 5, 23, 24, 30, 42–43, 101, 146, 152, 154
Modelling, 7
Montaigne dogma, 137–38
Multiple self, 6

Neoclassical (economics), vii, viii, ix, 1, 2, 4, 5, 7n, 14, 16, 17, 19–23, 26, 28, 35n, 38, 41, 51–59, 84, 100–105, 109, 146, 147, 149–54
New institutionalism, 147
No-action, 55
Norms, 4, 8, 56n, 82–83, 91, 92
Novelty, 47

Opportunity, 24, 87, 100, 101, 108, 134, 136, 139, 144, 146
   exploited in full, 20
   growing, 105, 108, 109, 133, 153
   unexploited, 9, 23, 30, 99, 100, 101, 105, 106, 108, 110, 133, 143, 152–54
Opportunity value, 14
Optimal(ity), 8, 20, 25, 53, 58
Ostracism, 94, 95, 100–102, 106, 132, 134, 144, 152, 153

Paradigmatic approach, 7–9, 27, 32, 33, 37–38, 39–45, 53–58, 71n, 80–82, 96, 99, 101, 104, 105, 109, 111, 125, 128, 149, 151, 152, 154
Paradigm(s), 7, 8, 16, 32–39, 41, 44–58, 62, 65–70, 80, 81, 87, 88, 91, 94, 95, 103, 105, 107, 108, 109, 114, 115, 117, 120, 124, 128, 142, 144, 145, 152, 153, 154
   assignment, 38n, 47–48
   social, 68, 71, 81, 83, 103

Paradigm seeking, 8, 47, 49, 54–58, 63, 65, 69, 72, 81, 114, 152
Peers, 61, 124, 132
Perception, viii, 4, 6, 7, 34, 49, 56, 137
Precedents, 52, 57, 58, 101, 152
Preference, 17, 21
   falsification, 89, 93
   reversal, 18
Price fixing, 82
Prisoner's dilemma (or PD), 60, 68n, 72, 74–79, 81, 82, 83n, 85, 86, 90, 95, 99n, 101
   latent, 108
   repeated, 79–80, 82, 95
Proficiency, 46, 93, 113, 114, 120, 125
Property rights, 9, 21, 141, 142–43

Rationality (or rational), 5–7, 9, 19–23, 32n, 41, 43, 53, 76, 81, 82, 91, 98, 99, 100, 110, 121, 150
Reason
   apparent, 96
   real, 96–97, 99
Reasoning, 6, 32
Relative deprivation, 4, 99, 140
Reliability, 50
Representative man, 71, 150, 151
Reputation, 4
Requirement of social interaction, 69–70
Resentment, 129–30, 138
Risk (or risky), 12, 18, 104
Routine, 2, 5, 7, 32n, 133, 144, 145, 153
Rule-governed behavior, 6, 25, 41n
Rule(s), 8, 14, 15, 34, 74, 85, 128

Satisficing, 25–26
Schema, 33
Science (or scientist), 34–38, 49–50
Selective attention, 6, 7, 30, 43
Selective vision, 39, 40, 42, 43
Selectivity, 39, 52, 152
Signalling, 121

Skill, 32
Social change, 8, 46n, 94, 106, 107n, 108, 109, 111, 133
Socialism, 110, 146
Spontaneous process, 69
Stability, 95, 96, 101, 105, 111, 124, 153, 154
Status, 4, 8, 112, 112–21, 124, 125, 133, 152, 153
 competition for, 8, 120, 123
 derived, 117
 seeking, 114, 121, 152
*Status quo*, 71, 91, 92, 97, 98, 104, 105, 124, 128, 129, 132, 136
Suboptimal(ity), 20n, 101, 103, 104
Sympathy, 2, 67n, 140

Taboo, 127
*Taqiya*, 89
Tradition, 4, 95, 96, 142, 146
Transaction cost, 21, 147
Transitivity, 18
Trembling hand, 43
Trial and error, 8, 50, 73

Tulip mania, 58
Tunnel vision, 62, 140

Uncertainty, vii, viii, 1–38, 45–56, 59, 63–69, 71, 81, 87, 88, 94, 95, 103, 105, 109, 117, 120, 124, 125, 128, 149–54
Unconventional, 8, 9
Understanding, 15, 31, 32, 39, 47, 48, 96, 151
Unpredictable, 51, 82
Urgency of action, 32, 35, 51
Utopia, 135

Veracity, 39

Wage rigidity, 127, 154
Wieser's principle of continuity, 42, 96n

X-efficiency (or X-inefficiency), vii, 2, 3n, 5, 21–23, 103–5, 149
Xenophobia, 94

Zero-sum game, 137

| DATE DUE | | | |
|---|---|---|---|
| ~~DEC 1 8 1993~~ | ~~MAY 1 0 1994~~ | | |
| ~~MAR 0 9 1994~~ | | | |
| ~~MAY 1 4 1995~~ | | | |
| ~~FEB 1 9 1996~~ | | | |
| ~~MAY 1 1 1999~~ | | | |
| ~~NOV 1 0 2003~~ | | | |

Printed in USA